ADVENTURES A[...]
THE EDGE

ISLANDEERING

OF BRITAIN'S
HIDDEN ISLANDS

LISA DREWE

WILD
THINGS
PUBLISHING

ISLANDEERING

ADVENTURES AROUND THE EDGE OF BRITAIN'S HIDDEN ISLANDS

Great Bernera p276

CONTENTS

THE ISLANDS

MAP OF THE ISLANDS

ISLANDEERING

slandeering is the adventure of circumnavigating our islands by walking, running, swimming, cycling, scrambling, coasteering, or kayaking around their periphery. Using your skills and wit, you need to get to an island and then travel around its outer edge to complete the circuit.

This book shares my favourite day walks and adventures around 50 islands off mainland Britain and, in the true sense of islandeering, explores the coast along the way. It gives details of sea caves, cliffs and geos to explore, secret beaches, wild swims, and the huge diversity of cultural and wildlife highlights that every island has to offer.

Many of the walks are free-range, following animal tracks around the outer edge or forging new routes along rocky foreshores and unexplored cliff tops. Some simply follow recognised coastal paths. There are usually easier inland options, but for the adventurous there is plenty of excitement, not least in getting to the island itself. Access may be via road bridges, epic crossings over quicksand and against fast tides, or via local boats and ferries. For the amphibious there is always the possibility of a swim across, or a kayak if preferred. That said, in this book there is just one island where it won't be possible to keep your feet relatively dry on the crossing.

ISLOMANIA

o many people, islands are very special places. For some of us they are an obsession. This obsession has a word of its own, 'islomania', first coined by Lawrence Durrell who defined it as a 'rare but by no means unknown affliction of spirit. There are people...who find islands somehow irresistible. The mere knowledge that they are on an island, a little world surrounded by the sea, fills them with an indescribable intoxication.'

Islands have captured our imagination throughout history. They have been the setting for great literary works such as *The Odyssey, Robinson Crusoe, Treasure Island, Swallows and Amazons, Lord of the Flies,* and *Utopia,* which introduced a new word into our language. Each explored our fascination with the effects of solitude on people and society, created a more beautiful world or conjured up a sense of escape. Islands have also played a central role in scientific literature. Charles Darwin in *On the Origin of Species* shared his theory of evolution after extensive research of island species. The Lundy cabbage instantly springs to mind as an example of this process at work.

So what is it about islands that generates this human affliction and touches our psyche more deeply? I think the answer is different for each and every one of us. Maybe it's because they are whole, delineated, and fathomable entities – some can even be walked around in a day. Perhaps we also look to places on the periphery for escape, inspiration, and freedom. The values of island life – self-sufficiency, the importance of community and being accountable to each other – also connect us more closely to what it is to be human. And maybe the answer lies in the elemental nature of islands. With the wind blowing through your hair, seabirds swirling above your head, the thick aroma of seaweed and ozone in your nostrils, you feel completely connected with the natural world.

Islands also give us one of the greatest immersions in the wild: a glimpse of what it is to not be human. Each is delineated from the ocean by a unique foreshore, its intertidal zone, the greatest wilderness left on Britain today. Here at the frontier between two worlds, the ocean reveals its secrets twice a day and offers a unique window into life beneath the waves. This is an extraordinary place for us terrestrial beings and the only place where most of us can touch, see, and experience underwater creatures and landscapes. Arguably, this is where we can feel the greatest connection to the ocean. Certainly this outer edge offers the simple uncluttered horizons that gives us a cognitive break and free the mind from the information overload of our daily lives. Research has long found that humans are pulled towards Mother Nature's blue for, in part, its restorative benefits. It comes as no surprise that islands are used as spiritual retreats – Holy Island off Arran, Lindisfarne, and Iona are some of the best. Their seascapes invoke a feeling of awe, a sense of the vastness of nature and the power of the oceans – so much greater than anything else on earth.

A walk around our islands is a celebration of our human history. You'll find ancient stone circles, abandoned villages, atmospheric ruins, and tales of mythical and legendary characters. The darker side is also in evidence with fortifications and strongholds, bloody battles, and sites where society separated the diseased and immoral. There are the secretive military places that few can access, like Foulness and Thorney, as well as the exclusive islands – places of sanctuary for people and wildlife alike.

Today's island inhabitants create colourful and vibrant communities that collectively celebrate their traditions, local food, and a life chiselled out by the powerful forces of nature. Their beat seems stronger the further they are from the mainland. Community life on islands such as Papa Westray, can be the height of self-sufficient fun. They are places of leisure and learning as well as places of adventure and physical challenge. Many have races, competitions, and festivals – some of which are downright bizarre.

Yet the islands of Britain are not just a celebration of people. They are a showcase of the most magnificent and diverse landscapes and extraordinary wildlife there is to be had anywhere in the world. They are conservation frontiers, hotspots of evolution and biodiversity, home to rare species, and rest stops for migrating birds. They are primal and elemental and may contain an explosion of life that is so often not seen on the mainland.

There is one thing you can be sure of in visiting the islands in this book. No two are the same. The essence of an island lies in its difference and self-sufficiency, and the sea in-between defines this. What may look like a rock in the distance cannot be judged from the mainland. You won't know its secrets until you have arrived and rolled up your sleeves to discover them.

To an islandeer every island is a treasure island.

IN SEARCH OF ADVENTURE

One of my earliest memories of adventure was being stranded on Asparagus Island in Cornwall. I was 12 years old and, as far as my parents were concerned, our family holiday at the seaside had taken a turn for the worse when the incoming tide threatened to cut us off from the mainland. But I remember being delighted with the idea of exploring my very own lump of rock, surrounded by sea with the remaining picnic to sustain us. What more could a girl of 12 really want?

With my appetite now seriously whetted for outdoor adventure, I grew up seeking challenge on some of the more distant mountain peaks and islands of the world. Then one summer, after sea kayaking around the Isles of Scilly for a week, I realised that I had returned in spirit to where my adventures had begun – a British island. Not only that, there were hundreds more islands to explore and they were all, relatively speaking, on my doorstep.

Much like climbing a mountain, where there is a real start and finish and rarely any point in aiming to go only halfway up, I discovered I felt exactly the same about islands. I wanted to get around their outside edge, to complete a circle, to know the place as a whole. And on the way I hoped to learn a few more things about myself as I experienced new terrains and needed different skills to complete my journey. My obsession fuelled, I soon had 130 island circumnavigations under my belt – achieved on foot, and by kayak, bike, and swimming.

I hope you get as much from the islands as I have, enjoying the freedom they offer as well as the sense that you are leaving the ordinary behind. I also hope you experience their different horizons, the warmth of their communities, and the excitement of getting to the islands and then around their perimeters. Some of these routes are challenging and not a straightforward walk. You will need to navigate geos and bogs, cross streams, and scramble up rocks, but in the words of Charles Darwin, 'Attitude is the difference between an ordeal and an adventure'. If you are looking for adventure, these islands will definitely deliver. Enjoy discovering more about the unique constellation of islands that lie off our shores and about the wild creatures and plants that share them. These are very special environments and they need our love and attention more than ever.

LISA DREWE

Eriskay p254

WHALE & DOLPHIN CONSERVATION

On my trip aboard the Scillonian III, the captain announced that a large pod of dolphins was surfing our wake. He might as well have shouted 'Abandon ship!' because each man, woman, and child dropped everything except their phones and cameras, and rushed to the rear of the boat to watch the spectacle. Islands are fantastic places to see whales and dolphins, whether from the boat out or from their cliff tops.

These air-breathing mammals, which straddle the terrestrial and oceanic worlds, arouse a sense of wonder. Yet things are changing rapidly for them as human activity takes its toll. None of this is intentional – with the exception of whaling – but is due to a lack of awareness and action. Scientific research continually provides new facts and figures about these wonderful creatures and our generation now has an opportunity to put things right. We can aim to restore their numbers to pre-industrial levels as well as improve their quality of life.

Whale and Dolphin Conservation (WDC) is the global charity at the forefront of this work. It campaigns to stop whaling and hunting, to end keeping whales and dolphins in captivity, and also to stop them getting caught unintentionally in nets. WDC are leading the global debate to understand and improve the oceanic environment for cetaceans and are pioneers in talking of them as sentient animals with a language and culture, and as having huge educational, emotional, environmental and economic value that deserves a greater regard from policymakers and commerce.

I feel beyond privileged to work with WDC as the chair of trustees and to play a part in the considerable impact worldwide this organisation has on protecting cetaceans and their oceanic environment. I am donating 10% of my profits from this book to WDC. I know they will spend it wisely and do the right thing to bring about their vision of 'a world where every whale and dolphin is safe and free'.

I have had some incredible whale and dolphin encounters on my journey around the islands of Britain and hope you will be as fortunate when you undertake your own explorations. Enjoy this gift from nature and thank you for buying the book and supporting something very special.

Learn more about WDC at www.whales.org.

FIVE WAYS TO STAY SAFE

1 Always check the weather. Fog can be problematic on the free-range routes, rain can make rocky foreshores slippery, higher waves (even at low tide) can make a route unsafe, and wind speed and direction can make clifftop walks more challenging.

2 Always check the tide times and depth. If you miss the low tide period do not attempt to cross when an incoming tide has covered or is about to cover your route. In a serious situation call the coastguard. If you have suitable clothing and shelter and it is safe, wait 6–9 hours (it may be less) until the next safe crossing.

3 Cross to an island when the tide is ebbing (going out). That said, there are a few instances where we recommend crossing on a rising tide to give you more time on the island – but be sure you know your timings.

4 Always let someone know where you are going, which route you are taking, and your expected return time. If you do have a problem and you have intermittent mobile reception or a low battery, you might be able to use the Emergency SMS service. It's important that you register your phone first: text 'register' to 999 and follow instructions on the reply www.emergencysms.org.uk.

5 Last but not least, always take a suitable map and compass with you, and a GPS for the more challenging routes.

ADVANCE PLANNING

TIDES: Many of the islands in this book are accessed via causeways, bridges or beaches that are safe to cross only at lower tides. Some of the routes also cross tidal sections, so ensure you are competent at reading tide timetables when planning your walk. These are available online at www.bbc.co.uk/weather/coast_and_sea/tide_tables. Tables can also be purchased for individual locations (www.tide-times.org.uk/all) detailing the tides for the whole year.

The tide tables use UTC (Universal Coordinated Time), which is the same as GMT (Greenwich Mean Time). In the UK, during British Summer Time, you may need to add one hour to the time stated for low water. Some tables do this automatically but others, such as BBC tide timetables, don't. Always check first.

When you are looking for the times of low tide, your window of opportunity for crossing to an island or navigating around some foreshores will depend on a number of factors. Spring tides, during the full and new moon phase, lead to the lowest of low tides (when the tide goes out further) and the highest of high tides (when the tide comes further up the beach or rocks). Neap tides, on the other hand, when the moon is at first or third quarter, lead to low tides that are higher than average, and high tides that are lower. Unusually high- or low-pressure systems, or prolonged periods of strong winds and larger swells, can also mean an incoming tide reaches you before predicted.

The most important thing to remember is that the depth of the low tide is not the same every day and the height, in addition to the time, needs to be checked. For some islands, the causeway can remain underwater even at low tide for most of a lunar month and the water level will drop to reveal the crossing only on spring low tides.

TIDAL FLOWS & RIP CURRENTS: If you are planning to swim across to islands or to jump in the sea, do be aware of the tidal flows and rip currents in that area. Generally, tidal flows are at their slackest at either high or low water. At mid-tide the flow is at its fastest. That said, topographic features will also have an effect. For example, tidal flows will be faster through narrow or shallow stretches and around coastal headlands.

Rip currents are slightly different. These are strong, narrow flows of water that move away from the beach and into the ocean as a result of local wave action. They can flow quickly, are unpredictable, and depend on the shape of the coastline. If you are unsure always seek local guidance.

WEATHER: The main thing to remember is that once you leave the mainland and head out to sea the weather generally gets breezier and cooler. Always look at the forecast but bear in mind that things can change more rapidly on an island and the weather can be very different between the leeward and seaward coasts.

Fog is the biggest challenge, particularly if you are on an island with a limited coastal path and you are relying on your navigation skills to circumnavigate, or if you are attempting one of the longer sand crossings. Always check the forecast before you head out. BBC Weather (www.bbc.co.uk/weather), Magicseaweed (www.magicseaweed.com) and XCWeather (www.xcweather.co.uk) are all good sources.

TIMING: Good timing is everything on islands, both to maximise your access period and get the most out of your visit. Here are a few tips:

WILDLIFE Many islands are blessed with some amazing birdlife but access can be restricted so always check before you go. If you hit key nesting time it can also be noisy, smelly, and painful. If you are intending to visit specifically to see wildlife then check out when the cetaceans or birds migrate to maximise your chances.

FERRY TIMINGS A number of islands have a regular ferry service only from Easter to September. Always check beforehand.

CALM SEAS If, like me, you have a delicate constitution, a rough crossing can create havoc. Check the forecast first. Many commercial ferries in Scotland and to the Isles of Scilly operate in all but the most extreme weather conditions and you may prefer not to be on them.

TOURIST SEASON & FESTIVALS If your island is a popular tourist destination there will be upsides and downsides. The upside is that everything will be open; the downside is needing to book well ahead. If the island is hosting an event, the facilities may be very overstretched.

GETTING TO THE ISLANDS: Getting to the islands is a big part of the adventure. To get to the departure points from the mainland I have used public transport as much as possible, and the car when tides and timings require it. Public transport options are listed, but it is always worth checking further to see what is available. Once at the departure point there are various options for travelling to the island:

CAUSEWAYS Many of these are tidal and safe crossing times are listed for the relevant island.

SAND CROSSINGS A few of the islands have short or long crossings of tidal sands, some of which are quicksand and where guides and local knowledge are essential to a safe passage.

FERRIES & BOATS The longer crossings to and between the islands of the Inner and Outer Hebrides, Orkney, and the Channel Islands are operated by CalMac (www.calmac.co.uk), Orkney (www.orkney-ferries.co.uk), and Condor Ferries (www.condorferries.co.uk) respectively. The Scillonian III to St Mary's is a legend. Other islands requiring boats use local ferries: details are included under each listing.

FLYING Sometimes, when the sea is very rough, flying is the only option to get to far-flung places. The Outer Hebrides, Orkney, Channel Islands, and Isles of Scilly have very small airports for very small planes, affectionately known as flying Land Rovers. The landings on beaches, small airstrips, and cliff tops are a lot of fun. It is also possible to get a certificate on the world's shortest scheduled flight, between Westray and Papa Westray.

KAYAKING For those competent at calculating and negotiating tides and flows, many of the islands can be reached by sea kayak. Coupled with a wild camp, this makes for a great islandeering experience.

SWIMMING For shorter crossings, this is the best way to arrive on an island.

MIDGES & TICKS In Scotland, midges appear from the beginning of June, reach a peak in July and August, and then disappear in mid-September. I have found the best repellent is Avon 'Skin So Soft' when I am walking. There are numerous repellents on the market, with most stores selling 'Smidge'. Ticks can be problematic in areas with high numbers of sheep and deer. They are picked up by walking through longer grass and bracken but can be largely avoided by wearing long sleeves and trousers. They are difficult to spot initially, but if you think you have walked through an infected area always check their target areas – armpits, groin, and just above the top of your socks. They are easy to dislodge with a specialist tick remover that can be bought from outdoor shops and many local outlets. Ticks can carry Lyme disease, which can become serious if left untreated. If you suspect infection see a doctor immediately.

Kerrera p220

HOW TO USE THIS GUIDE

DIRECTIONS: The route description gives enough detail to walk around the island and find the points of interest and is supported by an overview map. However, it is important to research each route fully using the online resource at islandeering.com. Here, you will find the latitude/longitude coordinates of the starting point, the detailed route descriptions, OS maps and downloadable GPX files. Many of these walks use free-range routes that follow animal tracks or require route plotting over the terrain. We always recommend that you plot your route on the relevant OS Explorer 1:25,000 map and take it with you on the walk along with a compass and, for the more challenging walks, a GPS.

ABBREVIATIONS: N, NE, E, SE, S, SW, W, NW refer to the points on the compass. Left (L) and right (R) relate to the turns from the walk.

TIMINGS: The timings used are those of a moderate pace (2.5–3 miles per hour or 4–5 kilometres per hour) with no stops. Do build in extra time to take in optional excursions and the points of interest of the island.

GRADING: The walks are graded 1–5 for difficulty of terrain, navigation, and access. Walks graded 5 are the most challenging.

GRADE	DIFFICULTY OF TERRAIN	NAVIGATION	ACCESS
1	Footpaths that are mostly on good surfaces	Well-marked routes	Non-tidal causeway or bridge
2	Rougher ground and animal tracks or beach crossings	Paths with limited signage	Public ferry
3	Rougher ground and animal tracks or beach crossings with stretches of boggy or muddy ground	Mix of unmarked paths and free-range routes	Short tidal causeway
4	Any terrain that includes rocky sections	Mostly free-range but in a landscape that is easy to read	Tidal crossing with a wait on the island during high tide required to do the walk; or long, committed tidal crossing
5	Rocky foreshores or scrambles on cliffs that require use of hands (and feet). Quicksand in the area	Mostly free-range requiring navigation with a map and compass. Possibly taking bearings to cross featureless ground or avoid geographic features	Swim or kayak/boat required to reach the island

Eriskay p254

WHAT TO TAKE

MAP, COMPASS, GPS, PHONE Many of the routes will require good navigational skills in the absence of an official coastal route. The same rules would apply if you were walking in the mountains. Visibility can disappear quickly and some routes are harder to find

WATER AND FOOD Make sure you have enough or check that you can replenish your stores on the island

WATERPROOF/WINDPROOF SHELL I can't think of many islands that haven't been at least a bit windy. Waterproofs and Scotland? Say no more

WARM LAYERS Including hats and gloves if necessary. You'll be spending most of the day out at sea where it is generally cooler. Bring an extra layer for the ferry trips, which can be quite breezy too

FOOTWEAR Trail shoes, walking boots, or beach shoes for mud and water crossings or a mix if there is variable terrain

SUNSCREEN, SUNGLASSES, SUNHAT It's easy to get burnt when the wind is blowing

TIDE & FERRY TIMETABLES Don't rely on being able to find out this information on the island or getting a good enough signal to Google it when you are there. Be safe. Take the timings along with you just in case

SWIMWEAR & SARONG Or something else to dry yourself and double as a picnic rug

FOR THE MORE ADVENTUROUS Take a wetsuit for swimming longer distances, dry bags, swimming goggles, wetsuit boots, and waterproof camera

St Agnes p32

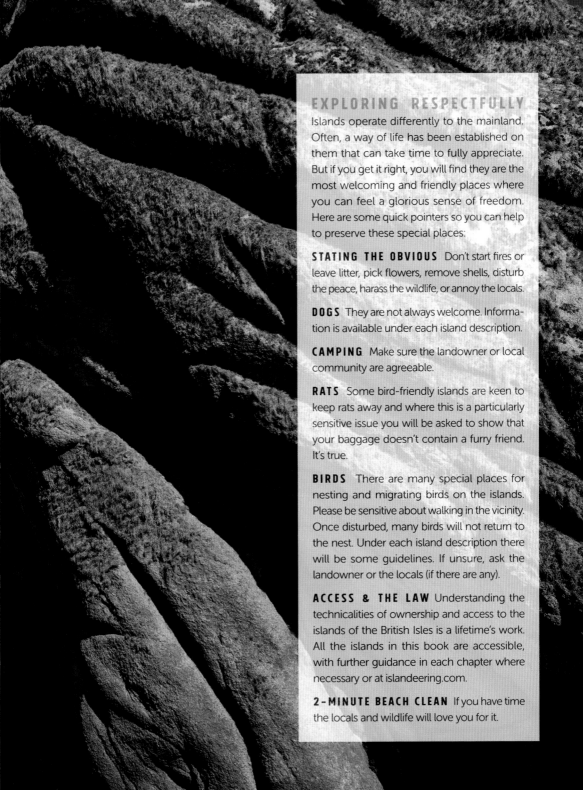

EXPLORING RESPECTFULLY

Islands operate differently to the mainland. Often, a way of life has been established on them that can take time to fully appreciate. But if you get it right, you will find they are the most welcoming and friendly places where you can feel a glorious sense of freedom. Here are some quick pointers so you can help to preserve these special places:

STATING THE OBVIOUS Don't start fires or leave litter, pick flowers, remove shells, disturb the peace, harass the wildlife, or annoy the locals.

DOGS They are not always welcome. Information is available under each island description.

CAMPING Make sure the landowner or local community are agreeable.

RATS Some bird-friendly islands are keen to keep rats away and where this is a particularly sensitive issue you will be asked to show that your baggage doesn't contain a furry friend. It's true.

BIRDS There are many special places for nesting and migrating birds on the islands. Please be sensitive about walking in the vicinity. Once disturbed, many birds will not return to the nest. Under each island description there will be some guidelines. If unsure, ask the landowner or the locals (if there are any).

ACCESS & THE LAW Understanding the technicalities of ownership and access to the islands of the British Isles is a lifetime's work. All the islands in this book are accessible, with further guidance in each chapter where necessary or at islandeering.com.

2-MINUTE BEACH CLEAN If you have time the locals and wildlife will love you for it.

Ynys Lochtan p168

Best for

EXPLORING CAVES, GULLIES, GEOS & STACKS

ADVENTURE UNDER, AROUND, AND ABOVE RUGGED COASTLINES

EPIC TIDAL CROSSINGS

RACE THE TIDE ACROSS VAST SANDS AND ROCKY CAUSEWAYS

TRAIL RUNNING

ISLAND CIRCUITS TO GET THE HEART PUMPING

Vallay p260

Best for

GLORIOUS BEACHES

WILD, SANDY BEACHES THAT YOU WON'T HAVE TO SHARE WITH TOO MANY OTHERS

FAMILIES

EASY ACCESS FOR KIDS AND MOSTLY FLAT ROUTES

CONTEMPLATION & RETREAT

PLACES OF PILGRIMAGE AND SPIRITUAL RETREAT

Sark p86

SKINNY-DIPS & SECLUDED SWIMS

STUNNING SWIMS IN REMOTE LOCATIONS

SPOTTING WHALES & DOLPHINS

WITH LUCK, YOU CAN WATCH THEM FROM THE SHORE

BIRDS, WILD CREATURES & FLOWERS

SPECIAL ENVIRONMENTS FOR NATURE

Great Bernera p276

RUINS & ANCIENT REMAINS

FROM SECRET MILITARY BUNKERS TO CASTLES AND STONE CIRCLES

WILD & REMOTE

FOR A TRUE WILDERNESS EXPERIENCE

CAFÉS, LOCAL FOOD & INNS

WELCOMING PLACES WITH TASTY BITES

ST AGNES

AN ISLAND TRILOGY ON BRITAIN'S WESTERN EDGE WITH TWO TIDAL CROSSINGS, ASTONISHING NATURAL ROCK FORMATIONS AND A FEELING OF COMPLETE PEACE

Swinging gently between two boulders on the campsite beach, in a hammock made of discarded fishing net and looking out to Bishop's Rock Lighthouse, the peace was absolute. With scoops of delicious Troytown Farm ice cream waiting just up the lane, the only real distraction was deciding which flavour to try next.

The most westerly of the inhabited Isles of Scilly, St Agnes stands on its own with an 'outer-edge' feel that will inspire adventurers. The abundance of natural rock formations around the heavily indented shoreline, the offshore islets and sublime beaches make an irresistible combination.

The route around St Agnes is on a reasonably flat coastal path that crosses some spectacular rock 'gardens'. Along the way there are optional spurs out to the various headlands to experience the full effects of the wild Atlantic that shaped these western shores. With the right tide it's possible to cross the sandbar to Gugh for a 4-kilometre free-range circular route of this island, as well as walk across the uneven boulders to Burnt Island.

There are a number of notable features on this walk. The most obvious is the squat light-house, visible from any point on the island. One of Britain's earliest lights – its lamp originally a coal fire burning in an open casket – it is also the site of the island's big murder mystery. Two squab-bling keepers tended the light but one disappeared without explanation overnight. Identified only by his teeth, the keeper was found forty years later buried a metre beneath the foundations of the adjoining buildings. The lighthouse is now a holiday home and no doubt has a ghost story or two to tell.

Immediately after the start of the walk, it's well worth making the crossing to the tiny island of

---

TERRAIN: Mostly easy coastal paths; free-range paths on Gugh, rock-hopping on Burnt Island

STARTING POINT: St Agnes Quay. Lat/Long 49.8960, -6.3401; SV 884 085

DISTANCE: 7.7km (ascent 324m); (4km Gugh)

TIME: 3 hours (St Agnes & Burnt Island); 1 hour (Gugh)

OS MAP: OS Explorer 101

DIFFICULTY: 2

NAVIGATION: 2

ACCESS: 2 (3 for crossing to Gugh and Burnt Island)

DON'T MISS:
- Exploring the incredible rock formations
- Swimming and snorkelling in The Cove
- Feeling the deep white sand between your toes on The Bar
- Sunset on some of Britain's most westerly beaches
- Indulging in Troytown Farm ice cream

GETTING THERE: Boats in season from St Mary's. Check St Mary's Boatmen's Association boards at the quay on St Mary's or their Facebook page for daily sailings.

FACILITIES: Food: Turk's Head; Covean Cottage Café, Higher Town; Coastguard's Café and High Tide Seafood Restaurant, Middle Town. Dairy products at Troytown farm shop; groceries at St Agnes Post Office store. Public toilets at New Quay.

The only holy well on Scilly can be found on the western shore above St Warna's Cove. The role of this saint (possibly female), who arrived by coracle from Ireland, was to direct ships away from the rocks. Occasionally, during hard times, islanders made offerings at the well in the hope that her protection would fail and the goods from wrecked ships might come their way.

Further along the west coast, through the ancient stone enclosures and around Long Point, the medieval turf and stone Troy Town Maze is a great spot for a full-moon foray. With no dead ends it is impossible to get lost.

Just inland from the maze, the Nag's Head is one of the island's most remarkable natural rock formations. Take a short detour to see this ancient granite stone, shaped like a horse's head and standing proud at 4.6 metres. After the Maze, enjoy a rest stop at the campsite beach with its idyllically sited hammock, and take in incredible views of the bird-sanctuary island of Annet, the 'broken' islands of Hellweathers, and the Western Rocks. Beyond lie thousands of miles of uninterrupted Atlantic.

Gugh for the fabulous views back across the crystal-clear waters to Porth Conger and St Agnes. You can also see the other islands to the east. There is a faint path around the island up to the highest point on Kittern Hill and past the impressive standing stone, The Old Man of Gugh, and Obadiah's Barrow. The landscape around the Old Man is littered with prehistoric entrance graves, cairns and hut circles. The beaches on St Agnes feel busy in comparison with Gugh, where you might not see another soul.

Once back on St Agnes, the route continues around The Cove where deep white sands give way to an underwater boulder field. This is a perfect place to snorkel and explore the rich marine life. Walking south, the wild, boulder-strewn landscape of Wingletang Down has Bronze Age cairns, characterful granite sculptures and is home to two rare plants, the orange bird's-foot and least adder's-tongue. Crossing the boulders at the top of Wingletang Bay there are views out to the jaws of Western Rocks where a Venetian ship was wrecked in the 17th Century. The beach, known as Beady Pool, was once a good place to find ceramic beads washed ashore from the ship's cargo.

At the campsite, a short diversion to sample the delights of Troytown Farm is a must. Probably the smallest dairy farm in the country, it punches way above its weight. Along with butter, clotted cream and scrumptious yoghurt, it sells the most delicious ice cream with flavours including rose geranium, banana Baileys, chocolate, and cherry sorbet. You might need more than one for the journey to Periglis in the north of the island. The sandy beach here, the most westerly in Britain and protected by the Western Rocks, is a wonderful place for a safe swim. At low tide it is possible to cross over to tiny, uninhabited Burnt Island, which has a surviving Bronze Age platform cairn.

Back at New Quay, the starting point, the excellent Turk's Head pub is the best place to sit and enjoy the view over to Gugh's sparkling white sand. If you are lucky you may spot the rare storm petrels that have recently returned to Scilly following a programme to eradicate rats, their main predators. These sparrow-sized birds – the world's smallest seabirds – nest in the cracks in the rocks beneath the pub. After this three-island trip there may still be time to explore the narrow lanes of Lower, Middle and Higher Town. Here you'll find a couple of cafés, a shop, and the charming stone cottages that huddle inland, away from the strong westerlies.

DIRECTIONS

》 For a clockwise route, start at New Quay (1) and walk past the Turk's Head. To visit Gugh, take the sandy path 200m beyond the pub and cross the sand bar (2), accessible for 3 hours before and after high tide. On Gugh, turn L and follow the faint coast path to the N end of the island, taking the detour to Obadiah's Barrow (3). Continue around Kittern Rock, passing the Old Man of Gugh (4), on the way to Dropnose Point. Follow the path past Hoe Point at the island's S tip then head back to The Bar.

》 Cross over to St Agnes, turn L and through trees above the shore, then after 540m drop down to The Cove (5). At the far end of the beach, climb

the stone steps and go over the stile, continuing on the path through the heathland and across the boulder field at the top of Wingletang Bay.

》 Head S to Horse Point then return to the main path and on to Porth Askin. Pass through the first set of stone enclosures and over a stone gate to pass St Warna's Well (6). Cross a number of stiles, gates and boulder fields, stopping to admire Nag's Head (7) on the way, and around 1km later reach the maze (8).

》 At the campsite, pass through the gates at either end of the camping field, or detour R, taking the track to Troytown Farm (9) for ice cream. Pass

the campsite shower block to find the track towards the church. Turn L at the surfaced lane towards Burnt Island (10) to cross the causeway at low tide, then keep to L side of the main rock outcrop.

》 Return the same way and continue on the coast path, keeping to L of the lake and walk round it or follow the stone wall on the R around the N tip of the island. Cross the stile and follow the track to the R side of the large stone wall, passing Kallimay Point and back to the quay. If time permits, follow the island lanes to explore the lighthouse (11).

SAMSON

IDYLLIC AND UNINHABITED, THIS TINY ISLAND HAS WHITE SANDS, CLEAR BLUE SEA, BIRDS, FLOWERS, AND 8,000 YEARS OF LIVING HISTORY

Stepping off the RIB into the sparkling, clear waters around Samson, I waded onto the deserted white beach, the engine noise of the ferry fading as it disappeared towards Bryher. A welcoming party of wild flowers nodded in the gentle breeze while the querulous cries of black-headed gulls sounded above.

After the bustle of St Mary's quay and negotiating the return pick-up time with the boatmen, a sense of peace enveloped me. The urge to just lie on the sands at Bar Point and listen to the gentle waves lap the shore would tempt even the strongest-willed, but the intrepid islandeer will press on to experience a fabulous trip. The free-range coastal route is mostly a scramble along the rocks of the foreshore combined with gentle strolls along the island's idyllic beaches.

Samson, Scilly's largest uninhabited island, is managed by the Isles of Scilly Wildlife Trust and justly celebrated for its rich array of nesting seabirds and wild flora. It is also is stacked with ancient ruins that bear witness to human activity dating back to Neolithic times. The island's two high points, North and South Hill, are joined by a sandy isthmus and accessed via paths that criss-cross the island. On both hills the stone chambers and alignments remain mysterious, even to the experts, and they continue to inspire the imaginations of those who take the time to explore.

A short climb up North Hill reveals a Bronze Age stone burial chamber – one of the best preserved on Scilly. This vantage point also offers a bird's-eye view of the Samson Flats where, at low tide, the Bronze Age field systems are still visible. At that time, when the sea level was much lower, the current

---

TERRAIN: Rocky foreshore and sandy paths

STARTING POINT: Bar Point, Samson. Lat/Long 49.9372, -6.3494, SV 880 131

DISTANCE: 3.8km (ascent 130m)

TIME: 1 hour 30 mins (plus time for exploring the rest of the island)

MAP: OS Explorer 101

DIFFICULTY: 2

NAVIGATION: 3

ACCESS: 2

DON'T MISS:
- Wild swimming at Bar Point
- Exploring the ruins of Neolithic sites
- Walking up North and South hills for wonderful views

GETTING THERE: Boat from St Mary's. Check the St Mary's Boatmen's Association boards at the quay on St Mary's or their Facebook page.

FACILITIES: No facilities. Take all food and water.

SPECIAL NOTES: No quay: visitors disembark the passenger boat by walking down a plank or by transferring to a small RIB. Do not attempt this coastal circuit at particularly high tides or in bigger swells and be aware that there is limited access to the foreshore from April to September when seabirds are breeding. Seals are also starting to pup here from August to December and shouldn't be disturbed.

ocean floor was cultivated land and the islands in the archipelago were the high ground of one large land mass called Ennor.

An ascent of South Hill reveals more prehistoric graves along with the ruined cottages of the last inhabitants. Although up to 40 people once lived here, the last two surviving families were known to have suffered from malnutrition before being moved to a neighbouring island by their landlord. This wasn't an act of kindness; he wanted to build a private deer park and you can still see its walls. But even the deer found life here too tough and swam to Tresco where the grass was definitely greener. Sitting by the fireplace of one of the cottages to eat my staple island lunch of oaty biscuits and cheese, I did feel slightly guilty about the unappetising diet of limpet and potato available to its previous inhabitants.

Between the two hills, the sandy paths at the isthmus weave through beautiful wildflower 'gardens'. Take time to visit the ruins and beaches of East and West Porth and stop by the boatsheds of the fishermen who once lived here. Although the island's past inhabitants seem forever present, Samson has returned to a peaceful wildness. This is a place for quiet exploration where you can soak up the unique, haunting atmosphere. Now for that chill-out on the beach.

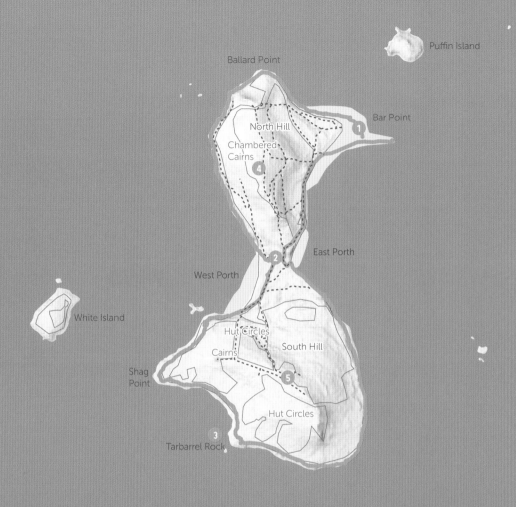

Puffin Island

Ballard Point

North Hill

Chambered Cairns

Bar Point

1

4

East Porth

2

West Porth

White Island

Hut Circles

South Hill

Cairns

Shag Point

5

Hut Circles

3

Tarbarrel Rock

DIRECTIONS

» For the free-range coastal route, start at Bar Point (1), the main landing beach. Head S on the beach for about 400m, find the footpath on the bank and reach the neck of the island and the ruins (2) between East and West Porth. Drop down onto the foreshore and rock-hop along the high water mark to reach the S tip of Samson, after 1.4km. Just after Tarbarrel Rock (3) leave the foreshore for the faint path along the grassy bank and round Shag Point before returning to the foreshore at West Porth. Follow the rocky foreshore to reach Samson's N tip with views across to Bryher. Walk around Ballard Point to return to Bar Point. The various inland walks to the ancient burial sites of North Hill (4) and South Hill, along with the ruined buildings (5), are illustrated on the Isles of Scilly Wildlife Trust's information board a short walk inland from Bar Point.

BRYHER

FIND ADVENTURE ON THE 'LAND OF THE HILLS' WITH CHASMS AND CAVES TO EXPLORE, EXTRAORDINARY HILLTOP VIEWS AND EXCELLENT LUNCH STOPS

On this island of dramatic contrasts, thundering Atlantic rollers pound the northern tip and the jagged coves of the west coast, while the south boasts wonderful sandy beaches. The tranquil east is full of character and the place to eat delicious island food. This coastal walk is thrilling enough, but for the adventurous there is the added excitement of scrambling or swimming through the tidal chasm onto Shipman Head, as well as exploring the longest cave in Scilly on the fearsome west coast.

This is an anti-clockwise walk that explores the hugely diverse coastline of Bryher and, although unmarked, the free-range path is easy to follow. You might be tempted, as I was, to make the expedition a little more challenging by stopping at the first island stall selling fresh produce. I completed the route carrying a plant, a bag of narcissus bulbs, a pot of freshly landed crab meat, and a bag of Veronica Farm Fudge!

This smallest of the inhabited Isles of Scilly was formed when the Atlantic Ocean rose by a few metres and Bryher and Tresco became separate islands. Today it is still possible to walk from Tresco to Bryher on a very low spring tide across the exposed ocean floor. It can certainly make for an adventurous start to the walk.

From Church Quay a peaceful path works its way north along Bryher's east coast, passing what were once bulb fields and the quaint cottages and gardens of The Town above. Bryher Boatyard, crammed with fishing nets, lobster pots and boat hulls, is an alternative starting point if you have arrived at the newer (Anneka) quay at Bar.

Within a few minutes, you reach the wonderfully situated Fraggle Rock Bar and Café, which is

---

TERRAIN: Paths of mixed grass and rock.

STARTING POINT: Church Quay, Bryher. Lat/Long 49.9528, -6.3496. SV 88111 14915

DISTANCE: 8.2km (ascent: 181m)

TIME: 2 hours

MAP: OS Explorer 101

DIFFICULTY: 2

NAVIGATION: 2

ACCESS: 2 (or 3 if crossing by foot from Tresco)

DON'T MISS:
- Watching Atlantic rollers thunder into Hell Bay
- Swimming the gully of Shipman Head
- Exploring the longest cave in Scilly
- Floating in the gentle waters of Rushy Bay
- Picking up home-made goodies at honesty-box stalls

GETTING THERE: Ferry from St Mary's or Tresco; for low-tide crossing from Tresco check tide times www.tresco.co.uk/enjoying/events/walking-tides.

FACILITIES: Food shops and café in The Town; Fraggle Rock Bar and Café on NE coast; Hell Bay Hotel on W coast. Public toilets behind Church Quay.

SPECIAL NOTES: Access to Shipman Head and to cave is dependent on tide and swell.

a great place to eat, especially if you like seafood. Close by, the small, sandy bay at the narrowest point of the Tresco Channel is a very sheltered spot and a favourite anchorage for visiting yachts. From here there are views to Hangman's Island and to Cromwell and King Charles's castles on Tresco.

Towards the north end of the island the landscape changes and bursts of purple heather and yellow gorse provide a colourful backdrop for exploring the prehistoric cairns that sprinkle the heathland. This atmospheric location is one of the largest Bronze Age burial sites in northwest Europe. From here, ancient settlers believed their dead ancestors could keep watch over the living.

Once you arrive at the northernmost tip of Bryher, the adventure begins. When swells are low, the steep-walled gully that cuts off Shipman Head is a thrilling place to jump or swim for the more experienced. At lower tides a large boulder protects its western end from the breaking waves, creating a spa-like bubble bath – although with no swell the water can also be quite still. You can also explore the large kelp bed at the eastern end of the gully.

Shipman Head itself can be accessed on foot at low tide for a short time via the jumble of rocks at the western end of the gully. It is an important nesting site for birds and access is restricted until the end of August. If it is not possible to pass the gully, it is still well worth dropping down to the rock platform above it to view the water surging through. Do take care on the steep descent; the rocks can be slippery.

Turning down the west coast the scenery gets ever more dramatic. Here the rugged coastline is exposed to the full power of the Atlantic and on a blustery day huge waves break over the tops of the tall granite rocks, the immense power dissipated into a foaming cauldron of spume. This is Hell Bay and the roar of the waves can be heard on the opposite side of the island.

Halfway down the west coast, the cliffs just north of Great High Rock are pierced by the longest cave in Scilly. With an entrance just 1 metre wide and nine metres high, it tempts you to explore further. But this is not a trip for the faint-hearted: access is via the rocks at the base of the cliffs but only on a low tide with a minimum westerly swell. For the adventurous, it is possible to access the cave by climbing the large boulder that obscures the entrance.

Further south you reach Great Pool above the protected cove of Popplestone Neck. This inland pool was formed following peat excavations and its calm, brackish waters are now home to a variety of waterfowl. You may be lucky enough to spot a rare migrant bird here, such as the large glossy ibis.

The route then takes in the two westerly points of Gweal Hill and Heathy Hill, both with easy scrambling, ancient cairns and fabulous views of the jagged Norrard Rocks and the untamed Atlantic. Just east of Droopy Nose Point's characteristic stack of rocks, a group of big boulders mark the site of a 'castle' defence against the Vikings. From here, the walk takes in the lovely, sandy, crescent bay of Stony Porth, which is a popular haul-out spot for seals.

Towards the southeast corner of the island, at the base of Samson Hill, Rushy Bay has fine white sands and is a great place for swimming and finding shells. This sheltered part of the island is also a haven for wild flowers, including the very rare dwarf pansy that grows in the sandy turf behind the beach. You might see plant lovers bending to look for this treasure alongside visitors crouching to create the pebble stacks or 'chortens' that stand sentry here.

Heading back north along the east coast, the tranquil track leads back to Church Quay. If time permits, take a short detour into The Town to sample some delicious island fare, including fresh seafood at Island Fish. At the well-stocked local shop you'll find great local produce such as the island speciality, tattie cake. Made from potatoes using a secret recipe handed down through the generations, it is not to be missed.

Returning to Church Quay the stained-glass windows of All Saints look even better from the inside. A colourful celebration of life on the island, they depict island scenes, such as the gig rowing out to save a wreck, as well as interpretations by a local artist. After the experience of the walk, you can relate to the images. Many other artists and writers have been inspired by the beauty of Bryher including Michael Morpurgo who set *Why the Whales Came* on the island.

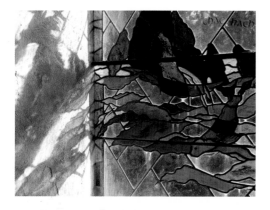

DIRECTIONS

» From Church Quay (1) walk inland, turn R at the public toilets (2) and follow signs to Fraggle Rock Bar and Café (alternatively, to pick up supplies head straight ahead to the church and follow signs to The Town). After 500m, meet the main island track, pass through the boatyard and walk uphill along the surfaced path, bearing R to reach the café and bar (3).

» Sweep L uphill for a short distance before turning R along the track signed Shipman Head. After crossing a stone stile, head uphill on the path through the bracken. Keep to the coast paths unless you wish to explore the prehistoric cairn cemetery (4). From the crest of Shipman Head Down, descend towards Shipman Head, skirting to L of the small hill immediately before the Head itself. At the island's N tip, access the rock platform closest to Shipman Head by continuing round on a narrow, descending path. Approach the steep gully (5) by crossing the rocks on the W side. Return by the same route and head S to climb the first hill along the W coast then down to an eroded cove before walking uphill again. Pass a large, natural wall of granite blocks where Great High Rocks form a cove to the S. For the cave (6) walk a short way down the grass bank to the rocks on the coast (see special notes below).

» Continue S, walking down towards Popplestone Neck and the Hell Bay Hotel (7) and to the right of Great Pool (8). Almost at the end of the lake, take the small grass track R towards the storm wall to walk around Gweal Hill (9). From here, cross the head of Stinking Porth and continue along the main track R of the hotel. After

Shipman Head

King
Charles
Castle

Cromwell's Castle

Hell Bay

4 Cairns

Shipman
Head
Down

Tresco

Great High
Rock

6

3

Fraggle Rock
Café & Bar

Low
Water
Quay

Vine Café

Gweal

Popplestone Neck

Bryher
Shop

Post
Office

9

Gweal
Hill

Great Pool

Quay

8

7

13 **2** **1**

Church

Stinking
Porth

Hell Bay
Hotel

Green
Bay

Merrick
Island

Great
Porth

Tresco Channel

Boatyard

Heathy
Hill

12

Droppy Nose Point

10

Samson Hill

Stony
Porth

11

Rushy Bay

Works Point

Samson

200m, where the track heads L uphill, continue straight ahead towards the artist's studio. Immediately after, take the small path through the bracken and walk the length of Great Porth.

» Take the R fork towards Heathy Hill's summit then around its outer edge to reach Stony Porth. Drop down from a small group of rocks

(10) to walk behind the beach and reach Rushy Bay (11) at the base of Samson Hill (12). Walk alongside the trees, continuing on the wider path around Works Point, then N up the Tresco Channel and after 400m reach a bigger track leading to a house.

» Turn R and keep to the main track, past the entrance to the boatyard. Pass Veronica Farm Fudge and after 100m where the main track bears L, take the smaller track R uphill to join the main island road. Just after the fire station turn R at the crossroads past the church (13) and then round to the R to return to the quay.

ST MARTIN'S

WALK A SWEEPING SHORELINE STRUNG WITH AWARD-WINNING BEACHES, ROCK POOLS AND SECLUDED SWIMMING SPOTS, STOPPING OFF FOR FABULOUS FOOD

On St Martin's there is definitely a sense of being on the edge of the archipelago. An island with a strong sense of community, it is full of hardy locals with a strong entrepreneurial spirit who make the most of what the land and sea provide. Taking in some spectacular scenery, this route is also a culinary and horticultural tour of the island. Place names such as Bread and Cheese Cove, Brandy Point, and Wine Cove whet the appetite for what's to come.

This is one of the longer walks on Scilly with sensational views throughout – either across to the rest of the archipelago or east to Land's End on the Cornish mainland. The coastal path weaves together vastly contrasting seascapes, creating one gem of a route for the islandeer, with the added attraction of exploring the uninhabited, tidal White Island.

St Martin's is a long narrow island, its coast fringed with spectacular white beaches and clear turquoise water. A small lane connects the island's two quays and the three charming settlements, aptly named Lower Town, Middle Town, and Higher Town. On the sheltered south-facing slopes narrow strip fields display colourful flowers, vegetables, and vines, in sharp contrast to the wild heathland areas of Chapel Down and White Island.

Starting at Lower Town Quay on the west coast, the route takes in great views of the uninhabited island of Tean, then the scenery becomes wilder as you approach Pernagie Point to the north. At low tide, the other-worldly landscape of granite strands holds vast and colourful rock pools that offer rare windows into the world beneath the waves.

Further around the headland, the extraordinary rocky foreshore continues across to White Island

---

TERRAIN: Undulating path; some rocky foreshore crossing to White Island.

STARTING POINT: Lower Town quay. Lat/Long 49.9658 -6.3040; GR SV 914 161

DISTANCE: 14.2km (ascent: 336m)

TIME: 3.5 hours (plus 45 mins for White Island)

MAP: OS Explorer 101

DIFFICULTY: 2

NAVIGATION: 2

ACCESS: 2

DON'T MISS:
- Swimming at St Martin's Bay, voted Britain's best beach
- Amazing hilltop views from the curious striped daymark
- Atmospheric ancient ruins on tidal White Island
- Local fish and chips and Island Bakery goodies
- Drinks on the Seven Stones terrace – the best pub view in the country

GETTING THERE: Boat from St Mary's in season. Check the St Mary's Boatmen's Association boards at the quay on St Mary's or their Facebook page for daily sailings.

FACILITIES: Restaurants, bakeries, Seven Stones Inn, and a well-stocked shop; honesty-box fruit, vegetable and cake stalls. Toilets at Higher Town.

at low tide. Crossing its boulder-strewn causeway feels like an audition for the Ministry of Silly Walks and the kittiwakes lining the shore make the perfect audience. The free-range route around the island features rarely visited and atmospheric sites including ancient chambered cairns, prehistoric field systems, and a dramatic geo (steep-sided cleft) called Chad Girt. There is also a superbly sheltered swimming spot on the long white, powdery stretch of sand at Porth Moran. I spent quite some time here hunting out the extremely rare gilt-edged lichen. Looking like a mini-cloud with a golden lining and more usually found in the warmer islands of the Azores, Madeira or the Canaries, its presence is a testament to the mild climate of this archipelago.

Returning from White Island, the route continues down the east coast past the magnificent white beach of Great Bay – recently voted the best beach in Britain. At the west end of the island the route ascends to the wild heathland of Chapel Down, home to one of St Martin's most distinct features – the red- and white-striped daymark. From this vantage point the views are incredible

and it's almost possible to imagine the lost land of Lyonesse, now engulfed by waves but – according to Arthurian legend – once stretched to Land's End. On Chapel Down you'll come across a number of ancient cairns and entrance graves as well as 'Billy Idol' – the local name for a metre-high standing stone with a carved head that looks a bit like a puffin.

The walk along the south coast is sublime, whether you stroll along the vast beaches at low tide or the dreamy footpaths through the once-thriving bulb fields. Make a short diversion inland around Higher Town and visit the vineyard, bakery, and flower farms or treat yourself at Adam's Fish and Chips. Eat fish caught by Adam from the boat he constructed, cooked in the restaurant he built and served with chips from the organic island potatoes grown by his brother. It doesn't get much more local than this.

Towards the end of walk the shallows near the Quay beckon. On my last trip I succumbed and took a last plunge into the refreshing clear water, a few stray notes from sea shanties drifting across from the Seven Stones Inn. It was a perfect way to end a perfect island day.

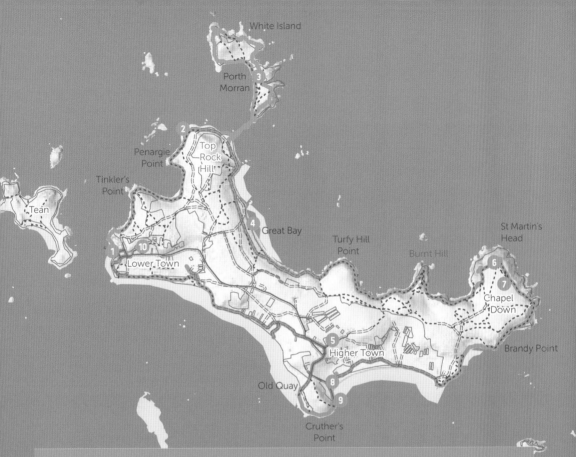

White Island

Porth
Morran   3

Penargie
Point

Top
Rock
Hill   2

Tinkler's
Point

Tean

1   10

Lower Town

Great Bay   4

Turfy Hill
Point

Burnt Hill

St Martin's
Head

6

7

Chapel
Down

Brandy Point

5

Higher Town

Old Quay

8

9

Cruther's
Point

DIRECTIONS

» From Lower Town Quay (1) find the small path in front of the Karma Hotel head N walking round Tinkler's Point and pass the rock pools of Pernagie (2). Continue on this easy path to reach the pebbly strand across to White Island (3). Cross at low tide and climb the grass bank onto the island. There are numerous faint paths to follow around its outer edge.

» Back on St Martin's, continue S along Great Bay (4). Towards the S end of the beach there are spurs up to the community hall and toilets, the Island Bakery (5) and the cafés of Higher Town. Continuing on the coast there is a short uphill section to Burnt Hill followed by a choice of routes up to the red-striped Day Mark

(6) – including the rockier coastal route. Pass the daymark and follow the smaller path along the coast.

» To explore the ancient ruins, including the carved standing stone (7), follow one of the many paths over the heath. From Chapel Down continue down through old field systems, derelict nurseries and small, succulent trees before reaching the E end of Higher Town Bay. The sandy path passes the vineyard and Adam's Fish and Chips before arriving at the cricket pitch and toilets (8).

» Turn L and follow the small road to Higher Town Quay (9), climbing up the grassy bank where the road ends onto the coastal path and walking around Cruther's Point to reach Old

Quay. Just beyond the quay follow the small lane inland, walking uphill through the cottages to Higher Town.

» At the junction with the 'main' road turn L, passing the Post Office and Stores after 100m, then turn L on a sharp R bend and follow the track. After about 200m, reach the first track to the L (to the beach). Ignore this and continue a little further to the next track L to the coast.

» Continue on the path just above the beach through the old nurseries, around Lawrence's Bay or walk along the beach to the surfaced paths of the Karma Hotel. For refreshments, head to the Seven Stones Inn (10) via the main island lane.

LOOE

EXPERIENCE NATURAL BEAUTY AND FOLLOW THE ISLAND DREAM OF TWO SISTERS

Looe Island sits less than two kilometres from Looe off the south coast of Cornwall. Now a nature reserve, it is a mix of woodland, grassland and beach, lovingly managed by the Cornwall Wildlife Trust. With a high point of 45 metres, its position in Looe Bay affords fabulous views of the coastline from the Lizard to Prawle Point in Devon. The gentle coastal walk along the only path will charm you, making the two hours allowed on the island seem far too short.

Atmospheric and steeped in legend, the island was said to be a stopping-off point for Joseph of Arimathea who landed here with the Child Jesus. Wild tales of free traders and smugglers also abound but it is the story of two sisters, Babs and Evelyn Atkins, that resonates so deeply with visitors today. Back in the mid-1960s they achieved their long-held dream of owning this island, where

they lived a happy, self-sufficient existence. Looe's magical atmosphere, ramshackle vegetable plots, and the wardens' tales of their home-made elder-flower champagne almost bring them to life.

The journey starts at East Looe on-board the Moonraker – reserve a space by jotting your name down on the passenger list the night before. Beware of the boatman's alluring West-Country drawl, which hides his sharp wit – he'll pull your leg for most of the way.

On just one or two days a year a very low spring tide allows the journey to be made on foot from Wallace Beach on the mainland across the rocky seafloor. You'll need to be speedy, though, as the tides come in fast. On arrival at the island's Main Beach the wardens, Jon and Claire, escort you across the spit of coarse sand and pebbles to give a short introduction in the Tractor Shed. They also

---

TERRAIN: Easy grass path.

STARTING POINT: Tractor shed.
Lat/Long 50.3381, -4.4501;
GR SX 257 516

DISTANCE: 1.5km (ascent: 57m)

TIME: 30 mins

MAP: OS Explorer 107

DIFFICULTY: 1

NAVIGATION: 1

ACCESS: 2

DON'T MISS:
- Living the island dream Babs and Attie-style
- Meeting the island's inspiring wardens
- Sitting in the bird hide, immersing yourself in the wildlife
- A swimming beach all to yourself

SPECIAL NOTES: Public trips allow 2 hours on the island. Longer trips can be negotiated with the boatman and it is possible to stay in the island's bell tent. No dogs.

GETTING THERE: Small passenger boat up to 2–3 hours either side of high tide, weather permitting. To confirm sailing contact the boatman, Dave Butters, on 07814 264514 or check the noticeboard on Buller Quay, East Looe, and sign up for the trip in the notebook. Boarding is from the floating pontoon, near the RNLI lifeboat station slipway in East Looe.

FACILITIES: Compost toilets.

hand out notes for a clockwise self-guided tour and a quick lesson on how to use the compost loo.

The track follows the northeast edge of the island past Smuggler's Cottage, home to the infamous brother-and-sister team, Finn and Black Joan. Said to be 'more like a man as she dressed like one, rowed a boat, smoked a pipe and could use her fists when required', Black Joan had at least one murder to her name. Spirits, silk stockings and tea came in from the Channel Islands via Looe Island – the perfect staging post for smuggling booty to the mainland. Fittingly, the cottage is currently used to ferment the warden's home-made wine and there are plans to turn it into a holiday let. Slightly further along the path is Babs' Meadow, a simple stone at the top of the field marking her grave. Her sister Attie is at rest in St Martin's church on the mainland.

Just before reaching the houses, the rustic vegetable gardens are a self-sufficiency enthusiast's dream and a veritable organic larder that nourishes the wardens through their seasonal residency. Onions, garlic, runner beans, artichokes, sweetcorn, raspberries, sunflowers and rhubarb flourish amongst the rickety array of poles. Grapes and kiwi vines grow behind the shed and the greenhouse is packed with chillies, melons and aubergines. Old apple trees, young plum and walnut trees also thrive on the island to complete the feast.

Next to the vegetable plots, Coastguard Watch House (now called Island House) failed to put a stop to smuggling activities – unsurprising given the divided loyalties of the excise men. In later years, the Atkins sisters lived here. Evelyn taught in Looe, where she remained during the week, leaving Babs alone with no means of communicating with the mainland other than flags and hand-signals. In periods of sustained rough weather, spending long winter nights cut off on an island reputed to be haunted must have required some nerve. Jetty Cottage, the barn the Atkins sisters used as a café and craft shop, is the wardens' accommodation. Below it, explore the rocky shore where rock pools and crevices teem with marine life.

After passing the sheep enclosure to reach the eastern tip of the island and the adjoining islet (not accessible to the public), there are views to the skerries. Known as the Ranneys, they are a popular haul-out for grey seals and home to the largest great black-backed gull colony in Cornwall. Beyond, there are great views across Whitsand Bay and to Rame Head. The waters here are a designated conservation zone, providing rich habitat for many fish species, pink sea fan, stalked jellyfish and cuttlefish.

Turning west along the south coast, you reach a small, green turf-roofed bird hide where you can observe the great black-backs, fulmars, herring gulls, cormorants, and shags. The seals you'll spot from here also have names, such as Lucille,

Duchess, Snowdrop and Sunrise. Inside the hide there is a helpful identification guide as well as shelves stacked with curiously coloured bottles of medicines used by previous inhabitants.

A hill occupies most of the island and as you ascend there are views of Eddystone Lighthouse, 19 kilometres out to sea. Below on the grass slopes and rocks, large numbers of seabirds breed and it can be mayhem in the springtime. From the summit, there are wonderful views across to the deep valleys and hilly coastline of the mainland. Here, too, in the shelter of the sycamores, is the islands' only accommodation – the bell tent. At the summit a few stones mark the site of a Benedictine chapel. Following the legendary visit to Looe by tin trader Joseph of Arimathea and his nephew, Jesus, the island became a place of pilgrimage for early Christians. Excavations have uncovered a Romano-British wooden chapel, which would at least make the island one of the earliest outposts of Christianity in Britain.

Downhill from the chapel there are views out to the Lizard Peninsula beyond, and around Dunker Point the cedars and pine trees add a Mediterranean feel. The route passes through the old potato field before it enters woods of sycamore, elder, oak and ash with dense fern adding a fairytale touch, before the path re-emerges at the Main Beach. If there is time, or if you are staying over, Main Beach is a good swimming spot. Back at the Tractor Shed there is a chance to catch up with the wardens and buy delicious home-made raspberry jam, apple juice and elderflower champagne, along with the books the sisters spent their long winter evenings writing.

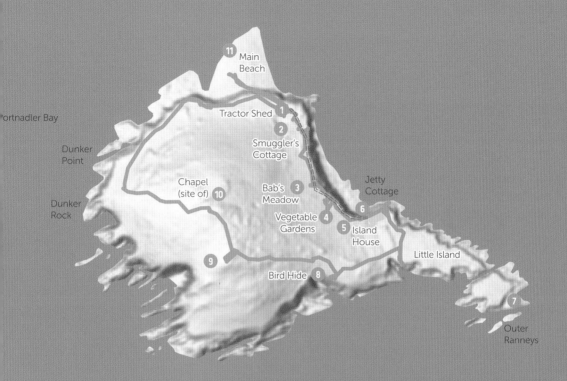

Main
Beach

11

Portnadler Bay

Tractor Shed   1

2

Dunker
Point

Smuggler's
Cottage

Chapel
(site of)   10

Bab's
Meadow   3

Jetty
Cottage

Dunker
Rock

Vegetable
Gardens

4

6

5   Island
House

Little Island

9

Bird Hide   8

7

Outer
Ranneys

DIRECTIONS

» From the Tractor Shed (1) follow the track along the NE shore past Smuggler's Cottage (2), Babs Meadow (3), the vegetable gardens (4), Island House (5) and reach Jetty Cottage (6), where there is access to the coast to explore the rocky shore.

» Continue past the sheep enclosure, reaching the E tip to view the seals on the skerries (7). Turn W and continue on the S coast, past the turf-roofed bird hide (8) and then uphill to a T-junction. Turn L for the viewpoint (9) and seabird nesting site or continue around the island to the summit (10).

» Continue downhill and around Dunker Point to return to Main Beach (11) and the Tractor Shed.

BROWNSEA

STEP BACK IN TIME AND EXPLORE A FLOURISHING WILDLIFE HAVEN WITH UNSPOILT BEACHES, LAGOONS, HEATHLAND AND WOODLANDS WITH RED SQUIRRELS

'L ife without adventure would be deadly dull', said Baden-Powell, who pitched his first Scout camp here, and a sense of adventure continues to permeate this island. Sitting serenely in Poole Harbour, it is just a hop yet also a world away from the glass-fronted mansions and urban foreshore of Millionaires' Row at the mouth of the harbour. Catch a ferry over and explore wooded coves, beaches and a very special nature reserve, or give yourself a challenge and swim or kayak across instead.

Once on Brownsea, easy paths wind through a wide variety of landscapes, and the island's pine-woods, heathland, sandy beaches, meadows, lakes and lagoons are crammed with flowers and wild creatures. It isn't surprising that this island was voted the best nature reserve in the UK. All around the walk there are stunning views north and east to Poole and Sandbanks, and the Purbeck Hills and chalk stacks of Old Harry Rocks to the south. With plenty of access to beaches for swimming and exploring the foreshore, there is too much to do in a single visit.

The island has been shaped by a string of eccentric owners. The most influential was Mary Bonham-Christie, known as the 'demon of Brownsea', whose motto was 'wildlife first, people second'. She banned hunting and fishing, visitors, and definitely Boy Scouts, and her prohibitions resulted in the flourishing habitat for wildlife we enjoy today. On Bonham-Christie's death, conservation campaigners, led by the National Trust (NT), tried to buy the island but the only affordable solution was a joint purchase with three other organisations. In partnership with the NT, the Dorset Wildlife Trust runs the northeast of the island,

---

TERRAIN: Easy island tracks; optional foreshore walking.

STARTING POINT: Quay on Brownsea Island. Lat/Long 50.6889, -1.9564; GR SZ 032 877

DISTANCE: 8.9km (ascent: 137m)

TIME: 2.5 hours

OS MAP: OS Explorer OL15

DIFFICULTY: 2

NAVIGATION: 1

ACCESS: 2 (5 if swimming or kayaking)

DON'T MISS:
- Spotting red squirrels in the pines and spoonbills on the lagoon
- Swimming off peaceful South Shore
- Spending a night under canvas in honour of the first Scouts

GETTING THERE: Half-hourly boat services depart Poole Quay (01202 631828) and Sandbanks (01929 462383).

FACILITIES: NT café; toilets at reception & visitor centre, Villa & outdoors centre.

SPECIAL NOTES: No dogs on the island. NT members free; non-members £6.75 adult. Entry to Dorset Wildlife Trust Reserve £2.00. Wild camping not permitted.

Through the open window of the hide unfolded a slice of lagoon life that can't be seen from anywhere else on the island. In the breeding season hundreds of common and sandwich terns nest just metres away on the lagoon's artificial islands. Along with the spoonbills, avocets, and godwits, the terns feed on the worms, crabs, and snails found on the vast dining table that is the mudflats of Poole Harbour. Beyond the hide, the Victorian vicarage known as The Villa has a small interpretation centre and is a red squirrel hotspot. If you don't see any high up in the pines there's always the stuffed one inside. Further into the reserve, a walk to the north coast is rewarded by fine pine-framed views of Poole – the noise of the Sunseeker Yachts churning through the waters a reminder of how close this sanctuary is to urban life.

On exiting the reserve and re-entering NT land, the next point of interest is Pottery Pier on the east coast. One of the island's previous owners, William Waugh, believed he could manufacture porcelain from the white clay deposits here but the quality was so poor he ended up making Victorian sanitary ware until his business went bust. Traces of these activities remain, and discarded ceramic fragments dot the shoreline. Waugh also built a miniature

including the large bird lagoon, while the John Lewis Partnership has a 99-year lease of the castle and grounds for staff holiday use. The Scouting and Girlguiding movements hold regular camps in the private grounds on the south of the island. All four organisations bring something different to the island and on this anti-clockwise walk you get some insight into their unique characters.

The walk starts at the landing stage on the east coast where the majority of the island's buildings are located, including the church, castle and café. Walking west to the wildlife reserve, the boardwalk hovers above creeks of dense black water and fern-cloaked logs, all with the feel of a primordial swamp. The sight of a red squirrel walking noncha-lantly along the planks ahead suddenly brings you back to the present.

After paying the entrance fee to the reserve I was told to 'watch out for the bearded tits near the hide', by the enthusiastic Dorset Wildlife Trust volunteer. Disturbing images started to swirl around my mind. I'd only come to see the spoonbills, and possibly a red squirrel or two, and wasn't sure what to expect when I eventually opened the hide door. The row of binoculars and camouflage jackets that greeted me was reassuring. Not a Panurus biarmicus (bearded tit) in sight, though.

village for his workers, known as Maryland and named after his wife. Sadly, Maryland was devastated by the Luftwaffe when fires to divert bombers destined for Poole lit up Brownsea. Waugh may have had big dreams but luck just wasn't on his side.

Along the south coast of the island, Baden-Powell's legacy draws hundreds of adventure-seeking Scouts and Guides to camp here every year. The opportunity to spend a night under canvas where the first Scouts camped over a hundred years ago is also available to the public. Although not true wild camping it comes pretty close, and you also get this spectacular island to yourself after hours. There are several access points to South Shore along this stretch of coast, but take care on the steep cliffs, which can be unstable. The beach here is quiet, even on busy weekends, and it's a good place to swim as long as you keep an eye on the strong current at certain tides. There are also great views from here of the other private wooded islands of Poole Harbour.

Returning via the visitor centre, across the well-tended lawns in front of the church, iridescent peacocks strut amongst the picnickers. They tend to harry the weak-willed for a crumb or two in exchange for a photo of their magnificent fanned tails. Finishing the walk with a large slice of cake in the NT café, you can understand why Brownsea is said to have inspired Enid Blyton's classic, Five on a Treasure Island. Scout's honour.

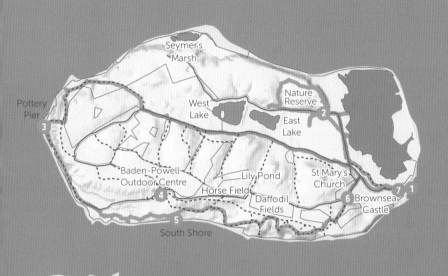

DIRECTIONS

» Arriving at the Brownsea Island quay (1), exit via the NT reception, and pick up a free island map. Turn L towards the clock tower and follow the path towards the Dorset Wildlife Trust Reserve, walking parallel to the Brownsea Castle garden wall and past the sculpture of Baden-Powell.

» After 150m turn R onto the boardwalk towards the nature reserve and continue until you reach the gravel track. Turn R and continue along the well-marked trails around the reserve (2).

» After 2km exit the reserve the same way you came in, return to the main track and turn R, passing the S tip of the two lakes and a wooden adventure playground. After about 1.3km, reach the four-ways junction and take the second path on the R towards Maryland and Pottery Pier. After 200m pass through the deer enclosure into Parkyn Copse and continue downhill, descending the steep steps to Pottery Pier (3).

» From here, walking the 2km of coastal route bearing L is possible only in dry weather, owing to a number of landslips. Follow NT guidance and take alternative paths inland if necessary. Passing through the ruins at William Pit, cross the grassy area past the flag pole and enter the woodland through the gate (avoiding the boardwalk), continuing on the paths that hug the coast. For simple refreshments or to visit the Scout Stone (4) walk uphill to the Baden-Powell Outdoor Centre.

» For the pebbly beach of South Shore (5), head uphill past the NT houses and follow the signs, passing the warden's cottage. At the beach, head immediately back uphill and turn R at the top to follow the sandy path. Along it are optional detours down to various points for views across to Shell Bay and Harry Rocks, as well as beach access. For a more direct route follow the larger paths along Horse Field and Daffodil Fields. Passing to the left of the enclosure and on towards the farm buildings, you arrive at the visitor and interpretation centre (6). Continue on the main path past the church and turn R along the main track back to the café (7) and quay.

LUNDY

GO ROCK-POOLING, SWIM WITH SEALS, EXPLORE SUBTERRANEAN PASSAGES AND LOOK OUT FOR PUFFINS AND BASKING SHARKS

Lundy lies off the North Devon coast, where the Atlantic Ocean meets the Bristol Channel. With nothing between it and America, this flat-topped granite outcrop of plunging cliffs is a place apart. With a chequered history of pirates, crooks, and failed businessmen, Lundy now makes an honest living as a holiday destination for those looking for peace or wildlife, or both. The island was named the UK's first marine conservation zone, and the richness of Lundy's underwater life is matched by the abundant wildlife on land.

Following an anti-clockwise circuit on an unmarked coastal path, the sheltered grassy slopes of the east coast rise to the windswept heathland plateau of the north. From the dramatic cliffs, stacks and granite outcrops of the west-coast section there are giddying views of the island's main seabird colonies. Short detours down the cliffs and further inland are possible to explore more of the fascinating historic and natural features.

On the voyage to Lundy in the charming *MS Oldenburg*, complete with original wood panelling and brass fittings, you might see harbour porpoise, common dolphins, bottlenose dolphins and Risso's dolphins. With luck, there may even be a glimpse of minke and pilot whales. Grey seals are often spotted too, as they forage for bottom-dwelling fish such as sand eels and flatfish. Each year (typically between May and August), basking sharks usually come to Landing Bay to feed on plankton. Many varieties of jellyfish and the beautifully iridescent comb jellies can also be seen above the kelp forests, on the surface of the shallow waters.

On arrival, the walk heads north along the east coast and soon the clamour of the day trippers following the main track to the village fades into

TERRAIN: Grass paths, steep, rocky walk at Gannets' Head; optional steeper sections.

STARTING POINT: Lundy Pier. Lat/Long 51.163030, -4.654250; GR SS 145 438

DISTANCE: 14.2km (ascent: 726m)

TIME: 4 hours

OS MAP: OS Explorer 139

DIFFICULTY: 2

NAVIGATION: 3

ACCESS: 2 (3 for Rat Island)

DON'T MISS:
- Famous Lundy puffins between April and July
- Exploring smugglers' caves and subterranean passages
- Climbing over to Rat Island to see the amazing rock pools
- Sampling the local brew at the legendary Marisco Tavern

GETTING THERE: *MS Oldenburg* from either Bideford or Ilfracombe in summer; helicopter from Hartland Point in winter months www.landmarktrust.org.uk/lundyisland/staying/staying-on-lundy/travelling-to-lundy/.

FACILITIES: Shop, pub, and toilets in main village.

SPECIAL NOTES: Dogs are not permitted on Lundy to avoid disturbance to wildlife.

the distance. The coastal path, lined with grass and bracken and the occasional Lundy cabbage, continues to cut through the side of the gentle slopes of the east coast. The only man-made features on this stretch are the buildings and workings of the former Lundy Granite Company, which once employed about 300 people. To explore further, make a detour from the coastal route around the Quarter Wall mark – one of the three stone walls that cross the island from east to west.

Further along the east coast, the path passes some spectacular rock formations. Lundy's unique 'white' granite sparkles with crystals of feldspar, mica and quartz. From here the North Devon coastline, Exmoor, and the Culm are clearly visible on a bright day. Towards the north of the island, Gannets' Bay is a spectacle and often filled with dive boats. Seals follow the neoprene-clad snorkelers, trying for a playful nip of their fins. The island is an important breeding site and seal pups can be seen all year round, although the main pupping season runs from August to December. The cliffs in the vicinity are usually packed with nesting seabirds in the spring and summer months.

The rocky path from Gannets' Bay ascends steeply to the plateau at the north end of the island, from where there are views to the Gower Peninsula in South Wales. At the northwest tip, the North Lighthouse makes for an exhilarating detour down steep stone steps and across two iron bridges. It was built not only to warn sailors but also to help ships from North America distinguish between the Bristol and English Channels. The ocean surges and sucks at the treacherous rocks below, even on a calm day. Atlantic seals rest on the rocks and you'll see breeding colonies of guillemots, razor-bills, and herring gulls. A large subterranean tunnel penetrates the whole north end of the island – it's inaccessible to all but the very determined.

Walking south along the west coast on the approach to the Threequarter Wall, the precipitous

rock structures and cliffs of St James's Stone and St Peter's Stone come into view. Lundy is a magnet for climbers, many heading for the Devil's Slide – a vertiginous 120-metre-high granite slab and a climbing classic.

Further south, just beyond Halfway Wall, the Pyramid marks the northern end of Jenny's Cove, the most popular destination – along with St Peter's Stone – for seabird watchers and the main observation point for the island's gregarious puffins. Between Halfway and Quarter Wall, the 'earthquake' is an adventurers' playground. With two distinct fissures 20 metres or so apart, this stretch has several chasms, ranging from a few metres to twelve metres deep.

Just south of Quarter Wall, a steep descent to Battery Point and the buildings hewn into the rock makes a very worthwhile detour. The historic fog signal station, along with two cannons used to warn shipping off the rocks, was built when the original lighthouse light flashed so fast it appeared to ships as a fixed light. Its position on the higher point of the island also left it frequently obscured by mist. Climb the cantilevered spiral staircase of the Old Light-house and enjoy fantastic views of the whole island from the deckchairs in the glazed lantern gallery.

On the approach to the prosaically named South West point, Montagu Steps run down the precipitous cliffs. The battleship *HMS Montagu* ran aground on the rocks around Shutter Point in 1905. During the salvage operation an aerial walkway was constructed from the top of the cliffs and a stepped path (Montagu Steps) made down the cliff-side.

After rounding South West Point and heading along the south coast towards the ruins of Marisco Castle, you come across Benson's Cave. Here, the grassy cliff slopes steeply to the south-east and a narrow path leads down to the opening. The cave is named after Thomas Benson – MP for Barnstaple, and merchant ship-owner turned smuggler – who is reputed to have constructed this cave to store his ill-gotten goods.

At the southeast extremity of Lundy, you can make the low-tide crossing to Rat Island for an atmospheric walk through the island's subterranean tunnel. Climbing to the top of the island – best achieved via the rocks on the south side and heading towards the South Light – it is possible to see as far south as Newquay in Cornwall as well as spot dolphins, whales and basking sharks.

Between Lundy and Rat Island, Devil's Kitchen is one of the richest places in Britain for seashore foraging. Here, the slate bedrock has been worn away to form a series of rock pools and gullies bursting with marine life. Brown, red, and green seaweeds, barnacles, and limpets, as well as beadlet, strawberry, and snakelocks anemones abound and for those who like to get their hands wet there are shore crabs, cushion stars, pipefish, gobies, and blennies living under the small rocks and seaweed. On the lowest tides it may be possible to see a Lundy speciality, the nationally scarce scarlet and gold star corals as well as jewel anemones, colonies of sea squirts, and clingfish, which can be found under damp rocks. Close by, at Mermaid's Hole, there is a low-tide rock pool with an inlet for sea water that is a wonderfully secluded spot to bathe. There are also other caves and tunnels to explore near the base of the nearby cliffs.

Once the exploration around the southern tip of the island is complete the route continues around the Marisco Castle, built by Henry III in 1243 after he had executed William de Marisco for treason. A deviation inland from the coastal route to 'downtown' Lundy is rewarded with a visit to the island's legendary pub, the Marisco Tavern. Once the old granite company's store and 'refreshment room', it serves the popular island brew, Old Light, and is the hub for the island's small community.

On the descent back to the Landing Bay to complete the walk, a calm sea may well tempt you to fit in a quick swim before being whisked back to the real world by the trusty *MS Oldenburg*.

DIRECTIONS

》 Walk uphill from the concrete pier (1) above the Landing Beach. After 0.6km turn R at a small building, just ahead of the walled garden. Go through the gate and follow the grass path along the E coast. Continue along the undulating path to Quarter Wall, past wind-sculpted oak and sycamore trees, a field of 'white' granite rocks, and a small stand of alder trees in a creek.

》 Once above Quarry Beach, keep to the level path through the granite quarry (2) passing the memorial to John Harmon. After 500m descend towards the coast on the R-hand path, joining a larger path, and continue N through towering rock formations. After a further 1km, go round the headland to find the rocky path ahead with Gull Rock and Tibbetts Point (3) in the distance.

》 Cross the stile on Halfway Wall and a little further go straight ahead at the crossroads. After several hundred metres take the path to R and head downhill towards the northern end of Halfway Bay (the path to L heads up to the cairn).

》 Make the steep ascent through the rocks adjacent to Gannets' Rock (4) and after 200m, just before the window in the rock, follow the faint path upwards over the rocks. After a further 100m or so, keep to the L and walk under the largest stack of rocks on L. Avoid any routes to R: there are steep drops. Turn L up the grass gully and at the top follow the faint path to reach the rectangular-shaped rock visible on top of another pile. At this point, the path bears R and follows a clear course to the summit of the promontory. From here, follow the path along the headland keeping as close as possible to the coast. Round the plateau at the highest point.

》 At a cairn, the main island path continues S along the W coast and there are opportunities to explore each headland and the dramatic cliffs via smaller paths that lead off. The first deviation takes you to the lighthouse (5), down steep stone steps and across two iron bridges.

》 Continuing S along the W coast, pass St John's and St Peter's Stones (6), crossing Threequarter Wall, followed by Halfway Wall, to Jenny's Cove (7) and reach the earthquake rock fissure (8). Keep on, crossing Quarter Wall to find a R-hand path alongside a precipitous wall for a detour to Battery Point (9).

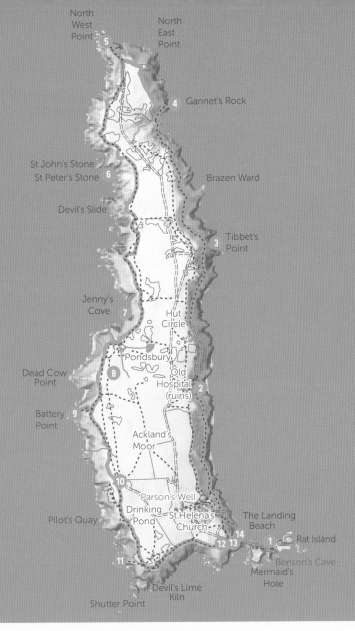

North West Point

North East Point

5

4 Gannet's Rock

St John's Stone
St Peter's Stone **6**

Brazen Ward

Devil's Slide

Tibbet's Point
3

Jenny's Cove **7**

Hut Circle

Pondsbury

Old Hospital (ruins) **2**

Dead Cow Point **8**

Battery Point **9**

Ackland's Moor

10

Parson's Well

Drinking Pond

St Helena's Church

The Landing Beach

Pilot's Quay

14

12 13 **1** Rat Island

11

Benson's Cave

Mermaid's Hole

Devil's Lime Kiln

Shutter Point

» Pass to the W side of the Old Lighthouse (10) towards Montagu Steps (11) and Southwest Point, then continue E along the coast path to reach the main island path, keeping parallel to the stone wall of the church. Before the end of the wall turn R to keep to the coastline and head towards the ruins of Marisco Castle (12), visiting Benson's Cave (13) on the way. Walk round the outside of the ruins past the garrison-like part of the building. For an optional visit to Rat Island (14), the Devil's Kitchen, and Mermaid's Hole, keep to the path along the cliffs.

» At the side of the old post-office building next to the ruin, turn R onto the track, then take the R fork downhill past a wooden chalet. After 200m, at the main gravel track to the village and on a sweeping L bend, take the hairpin path to R, descend to the main track and return to the pier.

STEEP HOLM

TAKE UP THE CHALLENGE OF GETTING TO THE ISLAND AND ENJOY PANORAMIC VIEWS FROM A FORMER MILITARY OUTPOST-TURNED-NATURE RESERVE

Bouncing towards the island over the waves on an exhilarating RIB ride from Weston-super-Mare, this mysterious lump of rock slowly reveals its character. Outlines of the ruined buildings of the hotel and inn emerge from the rocky cliffs, conjuring up images of smugglers, pirates and thirsty sailors swigging illicit liquor. Disused military installations remain on Steep Holm, which is now owned by the Kenneth Allsop Memorial Trust, set up in memory of the broadcaster and environmentalist. Devoted trustees manage the island as a nature reserve and bird sanctuary; they are also stewards of its military history.

Landing on the island requires two high tides in the daylight, almost flat-calm water, and low winds. With only twelve or so sailings a year, just getting here requires tenacity and planning. Circumnavigating the island may not take much time but it does offer challenges to those with a head for heights. The cliffs are sheer, with plenty of steep, exposed sections down to Rudder Rock Battery, 208 Steps, and Searchlight Battery. It is also possible to walk down to South Landing on the south coast and around the foreshore to East Beach out of bird nesting season, as long as you keep a watchful eye on the very strong tides.

After unloading the day's supplies of water, food and fuel for the generator – lovingly nicknamed Bertha – the first steps uphill are an introduction to the island's history. Known as the Zig-Zag path, the route follows the old cable-winched switch-back railway that was used to transfer goods from supply boats during World War II – a task previously performed by Indian Army Service Corps mules.

Steep Holm was probably first settled in the Iron Age; later, the Romans established a lookout post

---

TERRAIN: Easy path; optional steep and exposed steps down cliffs

STARTING POINT: East Beach. Lat/Long 51.3400, -3.1034; GR ST 232 607

DISTANCE: 2.2km (ascent 170m)

TIME: 45 mins; 12 hours exploration

OS MAP: OS Explorer 153

DIFFICULTY: 1 (4 for cliff diversions)

NAVIGATION: 1

ACCESS: 2

DON'T MISS:
- Culvert spiders in Split Rock Battery underground stores
- The rare wild peonies unique to the island
- Panoramic views of the Somerset and Welsh coastlines
- Scrambling down to the old searchlight posts

SPECIAL NOTES: Descent to Rudders Rock or 208 Steps is at your own risk: steps are slippery and exposed. Seek local guidance. Swimming is forbidden. Take litter home.

GETTING THERE: Access solely through trips organised by the Kenneth Allsop Memorial Trust (01934 522125 or steepholmbookings@gmail.com for reservations). Read restrictions and guidance before visiting.

FACILITIES: Detailed map of the main sites and footpaths can be purchased on the island. Hot and cold drinks, home-made cakes, beer, wine, and cider at the Barracks. Bring your own packed lunch.

here. With panoramic views back to the Somerset coast, across to the Welsh coast, and further west to the Quantocks – with the whole expanse of the Channel in between – few could evade scrutiny from this incredible vantage point.

The island's position in the Bristol Channel also made it attractive for religious retreats. St Gildas is said to have lived here in the 6th century and a small Augustinian priory operated between the 12th and 13th centuries. The friars were responsible for introducing the more unusual plant life to the island, bringing with them medicinal herbs such as caper spurge, a traditional 'violent purgative'.

Fortification of Steep Holm to protect the Bristol Channel began in Victorian times and continued through World Wars I and II. Today, Steep Holm is packed with signal stations, watchtowers, gun batteries, and underground munition stores. One of the barrack buildings now serves as the island's visitor centre. It has a fascinating museum and the knowledgeable trustees serve hot and cold drinks, home-made cakes, and beer in the tranquil gardens. Wildlife has also colonised the structures and between April and late August, Steep Holm is host to around two thousand pairs of nesting gulls that use the buildings as their HQ, screeching, squabbling, raising chicks, and dive-bombing the visitors. The gulls are also responsible for much of the island's plastic litter, which they collect and use for nest building. Chicken bones and half-eaten burgers,

too, are occasionally sighted. The gulls frequent the numerous takeaways strung along Weston-super-Mare's seafront and bring their booty home.

The rest of Steep Holm's wildlife reveals itself on the gentle walk around the island. If you're lucky you'll hear muntjac rustling or barking in the sycamore woods on the walk up from the beach, and maybe spot one of the giant slowworms wriggling in a crevice in the warm rocks. At low tide you can often see grey seals on Gooseneck Spit near the landing point. One of my favourite island beasties is the culvert spider, found in the underground munition stores. These large spiders suspend their eggs from the ceilings in large 'cotton-wool' sacks that look like Halloween decorations. Their glistening bodies can give you quite a shock when first picked out by torchlight.

In April to mid-May the vibrant, cerise flowers of the rare Mediterranean wild peony add a splash of bright colour to the island. Their striking pink and black seed heads also enhance Steep Holm's palette in autumn. As for the rest of Steep Holm's flora, it reads like a potent witches' brew: wild wallflower, stinking iris, and wild turnip – all seasoned with hemp and hemlock.

Twelve hours here might sound like a long time but you'll be lucky to have a moment to spare. Although a short walk in distance, for the curious it will take most of the day. Prepare to be surprised.

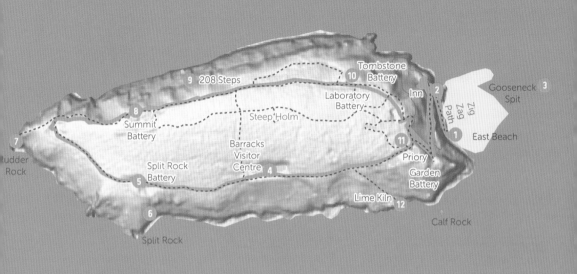

DIRECTIONS

>> Start at East Beach (1), the landing site for the RIB at high tide. Walk up the Zig-Zag path past the ruins of Cliff Cottage and the inn (2), then follow the rail tracks through the sycamore wood to the plateau. Gooseneck Spit (3) will be revealed at low tide from this point.

>> Continue clockwise along the S coast, past the Barracks (4) for toilets and refreshments, to arrive at the gun emplacement on Split Rock Battery (5). The underground, brick-lined ammunition storerooms can be accessed via the steps. After a further 100m, there are great views of Split Rock (6) and the nests of the great black-backed gulls.

>> The easy path continues to Rudder Rock Battery (7) and the searchlight post that stands on dramatic sea arches on the island's W tip. Access as far as the first platform is entirely at your own risk.

>> Rounding Rudder Rock, the perimeter path bears E east along the island's N coast and ascends steeply to Summit Battery (8). Further E, 208 Steps (9) and another searchlight post may be explored (again, at your own risk) before continuing towards Laboratory Battery and Tombstone Battery (10) in the NE of the island.

>> Reaching the E coast, ignore the Zig-Zag path back down to East Beach and head S to the priory (11) and Garden Battery to return to the Barracks. There is an optional descent down the steep path to South Landing (12) on the S coast to see the limekiln at the bottom. At low tide it is possible to rock-hop back to East Beach, but only if the birds have finished nesting.

LIHOU

PLUNGE INTO THE VENUS POOL, EXPLORE EVOCATIVE RUINS, AND BE AMAZED BY THE WEALTH OF MARINE LIFE

Here's a chance for a real adventure away from the mainland feel of Guernsey. As well as exploring the ruins of an old priory there is the chance to plunge into a deep, natural rock pool for an exhilarating swim before continuing around this bird spotter's and rock pooler's paradise. The walk starts on Guernsey and traverses the 400-metre cobbled causeway to Lihou, which is exposed at low tide. The sight of the exposed ocean floor and the beautiful rock pools is amazing. Once on the island the easy coastal circuit is along grass paths with breathtaking views back to the imposing Dalek-like fortifications of L'Erée, sweeping Rocquaine Bay and the scenic cliffs of the Pleinmont Headland.

From a distance, Lihou looks like an empty lump of rock, only revealing its beauty to those who venture across. It can be accessed for just two weeks a month when the causeway is uncovered at low tide. Although not inhabited, the population swells when Lihou House, a residential centre for groups, has guests. The island and its surrounds form an important marine reserve packed with fabulous creatures both above and below the water. Shore crabs, edible crabs, porcelain crabs, velvet swimming crabs, and hermit crabs scuttle among the rocks and pools. Squat lobsters, shrimps and prawns thrive alongside limpets, winkles, topshells, and dog whelks, leaving enough space for starfish and anemones to find their own niche. Over 200 species of seaweed of every size, colour and shape have been identified on these shores and pools, with some not found on any other site in the Channel Islands. Taking advantage of this seafood platter, oystercatchers, curlews, turnstones and redshanks wade on stilt-like legs in the shallow pools. On

---

TERRAIN: Tidal rock causeway; easy path on the island

STARTING POINT: Lihou Causeway. Lat/Long 49.4571, -2.6577; GR XD 524 509

DISTANCE: 4.1km (ascent 74m)

TIME: 1 hour plus swimming time

OS MAP: Bailiwick of Guernsey: States of Guernsey Official Map

DIFFICULTY: 2

NAVIGATION: 2

ACCESS: 3

DON'T MISS:
- Plunging into the depths of idyllic Venus Pool
- Rich and varied rock-pool life along the causeway
- Off-island adventuring away from bustling Guernsey
- Spotting waders and seabird colonies

FACILITIES: No water or food on the island. Public toilets at L'Erée Beach car park.

SPECIAL NOTES: Check causeway opening times (closed some days) and be aware of fast tides www.gov.gg/lihou. To protect the nesting birds, no dogs are allowed on the causeway or island.

GETTING THERE: Bus from St Peter Port, alight at L'Erée Bunker www.buses.gg/routes_and_times. By car, turn off the Route de Rocquaine at L'Erée Bunker. Follow green road signs to Lihou Island. Car park on L'Erée headland.

taller stilts, little egrets and grey herons search for larger fish in the deeper pools and shallows. On the western shore, Lihou's two small islets, Lihoumel and Lissroy, are important breeding sites for resident and migrating seabirds and are roped off during nesting season. The elusive peregrine falcon may also be seen swooping overhead.

Inland, plants flourish on the short turf, including wild carrot, violets, and campion. Very rare species such as sand crocus, dwarf pansy and sand quillwort have also been spotted and remain invisible to all but the experienced plant finder. Heading a little further north, a rocky path leads down towards the shore to the famous Venus Pool. This natural low-tide rock pool is deep enough to jump into and long enough for a swim.

This tiny windswept island also has a rich history with signs of prehistoric settlement. In the 12th century it was home to a Benedictine priory and the walk passes its haunting ruins – a protected monument. The monks of the Priory of St Mary farmed the land and kept bees for many years before the church was abandoned. The Governor of Guernsey destroyed the priory in 1759 to prevent French forces from capturing the island during the Seven Years' War. Islanders had been harvesting seaweed for fertiliser from the early 19th century and in the 1920s a factory was producing iodine from this abundant natural resource. Given the absolute peace and tranquility of the island today, it is hard to imagine any industrial activity here at all.

Today the island is owned by the States of Guernsey and the Lihou Charitable Trust is responsible for Lihou House and surrounding land. The house itself was rebuilt in the 1960s after it was used as target practice by German artillery in World War II. There are no facilities in the house beyond a borehole for water and solar panels for electricity, and it is mainly used for school trips and ecotourism.

On the return to mainland Guernsey there is plenty to see in the vicinity such as L'Erée German bunker, the legendary entrance to the fairy kingdom at Le Creux ès Faïes, and the views of the Martello tower of Fort Saumarez.

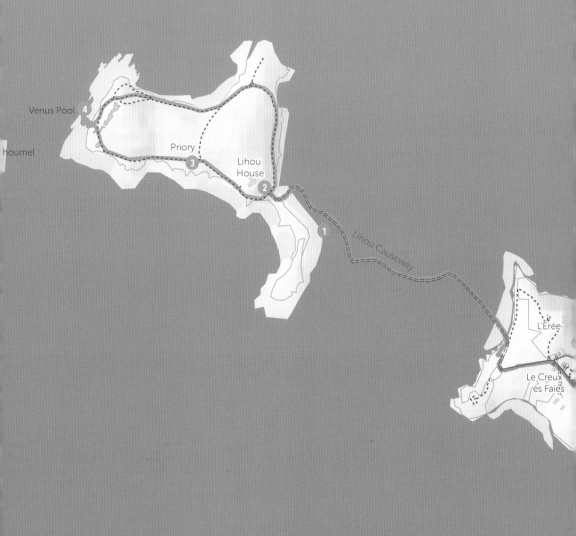

Venus Pool ④

houmel

Priory

Lihou
House

③

②

①

Lihou Causeway

L'Erée

Le Creux
ès Faïes

DIRECTIONS

» Start at L'Erée bus stop, walk around the bunker following the road sign to Lihou. Continue along the lane past the ecohouse on the R and towards the coast. Pass the car park on the L and sweep downhill following the road to the beach.

» After 600m walk along the causeway to reach the island's beach (1), then head towards Lihou House (2) and find the footpath to the L.

» Continue clockwise along the S coast to find the priory ruins (3) after 200m or so. After a further 100m, at

the most westerly point, descend the rocky path to the shore to visit the Venus Pool (4). Continue on the path around the N and E coasts, returning to mainland Guernsey via the causeway.

ALDERNEY

A FORTIFYING COASTAL PATH WITH DRAMATIC CLIFFS, EXUBERANT WILDLIFE, AND SECRET UNDERGROUND TUNNELS TO EXPLORE BY TORCHLIGHT

A night on the town in Alderney might be one of the wildest to be had in the Channel Islands. Walking on a side street, my torch picked out the big dark eyes and ghostly prickles of a native blond hedgehog. On summer evenings bats whizz overhead, hoovering up the insects that thrive in the pollution-free environment, and the night skies here are big and starry. Swimming among wave crests lit by bioluminescent plankton the dark hours here are touched with magic.

On this dramatic walk you experience both sides of Alderney. In the north, there is the greatest concentration of military fortifications and beaches, while in the south you'll see incredible wildlife and impressive cliffs. Following a well-marked coastal trail, there are some steep free-range paths and remote clifftop sections for the very best views and wildlife. The route passes most of the island's historic fortifications with plenty of opportunities to explore the secret rooms and tunnels. Along the beach sections there are good spots for swimming and foreshore foraging, an optional extra island visit, as well as stop-offs for delicious refreshments. Don't be surprised if it takes all day.

The closest Channel Island to both Britain and France, Alderney is the least well-known and the hardest to get to. Arrival is by small plane at the tiny, old-fashioned airport or by boat at laid-back Braye Harbour. With its unhurried pace of life and strong community spirit — possibly forged in one of the nine island pubs the locals call their second sitting rooms — this is a 'live and let live' sort of island with a distinct lack of stifling regulations.

Starting at Braye the route west passes the first of many Victorian fortifications reinforced when the German Army occupied the Channel Islands in

---

TERRAIN: Mostly easy coastal paths with free-range, steeper sections opposite Les Etacs

STARTING POINT: Braye Quay. Lat/Long 49.7240, -2.2004; GR XD 856 804

DISTANCE: 18.2km (ascent 473m)

TIME: 4.5 hours (not including time for exploration, swimming, and café stops)

OS MAP: Bailiwick of Guernsey: States of Guernsey Official Map

DIFFICULTY: 2

NAVIGATION: 2

ACCESS: 2

DON'T MISS:
- Peaceful swimming in Arch Bay
- Exploring the tunnels of Fort Tourgis and Bibette Head
- Observing the summer gannet colony at Les Etacs
- Post-walk treats in the restaurants and pubs of St Anne
- Dark-night safaris to experience the wildlife

SPECIAL NOTES: Take a torch to explore the underground bunkers, tunnels, and forts.

GETTING THERE: Aurigny has direct flights from Southampton and Guernsey www.aurigny.com. Direct sailings from Guernsey www.thelittleferrycompany.com. From the UK, Channel Seaways Ltd (01481 824484) run a freight service with limited passenger accommodation.

FACILITIES: Food and toilets around Braye and the harbour, Saye Beach Campsite, and Longis Bay.

CHAPTER 10

World War II. The rooms and tunnels of Cambridge Battery at Fort Tourgis can be explored with a torch. Just beyond, one of my favourite beaches on the route is Clonque Bay, home to over one hundred species of seaweed and a huge intertidal area that offers a wild, sandy beach and excellent rock pooling and foraging opportunities for samphire and shellfish at low tide.

Towards the western tip the flourishing gannet colony (active from March to October) of Les Etacs is best viewed from Giffoine Headland, after the very steep climb through the peaceful Vallée des Trois Vaux. Thousands of gannets live on the small, guano-whitened stack: their cries fill the air and their bodies plunge like missiles into the Swinge tidal race. Like most birdlife on the island, and the islanders themselves, they returned only after the war. From the west end of the island you also get the best views of Sark, Brecqhou, Guernsey, and Herm – with Burhou and its puffin and storm petrel colonies in the foreground. Close by, and in stark contrast, are the ruins of Lager Sylt, the only German concentration camp built on 'British' soil.

In the wilder southern half of the island you'll find heathland, woodland, dramatic cliffs, swirling birdlife, and the main agricultural area producing the island's deliciously creamy butter. The coast along the stunning southern cliffs between Telegraph Bay and the long, low sweep of Longis Bay is wild and inaccessible. South of the airport, on the cliff tops, the rare spotted rock-rose blooms in late April and May. The papery yellow flowers open in the morning sun then the petals drop as the light fades in the afternoon. With good timing, you might find it in bloom. Open fields, bluebell woods, and clifftop valleys lead eastwards to the Wildlife Bunker housed in the restored German radio communication centre. It is packed with information about the incredible wildlife on the island. From this vantage point, the French coast feels almost touchable and you may be fortunate enough to spot dolphins or basking sharks in the sea below. Further round, at the island's south-eastern tip, the wide, sandy crescent of Longis Bay is bounded to the east by the tidal Raz Island and Fort Raz – an optional excursion for the inquisitive.

Once back on the north coast, scenic Arch Bay is linked to the neighbouring Corblets Bay at low tide and connected to Saye Beach Campsite by a small tunnel. Rocky surrounds give it a secluded feel and protected water for safer swimming. At the east end of Saye Bay you come to Bibette Head, the location of a German stronghold. The tunnels here are great to explore by torchlight. Further along, the impressive 19th-century Fort Albert sits above Braye Bay.

Finish the round-island route at the family-friendly beach at Braye Bay, throwing off hot boots to walk the last few hundred metres on its sandy curve. Just beyond, the excellent restaurants and watering holes beckon.

Tranquil, wildlife-rich Alderney has points of interest around every corner, as well as culinary delights and a 'town' – St Anne – full of old-world charm. You'll need at least a week-end to explore

Burhou

4

Saye
Bay

Corblets
Bay

12 11

Fort Quesnard

Campsite

Mannez

Fort Albert

13

Fort Tourgis

Saline Bay

1

Braye
Bay

Roselle
Battery

Longis
Bay

Newtown

9

Essex
Castle

10   Raz Island

Fort Clonque

3

St Anne

Les Étacs

5

Airport

8

Telegraph
Bay

6   7

DIRECTIONS

» From Alderney Quay (1) turn W and follow the coastal route around Platte Saline to Fort Tourgis (2), reaching the causeway at Fort Clonque (3), which is cut off at high tide. Climb the zig-zag path above the causeway and, on a sharp L bend, follow the guide rope downhill to an underground bunker. Walk over the top of the bunker, on a faint path that runs parallel to the coast and Burhou Island (4). Continue along the undulating path to descend into the secluded Vallée des Trois Vaux, emerging to enjoy views to Les Etacs (5).

» Pass to the right of Telegraph Tower (6) and at the junction with the gravel track follow the coast path markers, passing the remains of Lager Sylt (7) on the L. Turn R on the track towards the coast and walk uphill S of

the airport. Just before the top of the hill take the faint path R marked by a small, white-painted stone. Follow the painted white rocks along the clifftop and continue along the coast path. Just before the isolated, large house reach the Wildlife Bunker (8).

» Continue to the road that leads to the island's rubbish tip and follow the coast path sign to Braye. After passing the telegraph buildings turn R at the road and walk downhill, past Essex Castle. For refreshments, the Old Barn Café (9) is on R just before the main road. Continue around Longis Bay with an optional low-tide crossing over the causeway to Raz Island (10).

» Follow the coast path marker to Braye, passing the converted Fort Quesnard and the black and white

Mannez Lighthouse, then bear R on a small path. Continue on round Veaux Trembliers Bay and the walls of Fort Corblets to reach Corblets Bay and Arch Bay before passing through the tunnel to Saye Beach Campsite, toilets, and café (11).

» Walk through the campsite and follow the track uphill to Bibette Head (12), bearing L uphill towards Fort Albert (13), then turn R halfway up to follow the coast-path signs and pass below the fort. At the top of the hill meet the gravel track that heads downhill, passing the arsenal buildings to the R, to join the main island road at the bottom. Turn R and walk along the road around Braye Bay to reach The Moorings restaurant. Turn R down Braye Street back to the quay.

CHAPTER 11

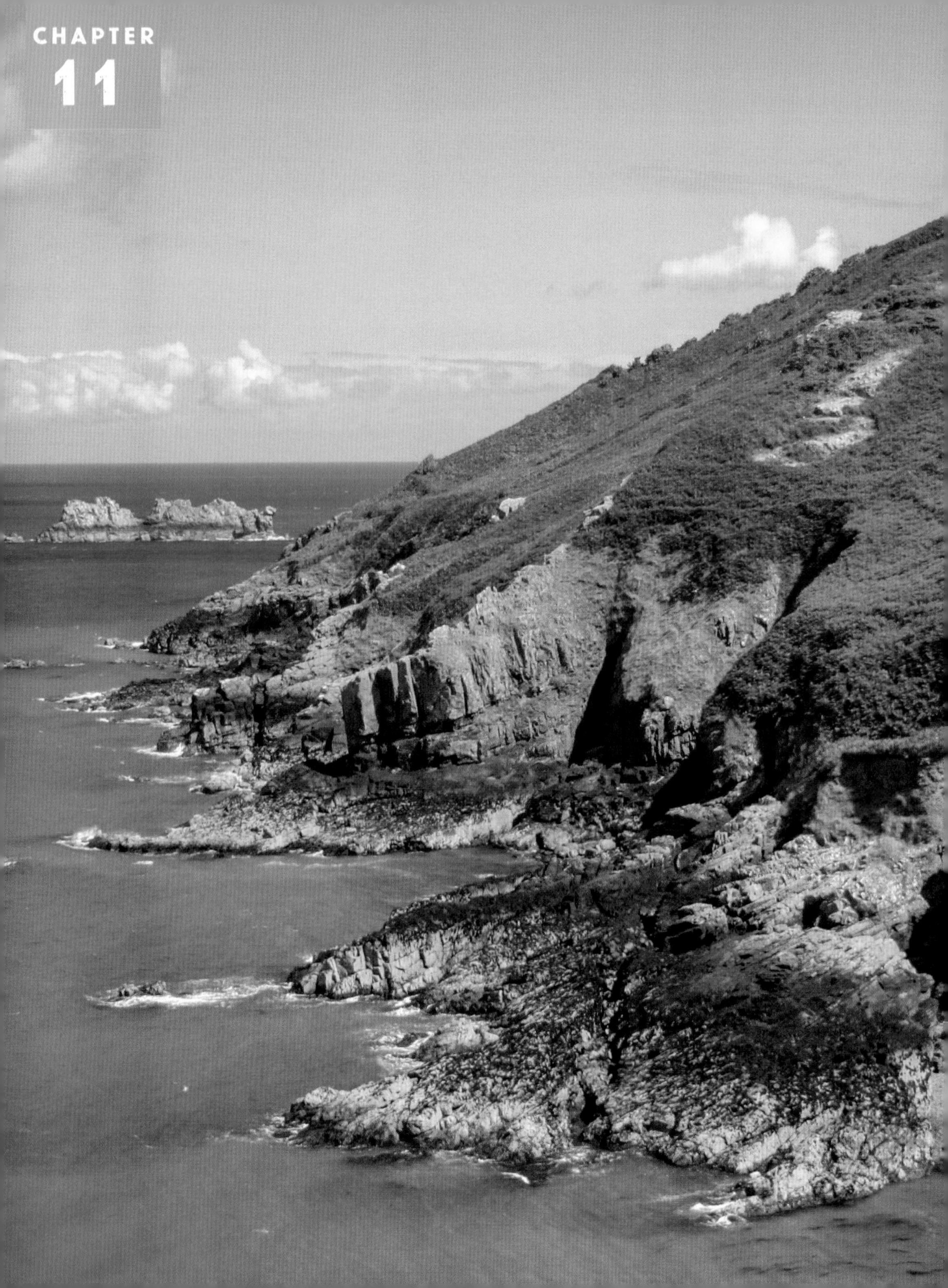

SARK

QUIRKY, TIMELESS ISLAND, ITS COASTLINE PACKED WITH CAVES AND SWIMMING SPOTS AND ITS NIGHT SKIES SPANGLED WITH STARS

Sark bills itself as 'a world apart' and there is no more apt description of this gem of an island. The skies are darker, the stars brighter, the sea cliffs higher, and the people more independent than on any other Channel Island. Once ashore, you seem to have inadvertently stepped into a time warp: this island has no cars, has its own parliament, and was one of Europe's last feudal states. Although most visitors come here to relax, the potential for a high-octane islandeering adventure among the cliffs, coves, gullies, caves, and beaches is huge.

The clockwise coastal path is mostly unmarked, although there is a clear route around the cliff tops across the generally private land of Sark and Little Sark. The route stays on top of the island's plateau, winding through farmland and past spectacular headlands, with optional descents to explore the many beaches, caves, and other points of interest. Crossing the dramatically steep isthmus of La Coupée to Little Sark, the route to the southernmost tip of the island passes excellent tearooms and restaurants.

Sark comprises two islands, Great and Little Sark, both with rugged cliffs and joined by La Coupée. It is the second smallest of the Channel Islands and the only way of getting here is by boat from Guernsey. Arrival for most holidaymakers means jumping on 'the toaster', the sturdy tractor and trailer that takes you and your luggage up Harbour Hill to the village. Luckily for the islandeer, the route leaves the tourist trail almost immediately, passing through Creux Harbour's old rock tunnel before making a steep ascent of the wild cliff tops.

Within a short distance, both Derrible and Dixcart Bays are relatively easy to access to

TERRAIN: Paths and island lanes; rocky sections in the detours

STARTING POINT: Creux Harbour. Lat/Long 49.4314, -2.3429; GR XD 752 478

DISTANCE: 17.3km (ascent 470m)

TIME: 5 hours

OS MAP: Bailiwick of Guernsey: States of Guernsey Official Map

DIFFICULTY: 1 (5 for some detours)

NAVIGATION: 2

ACCESS: 2

DON'T MISS:
- Vertigo-inducing crossing of La Coupée
- Exploring stunning caves and beaches
- Exhilarating dips in the Venus pool
- Stargazing under one of the UK's best night skies

FACILITIES: Café at the harbour. Refreshments along the walk (marked on the free tourist map). Public toilets at Harbour, Island Hall (centre of the island), and info centre.

GETTING THERE: Ferry (50 mins) from Guernsey (www.sarkshippingcompany.com). From Jersey the Manche Îles Express operate services from Granville and Carteret in Normandy to Sark, via Jersey, several times a week from April to September (www.manche-iles-express.com).

SPECIAL NOTES: Huge tidal range of 10m so take care and keep an eye on tide times when exploring beaches and caves.

explore the arch, caves, and beaches or to go for a safe swim. Between the two bays, Hogsback, the memorial to Major Appleyard who in 1942 led a commando raid to liberate the island, is a reminder of German occupation during World War II.

Further south, the route to Little Sark via La Coupée features an 80-metre drop down to Sark's most extensive sand beach, La Grande Grève. A challenge for those with vertigo, the causeway is just three metres wide, which seems to accentuate its spectacularly steep sides. At Port Gorey to the south, teams of Cornish miners once worked the four underground shafts, some extending under the seabed, for copper, silver, and lead deposits. Today, only derelict ventilation chimneys remain and these are slowly crumbling away. Nearby, a clamber down the rocks at the southernmost tip of Little Sark reveals the Venus Pool, a spectacular natural rock pool deep enough to swim and dive in. The best time to swim is two hours either side of low water.

After walking around Little Sark and recrossing La Coupée there are myriad unmarked paths and optional diversions to explore Great Sark's best stretches of coastline. Gouliot Headland, a lovely spot to watch the sun go down, is an internationally important wetland site with particularly rich animal and plant life. Above ground wild flowers, including the rare sand crocus, bloom in the spring meadows, while the accessible sea caves below are carpeted with anemones, sponges, soft corals, and sea squirts.

Beyond the headland, opposite the smaller island of Brecqhou, the route heads inland on one of the main tracks, passing the island store and the numerous cafés and restaurants that dot the iconic tree-lined Rue de Rade. Here you'll see horse-drawn carts taking visitors to island highlights, including La Seigneurie, home to Sark's feudal head, the Seigneur, since 1730. It boasts one of the best formal gardens in the Channel Islands. For spectacular views of Sark's coastline, take a short detour and follow the signs to 'Window in the Rock'.

Nearby, Port du Moulin is a great place to swim; go through the rock arch on the right to find the tiny cove beyond.

Continuing north, the day trippers thin out and you reach the open common at Eperquerie where a range of paths lead around the headland. For the adventurous, the Boutique Caves can be reached from the Eperquerie Landing via paths and steps in the cliff. There are various tunnels, shallow pools and wet and dry caves with beautiful light throughout. The small, pebbly bay just north of the landing is also good for a swim.

Heading back south along the east coast, towards Point Robert Lighthouse perched on the crags overlooking the nearby islets, you then descend back to Creux Harbour. For well-earned refreshment, head into one of the Village's taverns to meet more of the islanders and chat about life on this unspoilt isle.

Although the walk can be completed on a day trip from Guernsey, there is so much to see and do that spending a few days here is recommended and an overnight is a must. With little pollution and no cars or street lights, Sark became the world's first dark-sky island – an accolade taken very seriously by islanders who cover their torches at night with red cellophane to reduce light pollution. Comets, meteor showers, and bright constellations dazzle in the dark velvet sky and this is one of the few places in the UK where the Milky Way can still be seen in its full glory.

» Leave the harbour (1) on Great Sark, go through the tunnel, pass toilets and beach café (2) on L and start walking up the hill. After 95m take the signed footpath to L and continue uphill parallel to road. After 75m follow the footpath signs uphill to Les Laches through the woodland.

» At the small shack keep L on the track and after 200m reach the crossroads then follow the track to R through stone gateposts and head inland. After 160m follow the sign on L through the wooden gate to Derrible Bay (3) and Hogsback. Continue above Derrible Bay to T-junction and turn R, inland. Path on L leads to the Hogsback and the memorial (4) to Major Appleyard. After 220m continue on the track as it bends to L and heads downhill.

» Take the small path around the back of Dixcart Bay (5), down through the woods past a house then keep the stream to L. Take the R fork, climbing uphill towards the vineyards and turn L along the hedge between two vineyards towards La Coupée.

» Join the main track between the Village and La Coupée (6), turning L along the track to cross the causeway onto Little Sark. Pass the beach of La Grande Grève (7) on R and after 1.3km, at La Sablonnerie, take the track L to head S through a collection of small cottages and towards the two mine ventilation shafts (8). The Venus Pool (9) is a scramble down the headland at the southern-most point of the island.

» Return to the mine chimneys and continue on the coast path around Port Gorey (10) back to La Sablonnerie tearooms. Turn L to rejoin the track, cross back over La Coupée, and continue N to cross the Gouliot Headland (11). The caves can be explored on very low tides (less than 1m), by taking the steep path down to the R of the headland. Continue around the headland to reach the main track, Rue du Sermon. Pass the Sark Methodist church on the R and the island store (12).

» At the crossroads turn L towards La Moinerie, Port du Moulin, and Island Hall. Walk through the tunnel of trees on Rue de Rade, pass La Seigneurie (13) and 70m beyond follow the signpost to the 'Window in the Rocks' (14) for an optional detour. Further on, at the R-hand bend in the Rue de Rade, start the headland loop by walking straight ahead to follow signs to L'Eperquerie (15). Once on the common, choose any one of the paths that cir-

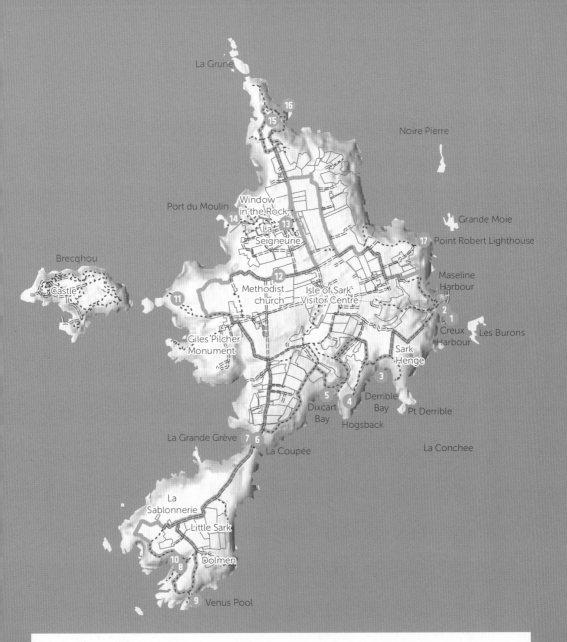

La Grune

La Gune

16

15

Noire Pierre

Grande Moie

Port du Moulin

Window in the Rock

14

13

17 Point Robert Lighthouse

La Seigneurie

Brecqhou

Maseline Harbour

Castle

12

Methodist church

Isle of Sark Visitor Centre

2
1

Creux Harbour

Les Burons

11

Giles 'Pilcher Monument

Sark Henge

3

5

4

Derrible Bay

Dixcart Bay

Pt Derrible

Hogsback

La Conchee

La Grande Grève

7 6

La Coupée

La Sablonnerie

Little Sark

Dolmen

10

8

9 Venus Pool

cumnavigate the northern tip of the island for great views and to explore the Boutique Caves near L'Eperquerie landing (16).

»   Return to the start of the headland loop and turn L (walking away from La Seigneurie) then, after 210m bear R and continue along the lane for 800m to a staggered crossroads. Turn L towards Point Robert Lighthouse (17) and La Grève de la Ville. After 160m, turn R at the junction and walk past the historic granite building. Continue on the track following signs to the Village. After 210m, where the track bends R, take the smaller track straight ahead with the stone wall on the L. Turn L, and on reaching a metal gate on L go through and follow 'Footpath to Harbour' signs to return to the start.

HERM

SNORKEL AND SWIM IN CLEAR WATER, STROLL ON UNSPOILT BEACHES, AND SEE EUROPE'S MOST SOUTHERLY PUFFIN-BREEDING COLONIES

Although very popular in the summer season, Herm has plenty of hidden corners and has to be one of the top islands for relaxing. No cars, no radios – just six astounding beaches surrounded by crystal-clear waters that almost disappear at low tide to reveal extensive rocky reefs. Offering good food and accommodation, this island makes a fantastic overnight stop and is even more peaceful once the last ferry has departed. The smallest of the publicly accessible Channel Islands, Herm is just a short hop from Guernsey. Its current tenants aim to retain the identity of the island whilst keeping it open for the enjoyment of all. Previous inhabitants include monks, smugglers, quarrymen, and Prussian princesses as well as occupying Germans. All have left their mark on this tiny island so there is plenty to explore.

The walk itself is as laid back as the island – a stroll in the park, with a gentle climb to the rocky southern plateau for lofty views of the stunning seascapes. It passes dramatic cliffs, fabulous dunes, white-sand beaches, and a large, wildflower-filled common. As well as swimming and snorkelling stops, there are opportunities to explore Neolithic tombs, follow winding inland paths, and treat yourself to delicious local ice cream. The circuit starts as soon as you set foot on Herm Harbour on the west coast where, according to local legend, the chairman of the Ford Motor Company – who once lived on the island – encased a pristine Model T within the stonework of the harbour wall itself. It's a mystery that won't be solved for a while.

Walking in an anti-clockwise direction to the south of the harbour, the palm tree-fronted White House hotel exudes small-island charm. With no

---

TERRAIN: Easy paths

STARTING POINT: Herm Quay (at low tide start from the base of Rosière Steps). Lat/Long 49.4697, -2.4537; GR XD 672 522

DISTANCE: 6.4km (ascent 257m)

TIME: 1 hour 45 mins

OS MAP: Bailiwick of Guernsey: States of Guernsey Official Map

DIFFICULTY: 1

NAVIGATION: 1

ACCESS: 2

DON'T MISS:
- Snorkelling in crystal-clear waters off Shell Beach
- Kayaking out to see Britain's most southerly puffin colony
- A night under canvas at peaceful Seagull Campsite
- Exploring Neolithic tombs

GETTING THERE: By Trident Ferry from St Peter Port Harbour, Guernsey www.traveltrident.com (01481 721379). Daily sailings from either the weighbridge or Inter-Island Quay depending on tide. Check in at the main kiosk before boarding the boat.

FACILITIES: Cafés and restaurants or take a picnic for the beach. Public toilets near Herm Quay.

HERM

Arriving at the southern tip, Pointe Sauzebourge, soak up the impressive seascape view of Sark and Brecqhou on the horizon, with many smaller islands and reefs in between. Further along the dramatic cliffs towards the southeast point of the island is a deep fissure in the rock face. This is Barbara's Leap, named after the girl who survived a 25-metre fall here and was carried up by locals in a heroic night-time rescue. From here, the path heading north up the east coast is wooded in places, climbing to a high point before descending towards the large island of Putrainez. Below is Puffin Bay, named for the characterful bird that can be spotted here in season.

clocks, televisions, or phones, this is definitely a place to switch off. In the grounds, a beehive-shaped building may be the world's smallest prison. It was built in the early 19th century and has room for just one mischief maker. Heading southwards, the coastal route offers wonderful views of the islands of Jethou and Crevichon. At the impressively crenellated Rosière Steps, which lead up from the low-tide landing point, the menacing Mouette and Percée reefs are visible offshore. From here the route climbs to the granite plateau at the steeper and rockier southern end of the island. This area was once extensively quarried for granite, some of it made into the kerbstones that still line the Thames Embankment in London.

The point at Caquorobert affords the first views of the stunning white sands of Shell Beach further north but first there is a surprise in store. Hidden Belvoir Bay doesn't reveal its beauty until you are almost upon it and on a summer's day this small beach with café, parasols, white sands, and turquoise sea feels like a tropical paradise. Beyond Belvoir, the extensive white sands of Shell Beach are framed by marram-fringed dunes. It is the jumping-off point for the Puffin Patrol kayaking trip which, in season, does exactly what it says on the tin. The beach has a small café and is a great place to relax, swim, or go snorkelling on the reefs in crystal-clear waters.

The north end of the island is dominated by a flat, grassy common where wild flowers flourish; there are also Neolithic tombs to explore. One mysterious 4,000-year-old tomb with large broken stones is known to the locals as Robert's Cross and is worth the short detour. On the northeast tip, Alderney Point is a fabulous place to view the expanse of Mouissonnière Beach below. To the west lies Guernsey, beyond Bréhon Tower atop its rock, while to the east are The Humps, a collection of sandbanks that is a haven for birds and seals.

The north coast itself is covered by wind-blown sand that hides an old, wave-cut platform, glimpsed as jagged, low-lying reefs offshore. Midway along this coast the stone obelisk breaks the otherwise

flat skyline. It was built to replace a huge standing stone that served as a daymark for local fishermen until quarrymen looking for prize pieces of Herm granite removed it. Arriving at Oyster Point on the north-western tip, a shallow, low-tide pool is all that remains of the oyster-fishing industry. Today, over a million shellfish are farmed further down the west coast at Fisherman's Beach and Bear Beach. Hermetier, also known as Rat's Island, lies between these two beaches. Cross its causeway at low tide to bag another small island.

From the coastal route you can make several interesting detours inland along grass tracks lined with pink dog roses, honeysuckle, fuchsias, and foxgloves. Manor Village in the centre of the island is a lovely stone hamlet with a chapel, farm, and 'power station'. St Tugual's Chapel has fine stained-glass windows featuring scenes including Guernsey cows boarding Noah's Ark and Jesus talking to the fisherman at Herm Harbour. Further east, the island's Seagull Campsite is temptingly located with

stunning views. The route finishes at the shops and restaurants near the harbour. The summertime bustle takes you by surprise after the peace and tranquillity of the island – until the last boat leaves, that is, and the island is yours again.

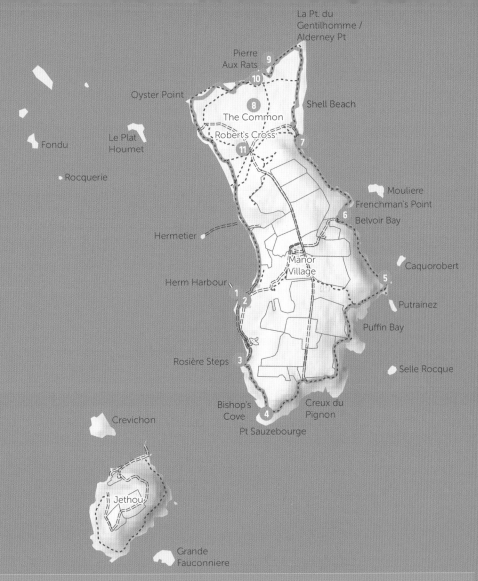

La Pt. du Gentilhomme / Alderney Pt

Pierre Aux Rats (9)
(10)

Oyster Point

Shell Beach

(8) The Common

Robert's Cross

Fondu

Le Plat Houmet

(11)

(7)

Rocquerie

Mouliere
Frenchman's Point

(6) Belvoir Bay

Hermetier

Caquorobert

Manor Village

(5)

Herm Harbour

Putrainez

(1)

Puffin Bay

(2)

Rosière Steps

(3)

Selle Rocque

Bishop's Cove

Creux du Pignon

(4)

Crevichon

Pt Sauzebourge

Jethou

Grande Fauconniere

›› Start at Herm Harbour (1) and follow the pier path to R just before the white 'sails' sculpture. Continue along the coast path in front of the White House (2).

›› Before descending towards the low-water landing pier at Rosière Steps (3), take the small path on L, climb the granite steps and head uphill to Pointe Sauzebourge (4). Continue along the undulating clifftop path, past Puffin Bay, to reach the headland at Caquorobert (5). Drop down to Belvoir Bay (6), then up the other side, following signs to Shell Beach and café.

›› Leave Shell Beach and café (7), bearing R on a path that heads N across The Common (8) and to the L of the dunes to reach the NE tip, La Pointe du Gentilhomme/Alderney Point. Turn L along Mouissonnière Beach (9) to reach the obelisk (10).

›› From the obelisk, continue past the Neolithic graves (11), to reach the main track and an optional low-tide visit to tiny Hermetier, then continue on back to the quay.

THORNEY

ESCAPE THE SOUTH-COAST CROWDS ON AN ISLAND HAVEN WITH A WILD-SWIMMING BEACH AND NATURE RESERVE

Crossing the bridge over the Great Deep you reach the MoD's barbed-wire fence with its CCTV cameras and intercom-controlled access. But once on the other side of the metal gate the contrast couldn't be sharper. Reclaimed mudflats open out, alive with the sounds of the creeping tides, the alarm calls of oystercatchers, and Brent geese taking flight. Earthy aromas of seaweed and salty mud drying in the sun soon fill your nostrils.

This clockwise walk on an easy coastal path, part of the Sussex Border Path, skirts the island's secretive military interior and follows the Thorney and Emsworth Channels. The lack of commercial development on the island makes this a wonderful haven for wildlife and the wild, sandy beach at the southern tip is a great place for a swim. The island is owned by the MoD and, although the large Baker Barracks buildings house the Royal Artillery, there are few other visible signs of the military's presence.

The walk starts at Emsworth Yacht Club and heads east to Prinstead before turning south along the east coast alongside the Thorney Channel. It passes Paynes Boatyard and Thornham Marina to reach the remote-controlled MoD security gate at the other side of the Great Deep, which separates Thorney from the mainland. Before the tidal mudflats were reclaimed in 1870, the only crossing was via an ancient causeway from Emsworth. Although the walkway no longer exists, records suggest that it was 'nearly a half-leg deep at low water'. Many misjudged the crossing and drowned in the strong currents of the channel.

The MoD's ownership of the island is the result of a chance event in 1933. When a Hawker Fury biplane came down on the island, officials inves-

---

TERRAIN: Easy path; S of W. Thorney path often overgrown and muddy, to N higher tides may hinder progress

STARTING POINT: Emsworth Yacht Club. Lat/Long 50.8428, -0.9303; GR SU 754 053

DISTANCE: 13km (ascent 54m)

TIME: 2 hours 45 mins

OS MAP: OS Explorer OL8

DIFFICULTY: 1

NAVIGATION: 2

ACCESS: 1

DON'T MISS:
- Ospreys in autumn at Pilsey Island Reserve
- A warm summer swim off Pilsey Sands
- Wildlife-rich waters of Chichester Harbour
- Atmospheric St Nicholas' Church, the soul of the island

SPECIAL NOTES: Access only via MoD gates and then limited to coastal path. Access to S tip of Pilsey Island only via Pilsey Sands and not through reserve.

GETTING THERE: Train to Emsworth Station and short walk to start. By car leave Emsworth on A27, go over bridge and take first R after Sussex Brewery. After 500m turn R onto Thorney Road and R into Mill Quay.

FACILITIES: No facilities on the island. The Deck café at Emsworth Yacht Club serves a full range of food; Scout Hut at Prinstead serves teas on weekends (April–October); basic snacks are available at Thornham Marina.

At Thorney's southern tip, the RSPB's nature reserve at Pilsey Island affords great views to West Wittering. Passing ospreys and avocets, as well as overwintering wildfowl and waders, seek refuge here and its bird hide, at the halfway point of the circuit, is a good place to shelter if the weather is bad. The large sand and shingle beach of Pilsey Sands, backed by sand dunes, is exposed at low tide, and outside the nesting season you can walk to the southern tip of Pilsey Island. This beach is a particularly good place to swim on a sunny day when the waters of the incoming tide are warmed by the mudflats.

tigating the crash scene decided it would be the perfect site for an airbase and life in the previously isolated village of West Thorney changed forever. The island was well used by the RAF during World War II and remained an active base until 1976. During the late 1970s it was a safe haven for the refugees dubbed the 'Vietnamese boat people'.

On the walk southwards, you can enjoy the wonderful sights and sounds of the tidal mudflats. A little over halfway down the east coast in the tiny hamlet of West Thorney, the graveyard of St Nicholas' Church is the resting place for World War II servicemen, both Allied and German, who now lie side by side. Continuing on, you see the long, grey smudge of the disused runway in the centre of the island.

On the route up the west coast along the Emsworth Channel, there are great views of Hayling Island. Alongside the path there is a poignant memorial to two SAS soldiers who lost their lives in recent conflicts. After a blissful circuit of this tranquil island, the exit through the west security gate brings you back to reality with a jolt. Although intimidating, the intercom and its disembodied voice mark the threshold of an amazing, wild world.

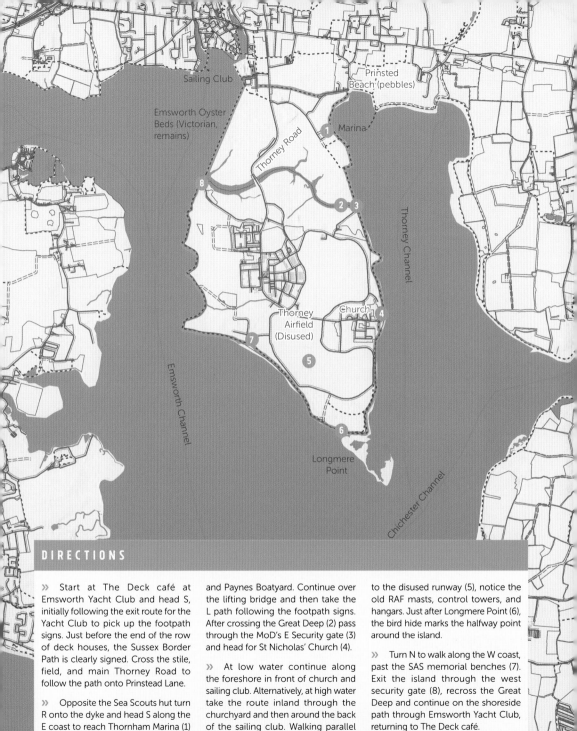

Sailing Club

Prinsted Beach (pebbles)

Emsworth Oyster Beds (Victorian, remains)

Thorney Road

1 Marina

8

2 3

Thorney Channel

Church 4

Thorney Airfield (Disused)

7

5

Emsworth Channel

6

Longmere Point

Chichester Channel

DIRECTIONS

» Start at The Deck café at Emsworth Yacht Club and head S, initially following the exit route for the Yacht Club to pick up the footpath signs. Just before the end of the row of deck houses, the Sussex Border Path is clearly signed. Cross the stile, field, and main Thorney Road to follow the path onto Prinstead Lane.

» Opposite the Sea Scouts hut turn R onto the dyke and head S along the E coast to reach Thornham Marina (1)

and Paynes Boatyard. Continue over the lifting bridge and then take the L path following the footpath signs. After crossing the Great Deep (2) pass through the MoD's E Security gate (3) and head for St Nicholas' Church (4).

» At low water continue along the foreshore in front of church and sailing club. Alternatively, at high water take the route inland through the churchyard and then around the back of the sailing club. Walking parallel

to the disused runway (5), notice the old RAF masts, control towers, and hangars. Just after Longmere Point (6), the bird hide marks the halfway point around the island.

» Turn N to walk along the W coast, past the SAS memorial benches (7). Exit the island through the west security gate (8), recross the Great Deep and continue on the shoreside path through Emsworth Yacht Club, returning to The Deck café.

CHAPTER

14

TWO TREE

A PEACEFUL SALT MARSH WILDERNESS ALMOST ON LONDON'S DOORSTEP

Salt marsh, mudflats, and tidal creeks are dotted with plantlife and the cries of migrant birds drift across the estuary. On this island walk of two halves, the eastern section is dominated by the reed beds of Leigh Marsh and the unmarked path along the wild foreshore is faint. On the busier western half of the island, the route follows surfaced paths around the sea wall.

Two Tree Island lies northeast of Canvey Island and southwest of Leigh-on-Sea, just over 54 kilometres west of London. Connected to Leigh by a bridge, this piece of land was reclaimed from the Thames Estuary in the 18th century and had rather inauspicious beginnings as a sewage works and landfill site. The Essex Wildlife Trust now manages the island and the eastern half is part of the Leigh National Nature Reserve, while the western half has two bird hides. The south shore of the island, at the end of the island road, is a popular place for water-based activities.

The walk starts on the mainland at Leigh-on-Sea railway station and heads out westward on the Thames Estuary Path parallel to the north shore of Leigh Creek. Separating the island from the mainland, this tidal stretch of water is dotted with 'ghost' boats, left to rot and long forgotten as they lie lopsidedly waiting for the sea to claim them. Of note is the 'Graveyard of Lost Species', an art project that celebrates the local tradition of wrecking boats on the salt marsh. It records and recognises the wildlife, people, dialects, and folklore that once flourished in the Thames Estuary. The names of these 'lost species' are carved on the decks of the Souvenir, a decaying boat now lying in the intertidal zone between Hadleigh Marsh and Two Tree Island. A short detour from the route takes you there.

TERRAIN: Some slippery, wet sections on the foreshore otherwise easy paths

STARTING POINT: Car park on Two Tree Island. Lat/Long 51.5376, 0.6296; GR TQ 825 854

DISTANCE: 8.6km (ascent 61m)

TIME: 3 hours

OS MAP: OS Explorer 175

DIFFICULTY: 2

NAVIGATION: 3

ACCESS: 1

DON'T MISS:
- Avocets on the lagoon at the western tip of the island
- Post-walk seafood feast at Leigh-on-Sea
- Exploring the wild salt marsh from the eastern foreshore

SPECIAL NOTES: Avoid the foreshore section of the walk on high spring tides and during bird migrating season from April to November.

GETTING THERE: Train to Leigh station from Fenchurch Street or numerous buses from Southend. Plenty of parking on the island.

FACILITIES: None. Small café at Leigh station and a range of facilities at Leigh-on-Sea.

On crossing the road bridge to Two Tree, the clockwise route tracks the eastern foreshore and nature reserve. Via a short extension into Leigh Marsh, you can experience the rich marsh habitat, a shell beach, and views across Leigh Creek to the old wharves hidden below the popular seafood eateries of Leigh-on-Sea. During summer on the salt marsh – one of the best surviving examples in the Thames Estuary – the yellows of the golden samphire, greens of the edible sea purslane, and the mauves of the sea lavenders and sea asters add vibrant colour to the glistening greys of the creeks. The intertidal mudflats are home to thick beds of eel grass – manna to the vast flocks of dark-bellied Brent geese that arrive in autumn from their breeding ground in Siberia. Leigh Marsh is a conservation site of international importance and is protected from erosion by brushwood faggots that slow the tides and increase the deposition of silt.

Halfway around the island, the slipway at the south end of the road juts out through Hadleigh Ray, its mud the consistency and colour of crème caramel. There are great views from here south to Canvey Island and you can enjoy a peaceful wild swim. The best time to plunge in is just before high tide, though the currents can be strong. From here, the route follows the western sea wall and leads to two bird hides – good places to spot avocets on the man-made lagoon. There are a few present all year around but the migrating birds arrive in greater numbers during the summer months.

This route would not be complete without visiting one of the numerous seafood shacks on the mainland along the shore of old Leigh-on-Sea. Eating a dish piled high with cockles seasoned with vinegar and pepper, while watching the swimmers and the promenaders from the sea wall outside the Crooked Billet is a firm weekend favourite.

Hadleigh
Marsh

Leigh-on-Sea Station

Leigh Golf
Range

Marina

1

2

3 Leigh Marsh

Bird Hide

4

Southend
Radio Flying Club

5

Bird
Hide

7

Two Tree Island
Scout Group

Slipway

6

DIRECTIONS

» Turn R out of Leigh-on-Sea railway station and head downhill towards the railway car park. After 100m walk onto the raised Thames Estuary Path past the marina, then after 987m reach the tarmac road and turn L over the bridge onto the island.

» Walk along the island road for 200m, then take the track over the grass bank into the trees. After a further 100m or so pass between the fence and the sign for Two Tree Island Nature Reserve. Follow the clear path through wild roses, brambles, and elders.

» After 1.4km take the L fork in the path, then after 30m take the R fork (looks like the main path). After 180m drop down onto the foreshore and follow the faint path through the reeds, which may be slippery underfoot. The route runs E along the shore parallel

to the walk from Leigh-on-Sea station, initially along the high-tide mark and then on the concrete sea wall. After 250m pass the ponds (2) and bird hide.

» At the end of the concrete sea wall, drop back down onto the foreshore and turn SE. After a short distance, and immediately after crossing the fence line, a path on L leads NE out into Leigh Marsh (3). After this detour, return the same way and continue along the foreshore towards the information point (4).

» At the information point, continue SW over the fence line initially along the foreshore and then after 400m or so go up on the grass embankment to meet the main path and on past the inland lagoon, the borrow dyke (5). At the end of the lagoon, walk up the steps to the car park towards the slipway (6).

» Continue W along the sea wall of the S coast, passing the first bird hide (7) after 900m to reach the second hide on the lagoon at the W tip of the island. At the end of the lagoon there is a tidal crossing (N) back to the mainland at Hadleigh Marsh, but the circular route continues on the path that veers E and along the N coast to pass the 'tree stump graveyard' (8) and the model-aircraft flying field. Join the main gravel path, then after 200m or so take the grass path on the L that leads straight on to stay parallel with the creek.

» At the main island road, pass through the gate and turn L to retrace the route back to Leigh-on-Sea.

CANVEY

QUIRKY, INDEPENDENT, AND DEFINED BY THE THAMES ESTUARY, CANVEY OFFERS WILD MARSHES, ANCIENT INNS, ARTY PROMENADES – ALL WITH A DASH OF R&B

The extensive shell banks at Chapman Sands east of Canvey Point are not the only place of wilderness and beauty on an island that has some of the richest sites in Europe for bugs, birds, and plants. Yes, much of it exists in the shadow of the petrochemical industry, but for open-minded adventurers this just adds to its special sense of place. Canvey lies on the north bank of the Thames between Basildon and Southend-on-Sea and is just 40 kilometres from London. Most of this heavily populated island is below sea level yet there is a surprising amount of open space and two important nature reserves.

This clockwise walk or bike ride follows a flat, well-marked trail along the sea wall that protects the island. Much of the route hugs the creeks, winding through the peaceful green marshes in the north and along the glistening, bird-filled mudflats

exposed at low tide in the south. After a colourful section along the sea wall of the Thames, with its art-deco café and murals, you'll get a fascinating insight into the island's petrochemical heritage and visit Britain's first nature reserve for bugs at Canvey Wick.

From Benfleet Station on busy Ferry Road, the roar of traffic is soon replaced by the sounds of wild estuary life along Benfleet Creek and Hadleigh Ray. Here there are extensive views across to Hadleigh Castle, the marshes of Two Tree Island, and out as far as Southend-on-Sea. At the island's eastern tip the walk out to Canvey Point, if tides permit, is well worth the detour. The extensive Chapman Sands sandbank was the last natural hazard for ancient mariners before entering the safer waters of 'Old Father Thames'. Today they form a surprising area of wilderness with gentle shell-bays and unusual

---

TERRAIN: Marked tracks

STARTING POINT: Benfleet Station. Lat/Long 51.5439, 0.5614; GR TQ 777 859

DISTANCE: 26km (ascent 100m)

TIME: 6.5 hours

OS MAP: OS Explorer 175

DIFFICULTY: 1

NAVIGATION: 2

ACCESS: 1

DON'T MISS:
- Explore wild marsh and sands at Canvey Point
- Infamous and historic Lobster Smack Inn
- Colourful murals along the sea wall near Concord Beach

SPECIAL NOTES: Synchronise your walk with low tide for the short walk out to Canvey Point.

GETTING THERE: Train to Benfleet station. By car, take M25, leave at junction 29 and head E on A127 (direction Southend-on-Sea) for 21 kilometres, then A130 S onto Canvey Island. At first roundabout, take L to Benfleet station.

FACILITIES: Lobster Smack, Windjammer pubs; Labworth and Concord Beach cafés.

low-lying mud sculptures etched by the timeless tides. Locals often wade way out beyond the path's head to collect the cockles, clams, mussels, and samphire that sit abundantly on the banks.

The walk along the south-east coast to Thorney Bay is the island's main promenade, strung with benches, lidos and cafés, including the Grade II listed art-deco Labworth, which resembles the bridge of the *Queen Mary*. Its architecture and views are as much of a pull as its menu. This part of the walk is dominated by the large blue sea wall decorated with eclectic and arty murals that reflect the history of the island, including scenes of the devastating North Sea flood of 1953 when fifty-nine islanders died. The murals also pay homage to the island's most famous natives, legendary 1970s R&B band, Dr Feelgood.

The island is affectionately known as 'oil city' and as the route continues along the south-west coast, past the sandy beach at Thorney Bay, the legacy of Canvey's petrochemical industry looms large. In the far distance, the huge cranes of the Thames Gateway's container port underline just how much this mighty river has shaped the island's character throughout history. Tankers offload at the oil-storage depots with their pipe-lined jetties on this 1.5-kilometre stretch of coastline before the ancient Lobster Smack comes into view. Perhaps the most famous, this is certainly the oldest building in Canvey and parts of it date back to the 16th century. The inn was notorious for its illegal bare-knuckle fights and a popular haunt of the island's smugglers.

Further west, Canvey Wick Nature Reserve on land at Hole Haven forms one of Europe's most important areas for bug life. Prototype structures built to store imported liquid natural gas from America were later dismantled after the discovery of gas in the North Sea. Today only the dilapidated 1.5km-long pier remains. Across the water, on the mainland, the view of the towers, silos, and flare stacks of the oil refinery at Shell Haven are softened by the mudbanks and the low profiles of Lower and Upper Horse Islands nestling within the creek. As the route turns north to East Haven Creek, the huge tide barriers and sluice gates are testament to the scale and complexity of the effort needed to keep flood water at bay. Walking parallel to the creek, the landfill site on the mainland crawls with bulldozers and lorries, while a short distance away wildlife thrives on the salt marsh and mudflats of West Canvey Marsh Nature Reserve.

Nearing the end of the walk, cars rush overhead on the A130, their occupants oblivious to the natural beauty below. The route then hugs Benfleet Creek, where egrets stand statue-still in the shallows, before returning to the road bridge and Benfleet station.

CANVEY

Benfleet Station
1
Hadleigh Castle Country Park
Hadleigh Marsh
Leigh-on-Sea
West Canvey Marsh Nature Reserve
Two Tree
East Haven Creek
9
Tewkes Creek
Canvey Heights Country Park
Oyster Creek
2
Canvey Wick Nature Reserve **8**
Canvey
Canvey Point
7
Leigh Beck
3
4 Labworth
The Lobster Smack **6**
5
Thorney Bay
River Thames

DIRECTIONS

» From Benfleet station turn L past the bus stops along Ferry Road (1) and after 340m cross the bridge onto Canvey Island, keeping to the L-hand bike/walkway. After a further 150m or so leave it and turn L onto a smaller gravel track through the grass park past the Canvey Gateway information board, with Benfleet Yacht Club to L.

» Continue straight over the road leading into the marina to follow a post marked with three white stripes. Pass the allotments and golf course and continue around the sea wall with the Benfleet Yacht Club to L. Follow the sea wall through the marshes, over Tewkes Creek sluice gate, and continue around Canvey Heights Country Park towards the marina at Oyster Creek. Cross the track to the

marina, turning R uphill for a few metres, through the metal gates and then immediately L to follow the sea wall that wraps around Oyster Creek to the car park of the Canvey Yacht Club.

» Follow the footpath sign, between the buildings of the club and yacht yard, to Canvey Point (2). Return to the sea wall and continue S along the wide bike/walkway. After 480m, or so, when the sea wall turns sharp R (W) use the stairs to drop down to the lower path for views of the estuary and to enjoy the artwork (3). Pass Concord Beach café and reach the Labworth (4) 400m further on.

» At Thorney Bay continue along the outside of the sea wall, keeping L towards the industrial buildings and past the large caravan site. Cross

various metal gates and bridges past the old petrochemical works (5).

» At the Lobster Smack (6) continue along the sea wall to reach Hole Haven Sluice and its dilapidated jetty (7) and then Canvey Wick Nature Reserve (8) after a further 600m. Bear R at the shipping sign for the tide barriers and after 100m cross the track, continuing on the grass embankment to follow East Haven Creek and West Canvey Marsh Nature Reserve (9).

» Pass underneath the A130 flyover and continue on the grass bank parallel to East Haven Creek and Benfleet on the mainland. Cross Canvey Road and continue along the bike/walkway back across the island's bridge to return to Benfleet station.

CHAPTER 16

FOULNESS

ESSEX'S BEST-KEPT SECRET AND JUST UP THE COAST FROM SOUTHEND-ON-SEA IS ACCESSED VIA THE 'DOOMWAY', A TREACHEROUS PATH THROUGH THE SANDS

Stepping out onto Maplin Sands to follow the legendary Broomway where the incoming tide is faster than most people can run, certainly requires some planning and can also test your nerve. What's more, the MoD, who own the land, like to fire missiles out across the sands, and don't exactly welcome casual visitors. But the reward for the few who do attempt this walk is a fabulous wilderness experience.

The entire route is on public rights of way, although these are generally closed every weekday between 8 a.m. and 6 p.m. Plan a weekend walk instead, particularly on the first Sunday of the month between April and the end of September when the Heritage Centre is open to the public.

The route itself starts from Wakering Stairs and tracks along the sands of the Broomway to Fisherman's Head on Foulness. Once on the island the paths and minor roads are easy to walk, with one long stretch along the sea wall bordering the rivers Crouch and Roach with great views across to Burnham-on-Crouch and Wallasea Island. Paths through farmland lead back to the sea wall at Asplins Head for the return across the sands. The route may be shortened using the various well-marked rights of way on the island.

On Foulness, the largest island in Essex and the fourth largest in England, civilians and military coexist. During the week, when the red flags are flying, various missiles, armaments, and torpedoes are tested to destruction, with the bangs and booms heard in Southend and beyond. The landscape is dotted with watchtowers, launch towers, strange domes, fenced compounds, and low-rise buildings that keep their secrets tight. Possibly the most secure place to live in Britain,

---

TERRAIN: Foreshore walking on Broomway; easy tracks and paths on the island

STARTING POINT: Wakering Stairs, Lat/Long 51.5485, 0.83966; GR TQ 970 871

DISTANCE: 29km (ascent 123m)

TIME: 6 hours (plus time to visit Heritage Centre)

OS MAP: OS Explorer 176

DIFFICULTY: 2

NAVIGATION: 5

ACCESS: 4

DON'T MISS:
- Trying to walk in a straight line along the UK's most hazardous public right of way
- Experiencing the surreal world of Maplin Sands
- Bizarre displays and delicious cakes at the Heritage Centre
- Learning a couple of words from the local dialect

FACILITIES: Cakes, sandwiches, hot and cold drinks at the Heritage Centre, first Sunday of month Apr–Sept.

GETTING THERE: Bus, line 41, from Southend-on-Sea to Foulness, Mon–Sat. By car, leave Great Wakering along New Road to Stairs Road. Report to QinetiQ reception (01702 383388) and ask for access to Wakering Stairs.

SPECIAL NOTES: Always check the QinetiQ website (www.shoeburyness.qinetiq.com) and call range control to check access (01702 383211/383212). The Broomway is always wet, wear wellies and carry your walking shoes.

Foulness is guarded 24 hours a day and access to unofficial visitors is restricted.

Accustomed to the weekday din, the 150 or so islanders who inhabit this place of wild beauty live in quaint weatherboard and brick homes. At Churchend, the island's centre, there is a single shop, a dilapidated church, a disused pub, and the Heritage Centre, which is housed in the former school. Here, eclectic displays, including wedding gowns and gas masks, tell the island's story through the ages, and there are poignant images from the unforgettable Great Flood of 1953. This is a great place to meet the friendly inhabitants whose local dialect, an Australian-like twang, is peppered with native Foulness terms such as 'stringies', 'cadgers' and 'doggies'. They sell delicious home-made cakes, too.

The 9.7-kilometre-long Broomway that crosses the flat expanse of Maplin Sands is thought to date back to Roman times. It is also known as the 'Doomway' in memory of the hundred or so who have perished here, disorientated by the creeping mists or outwitted by the fast and stealthy tides. Until the building of the military road in the 1920s, it was the only means of access to Foulness and the name refers to the branches of broom that marked the way. Today, there are no markers and the islandeer must rely on map and compass, with a GPS system also recommended as backup. If there is any hint of mist or rain in the forecast, excellent navigation skills will be required. The Broomway is inaccessible and dangerous for three hours either side of high tide (maybe longer with easterly winds or a high spring tide). A good plan is to leave Wakering Stairs at low tide (or earlier) if you are confident of covering the 9.7km in two and a half hours on an incoming tide. This allows enough time to explore the island at high tide, before you return on an ebbing tide three hours after the high.

At Wakering Stairs, the start of the walk, the causeway and the rubble extending beyond it offer firm passage over Maplin Sands' Black Grounds – areas of softer black mud that are easy to get stuck in. On the harder sands of the Broomway, the flatness of this vast, surreal seascape is interrupted only by the squiggles of thousands of worm casts and tangles of oyster, mussel, cockle, and clam shells. The earth and the sky are monochrome here and meet at the thin silver line of a sea that seems so distant at low tide that the North Sea container ships appear to slide along the sands, their size doubled by the mirror effect of the water. This foreshore is an important site for migrating birds that form lines when feeding – good markers of the position of the incoming tide. There are few notable features on the foreshore except the hull of a wrecked boat, the 'maypole' marking the entrance to Havengore Creek and a large ring of concrete. Further on, a ring of wooden poles marks the old fishing grounds.

When trialling the route I made it to Fisherman's Head with only 20 minutes to spare before the tide swept in. For most of the walk the distant sea was far from my thoughts, then it was upon me in minutes – the sounds of the feeding birds interrupting the trance-like state the serene, wild sands had induced. Detained on the island by high tide, I had plenty of time to walk the inland route before the low tide allowed me to retrace my steps over the sands.

DIRECTIONS

» Walk down the causeway at Wakering Stairs, continuing for approx. 400m to reach a small metal stake. Turn L here onto the Broomway, and follow a compass bearing of 61 degrees. Continue towards two distant poles, the course veers to the L of the L-hand pole, the 'maypole' (1), which marks the entrance to the creek. On drawing parallel with this telegraph pole with reflectors and numerous cross-pieces, reset the compass bearing to 50 degrees. After 3.7 km pass the first route inland to Shelford Head, then 800m later pass the second to Asplins Head, marked by two low metal posts. After 300m reach the low-rise concrete circle (2) with dilapidated metal pipes. After 5.9km, there is access to Rugwood Head and then at 7.42km, to Eastwick Head. Churchend can be reached via all these inland routes if you need to cut the Broomway section short.

» To follow the described route, turn off the Broomway after 9.8km via the slipway at Fisherman's Head (3). Pass the rusting bombs at the side of the slipway and continue over the sea wall past the watchtower onto the tarmac road. After 460m, at a L-hand bend in the road, continue straight ahead on the grass track to the side of a drainage channel. After 200m follow the footpath signs to the R for 500m then cross the concrete road into The Chase and pass houses on R. After 240m take the L fork in the road and then at the T-junction turn R along the tarmac road past clapboard houses. Cross the concrete road and head towards the sea wall at Crouch Corner (4). Walk E on the gravel track at the base of the sea wall for 3.7km to arrive at the Quay (5).

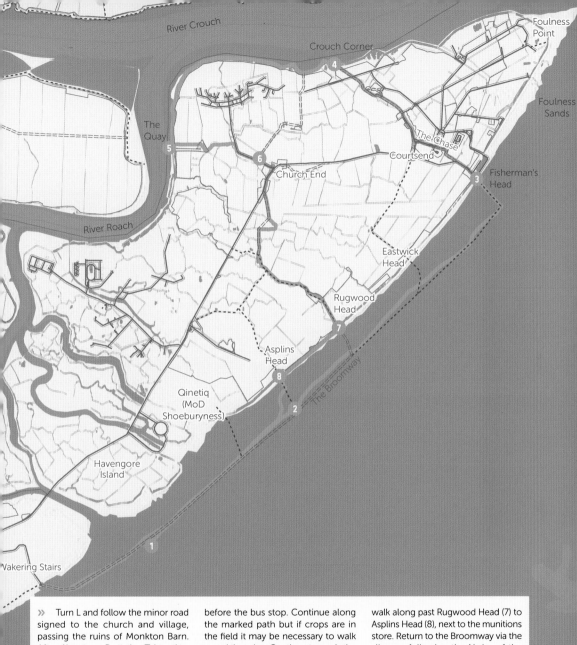

River Crouch

Crouch Corner

Foulness
Point

4

Foulness
Sands

The
Quay

5

6

The Chase

Church End

Courtsend

3

Fisherman's
Head

River Roach

Eastwick
Head

Rugwood
Head

7

Asplins
Head

8

The Broomway

Qinetiq
(MoD
Shoeburyness)

2

Havengore
Island

1

Wakering Stairs

» Turn L and follow the minor road signed to the church and village, passing the ruins of Monkton Barn. After 1km turn R at the T-junction with the main road. Pass the Heritage Centre (6) and church and after 170m, opposite the disused pub and shop, turn R onto the main road heading S off the island. After passing the village houses of Churchend, take the clearly marked footpath on the L, just before the bus stop. Continue along the marked path but if crops are in the field it may be necessary to walk round the edge. Continue towards the buildings of Rugwood Farm, turning L at the farm lane and carry on to a L-hand bend in the lane. Go straight ahead through the blue metal gates, pass a military area on L, and head directly towards the sea wall. At the sea wall, climb the steps, turn R and walk along past Rugwood Head (7) to Asplins Head (8), next to the munitions store. Return to the Broomway via the slipway, following the N rim of the concrete circle you passed on the route in, and return to the slipway at Wakering Stairs.

MERSEA

FOLLOW IN ROMAN FOOTSTEPS ON A FOODIE TRAIL OF OYSTERS AND FIZZ AROUND THIS UNDISCOVERED WALKERS' GEM

On this gentle walk around an island surrounded by silent tidal creeks and estuaries, village houses soon give way to wild salt marsh and mudflats packed with wading and migratory birds. Following the sea wall along the north coast alongside the Strood and Pyefleet Channels and round the eastern tip of the island, the route passes low Jurassic cliffs and woodland. Holiday parks and rows of pastel-coloured beach huts mark the return to civilisation at West Mersea.

Mersea is the UK's most easterly inhabited island, bound to mainland Essex via the Strood, a causeway that stretches across the tidal channels of Strood and Pyefleet. It lies in the Blackwater and Colne estuaries to the south-east of Colchester. The island is split into two main areas, the populated and seafaring West Mersea and the more rural East, which includes Cudmore Grove Country Park.

Famed for its native oysters, Mersea is a foodie destination that boasts its own vineyard and brewery.

The walk starts in bustling West Mersea, which has a marina, two yacht clubs, oyster yards, restaurants, and inns. Here you'll see sailors in their buoyancy aids coming and going along Coast Road, foodies tucking into a mountain of shells outside one of the lively eateries, and oystermen in their waterproof bibs busily sorting their catch. A visit to the island's legendary The Company Shed, a wooden shack where shared tables are adorned with just salt, pepper, and Tabasco sauce, is not to be missed. At this bring-your-own heaven you supply wine, bread, and anything else you fancy to accompany some of the best British seafood. I can vouch for the oysters and the plate of succulent scallops with crispy bacon. In season it's best to avoid the worst queues and get there before 11 a.m.

TERRAIN: Flat grass paths

STARTING POINT: Coast Road car park, opposite West Mersea Yacht Club. Lat/Long 51.7792, 0.8989; GR TM 000 129

DISTANCE: 21.5km (ascent 50m)

TIME: 6.5 hours

OS MAP: OS Explorer 184

DIFFICULTY: 1

NAVIGATION: 2

ACCESS: 1

DON'T MISS:
- Shucking meaty native oysters at The Company Shed
- English fizz and unique Champale at the vineyard
- Swimming across to Packing Shed, Cobmarsh, and Sunken Islands
- Enjoying the birdlife that thrives in the creeks

SPECIAL NOTES: The Strood is closed at certain high tides. Avoid driving over the bridge at tides greater than

5m, allowing up to 1.5 hours either side of high tides to get on or off the island safely. www.tidetimes.org.uk/west-mersea-tide-times.

GETTING THERE: From Colchester take the B1025 heading S.

FACILITIES: Seafood shacks and inns in West Mersea; café and vineyard between West and East Mersea; snacks and toilets at Cudmore Grove Country Park.

The 'common' rock oysters are available all year round here but the draw for the connoisseur is the native rock oyster. Sourced from local waters and brought to the laying beds around the island to grow naturally, they have been cultivated here by the same family since the 1700s. The current eighth generation of the Haward family export their prize-winning oysters to far-flung places as well as London's Borough Market.

Leaving the bustle behind, the walk heads past the charming black clapboard houses of the village to the wild north coast of the island. Here the only sounds are the oystercatchers' cries and the trickling tide filling or emptying creeks that carve up the salt marshes into jigsaw pieces of sage green. You'll pass forests of samphire growing on the mud banks and see the low-lying landscape of Ray Island rising slightly above Strood Channel to the north.

Among the variety of boats strung along the channel, the traditional red-sailed oyster smacks and Thames barges stand out. The smack was an oyster-dredging boat while the larger, flat-bottomed, Thames sailing barge transported goods around the coast and up the Thames Estuary. Now used as leisure craft, they sail once again along their home waterways and add a nostalgic touch.

The walk along the north coast is intersected by the Strood, a Roman causeway that links the island to the mainland. This bridge floods at high tide, baffling those expecting barriers. Common sense doesn't always prevail and cars are regularly stranded. The flooded Strood is also the highlight of the round-island dinghy race during Mersea Week in August, when volunteers help haul the boats over the bridge to complete the circuit.

Continuing along the Pyefleet Channel, past the Colchester Oyster Fishery building, you arrive at the eastern tip of the island. Here a sand and shingle spit known as Mersea Stone extends towards Brightlingsea to the north. Regular ferries connect the two in the summer months. Rounding the eastern tip the views open out to the waters of Brightlingsea

Reach and the small woods, beaches, and cliffs of Cudmore Grove Country Park. A popular destination for families, the park also features pillboxes and artillery emplacements from World War II. Yet its historical significance goes back much further and the small cliffs and foreshore have yielded a number of important geological finds. The bones of animals including hippos, macaque monkey, wolf, and bear paint a picture of the creatures that inhabited these Essex clays 300,000 years ago. For the fossil hunters, it is allegedly still possible to find sharks' teeth.

From Cudmore Grove the walk tracks the foreshore of the south coast all the way to the neat rows of holiday homes of Park Resorts. From here there is a permanent diversion inland to avoid the rapidly deteriorating sea wall. The diversion is recommended but you can continue on the path to the side of the sea wall, although this can get muddy after rain. On the plus side, the diversion passes the island's vineyard, brewery and tearoom.

Vineyards were first established here by the Romans and today's growers produce three whites and a sparking wine that flies off the shelf with the speed of a champagne cork. The vineyard is also home to the island's microbrewery. Its fine ales include Mersea Mud and Oyster Stout – the latter uses one famed local product; hopefully, the former

does not use the other. The brewery's best-known tipple is Champale, made with traditional malted barley and champagne-style yeasts to add fizz.

After the diversion and refreshments there are more holiday parks and beaches, including a string of beach huts painted in pastel colours reminiscent of the edible candy necklaces of childhood. Featuring small, nautical-themed stained-glass windows and ornate railings, they evoke the modesty of Victorian bathing. Today, they are the ultimate seaside home from home, a refuge from inclement weather, and the perfect place to make your own cuppa. Nearing the end of the walk you pass ramshackle houseboats moored at Monkey Beach – a community of bohemian residents and holiday renters. Just beyond the boats you can eat more fresh seafood at the West Mersea Oyster Bar.

Although Mersea Island will take most of the day to walk around, spending more time here will allow you to explore the other islands off its coast. You can hire paddleboards or kayaks or simply swim across. To the west, Cobmarsh, Sunken, and Packing Shed islands are all accessible by strong swimmers with a good knowledge of the tides and flows, as is Ray Island in the north and Pewit island in the Pyefleet Channel. If you want to stay dry, take the boat trip to watch the annual oyster-dredging match at Packing Shed Island – a glass of bubbles is included.

DIRECTIONS

» From the Coast Road car park (1) walk N past The Company Shed (2) to the shingle path to the R of the Dabchicks Sailing Club. Follow the footpath above the foreshore towards the Strood (3).

» At the B1025 turn L, walk along the hard shoulder for 0.5km, then turn R on the road to East Mersea. Continue on it for 300m then follow the footpath sign to L over a small bridge (there is no access via the path on the outer sea wall, which has been breached). After 10m or so drop down to the R of the sea wall for easier walking along the field margin, continue for 400m and pass through a line of scrubby trees on the footpath. A little further on the path curves to R through a small copse and around the head of a small inlet. The route then continues along the sea wall to the main Pyefleet Channel, through Maydays and Reeveshall marshes and around a larger inlet.

» Pass the Colchester Oyster Fishery building (4) and lagoon, cross the slipway track and continue through the gate along the sea wall to the E tip and Mersea Stone (5). Continue on the asphalt path along the coast towards Cudmore Grove Country Park (6). At the open area drop down onto the beach and walk below the small cliffs if the tide is low; at high tide stay at the top of the cliffs, keeping to the immediate R of the coast and wire fence. There are toilets (7) at the other side of the copse.

» At the W end of the copse drop down onto the beach, cross a small steam and continue along the shingle and sand with the holiday camp to the R. After 800m, at the end of the beach, take the concrete path to the R of the sea wall past another large holiday camp.

» At the camp bar (8) turn R through the car park along the track that passes the play area. At the crossroads continue straight ahead for 700m towards the church (9), past the entrance to Coopers Beach Holiday Park. Take the marked path to the L opposite the East Mersea parish church car park and continue W through the fields.

» At the farm, turn L past Rewsalls Farm and stay on the lane for 300m to the vineyard (10) and tearoom. Continue down the lane to enter the youth camp. Coastal erosion prevents access via the path marked on the OS map; instead follow signs to the overflow car park and the diverted footpath signs to reach the fields beyond the large green silo. Turn L and walk back to the coast.

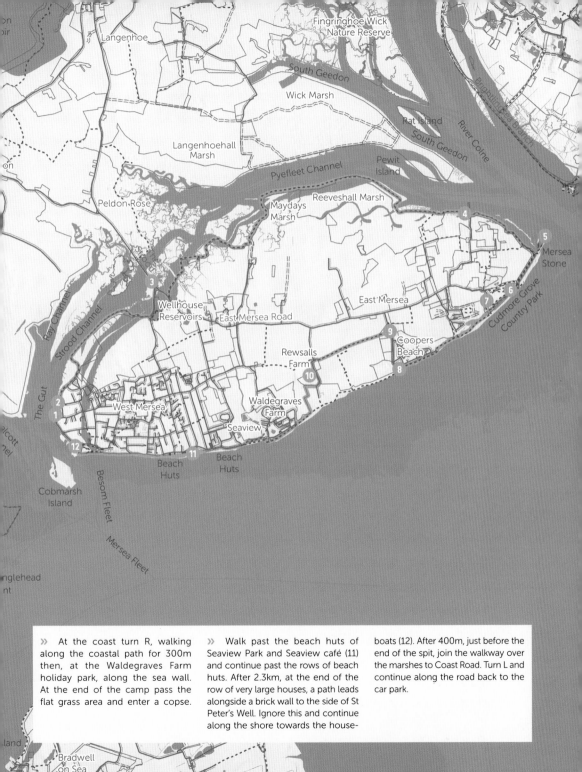

Langenhoe

Fingringhoe Wick
Nature Reserve

South Geedon

Wick Marsh

Langenhoehall
Marsh

Rat Island

South Geedon

River Colne

Pyefleet Channel

Pewit
Island

Peldon Rose

Reeveshall Marsh

Maydays
Marsh

4

5

Mersea
Stone

6

7

Cudmore Grove
Country Park

Wellhouse
Reservoirs

East Mersea Road

East Mersea

3

Roy Channel

Strood Channel

9

Coopers
Beach

Rewsalls
Farm

8

10

The Gut

2

1

West Mersea

Waldegraves
Farm

Seaview

12

11

Beach
Huts

Beach
Huts

Cobmarsh
Island

Besom Fleet

Mersea Fleet

nglehead
nt

Bradwell
on Sea

land

» At the coast turn R, walking along the coastal path for 300m then, at the Waldegraves Farm holiday park, along the sea wall. At the end of the camp pass the flat grass area and enter a copse.

» Walk past the beach huts of Seaview Park and Seaview café (11) and continue past the rows of beach huts. After 2.3km, at the end of the row of very large houses, a path leads alongside a brick wall to the side of St Peter's Well. Ignore this and continue along the shore towards the house-

boats (12). After 400m, just before the end of the spit, join the walkway over the marshes to Coast Road. Turn L and continue along the road back to the car park.

SCOLT HEAD

FORAGING, WARM SUMMER SWIMS, MUD GLORIOUS MUD, AND A WILD WALK ON ONE OF NATURE'S GREATEST BEACHES

There are a number of options for this walk depending on the level of adventure you're after. You'll cross two tidal creeks to get to the island then wade along the main channel around the southern length of Scolt Head. Even at low tide there will be water in most of the creeks, but it is fairly shallow – no more than ankle- or knee-high. The full route continues to the western tip before returning along the north shore of wild sand dunes and shingle. The shorter route, the one that has been written up here, diverts to the north shore before the western tip. But if you prefer to keep your feet dry, take the seasonal ferry from Burnham Overy Staithe and enjoy an uplifting, wild walk along the north shore.

Scolt Head sits between Brancaster and Wells-next-the-Sea on the north Norfolk coast. Owned by the National Trust, this small paradise of sand dunes,

salt marsh, mudflats, and shingle is internationally important for its birdlife. There are just two buildings on the island: one at the western end and the other more centrally situated towards the southwest end of the dunes.

The walk out to the island starts at Burnham Overy Staithe, an idyllic harbour with a historic boathouse, gorgeous flint-faced village houses, and a string of colourful boats bobbing at anchor along its peaceful creek. This is the place that inspired one of the area's more famous residents, Horatio Nelson, to learn to sail. The harbour is almost deserted at low tide, with activity building to a crescendo at high tide when picnic-laden dinghies, kayaks, crabbers and motor boats head out to Scolt Island.

The crossing of Overy Creek is straightforward at low tide; at high tide you'll need to swim. Either

---

TERRAIN: Creek beds, sand and mudbanks, sand-and-shingle beach

STARTING POINT: Burnham Overy Staithe quay, Lat/Long 52.9650, 0.7462; GR TF 845 444

DISTANCE: 13.8km (ascent: 243m)

TIME: 4 hours (for the short route)

OS MAP: OS Explorer 250 & 251

DIFFICULTY: 2

NAVIGATION: 5 (3 if arriving by boat and walking to the N shore)

ACCESS: 4 (2 if arriving by boat)

DON'T MISS:
- Exploring the wild creeks of the south shore
- Walking the extensive sands of the north shore
- Foraging for samphire
- Secret swimming in the warm pools of the creek

SPECIAL NOTES: Only attempt Norton Creek route at low tide (passable 2 hours before/after). Beware of fast tides which flood E and ebb W in the creeks. Swim back only

on flooding tide. Car park may flood at high tides. GPS device recommended.

GETTING THERE: Seasonal ferry from the quay runs 1.5 hours before and after high water (daylight hours, Apr-Sept). Check times at boathouse (07836 523396).

FACILITIES: No facilities on island. Burnham Deepdale has an excellent café, campsite and, shop. The Hero pub (Burnham Overy Staithe) serves good food and has rooms.

way, you get your first taste of the glorious mud to come. The path then meanders through the salt marsh, past tidal hollows imprinted with the footprints of birds, deer, rabbits, and children. The salt marsh here and on the island is considered one of the finest in the UK with a wealth of wild plants including samphire, sea lavender, and sea purslane in the creeks.

At Overy Cockle Strand, the main crossing point to the island, there are showstopping views to the broad sweep of golden sand and high, marram-topped dunes that form the spine of Scolt Head Island. At low tide you can walk to the island; at high tide the sun-warmed mud and sand make the water here the perfect temperature for swimming.

Once on the island the main navigational challenge begins. The quest is to find the head of Norton Creek amongst the maze of waterways that feed the salt marshes of the south of the island. The creek beds make the best and easiest walking routes, avoiding the delicate habitats and notoriously slippery mudbanks. Underfoot, the surface varies between soft sand, shell, shingle, and mud. On the creekbanks, birds search for shellfish and succulent salt marsh plants flourish, including samphire, its small, vibrant green stalks pushing up through the mud like miniature pine trees. With its distinctive salty crunch, this asparagus-like plant is a forager's delight. Small crab shells indicate an abundance of marine life, but also a perilous one for crustaceans surrounded by hundreds of hungry terns and gulls.

Norton Creek is much wider than the creeks encountered so far. It feels more like a boat channel and the south bank is marked with navigation stakes. There are plenty of pools, warmed by the sun, that make perfect secluded swimming spots all along this stretch. Just south of Hut Marsh the creek widens, offering sweeping views to the woods and fields of the mainland and across the vast, bird-filled sandbanks to the Hut.

For the full circumnavigation the route continues around the southern foreshore, across wide Cockle Bight and below the modern Ternery Hut to the western end of the island. At least five species of tern return here annually and it is out of bounds during breeding season (April to August). Visit at other times for views to Brancaster and to see the rusting wreck of the *SS Vina*, towed there by the military in 1944 and used by the RAF as target practice for the Normandy landings.

If time, tides, or wildlife restrictions do not allow for the full circumnavigation of the island, a shorter route is possible through the magical flower-filled marsh of Butchers Beach to the Hut. This pretty listed building is clad with weathered Norfolk oak, roofed with lichen-crusted cedar shingles, and

sports a tall, pebbled chimney. Sitting on the edge of the high dunes, it blends perfectly with its environment. It was built in the 1920s for the island's first warden and is the best place to observe the birdlife in the marsh and creek below. Just north of the Hut, at the top of the dunes is the island's high point. Enjoy the spectacular views and watch the North Sea rollers break along the full six kilometre length of the sand and shingle beach.

The walk along the north coast is as wild as it gets. The orange-brown tint of the North Sea adds a touch of colour to the parallel strips of blue sky, golden sand, and green grass-topped dunes. Large, sun-warmed pools of water left behind by the previous high tide make perfect, calm swimming holes away from the surf. The dunes are a rich tangle of colonising grasses dotted with sea holly, birds-foot trefoil, and pyramidal orchids, while on the shingle bank you can spot biting stonecrop, sea

campion, yellow horned-poppy, sea thrift, sea beet, sea wormwood, sea lavender, and shrubby seablite. And of course there is rich and varied birdlife here, too, their beautiful song sometimes drowned out by the pounding surf.

At high tide, the beach on the eastern tip of the island is the destination for the flotillas heading out from Burnham Overy Staithe. A variety of brightly coloured boats land their occupants on the beach here for a picnic and swim.

The return route back across both creeks depends on the state of the tide. In season, the ferry is the easy way back but I find a swim the most refreshing way to finish the walk. Let the incoming tide carry you all the way back from the island to the car park as you glide past the people in deckchairs and camper vans, all assembled to watch the high-tide spectacle.

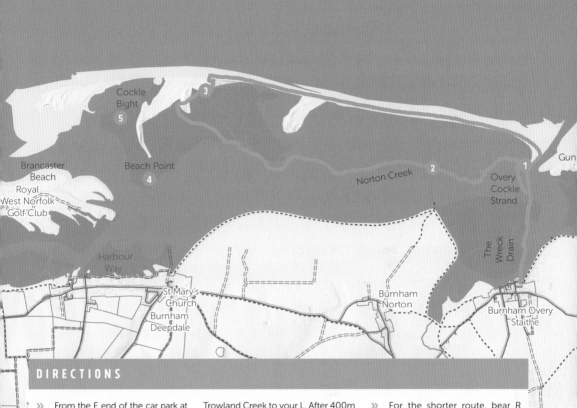

Cockle
Bight

5

3

Brancaster
Beach

Royal
West Norfolk
Golf Club

Beach Point

4

Norton Creek

2

1

Overy
Cockle
Strand

Gun

The
Wreck
Drain

Harbour
Way

St Mary's
Church

Burnham
Deepdale

Burnham
Norton

Burnham Overy
Staithe

Muckleton

DIRECTIONS

» From the E end of the car park at Burnham Overy Staithe cross Overy Creek keeping L of an obvious drainage creek on the opposite bank. Walk N along the wide mud path towards the E edge of the marshes. After 940m cross the first of two wooden footbridges over the smaller creeks, and after a further 260m reach Cockle Strand. Walk across the sands towards the white sign on the island (1).

» Cross the creek to the island and turn L to start the clockwise circumnavigation. Head W, then take the R fork along the creek bed towards the dunes of the island. After 600m avoid the inlet to the R that penetrates Great Aster Marsh and at the sharp R bend in the creek, walk up onto the S (L) bank and head S across the sands towards the mainland for 20m or so. Turn W and continue along the sandbank keeping the mainland and water of

Trowland Creek to your L. After 400m or so cross a creek and continue along the sandbanks and creek bed. After a further 100m turn R into the large sand estuary of Norton Creek (2) – probably dry for the first 100m or so and with sticks marking its S bank.

» Pass the 8 knots sign and after 500m the Hut (3) comes into view as the estuary sweeps to R. Continue wading along Norton Creek for 1.6km to reach the oyster beds and the path that crosses from Burnham Deepdale on the mainland.

» For the full circumnavigation, continue along the foreshore to Beach Point (4) and then cross the sands of Cockle Bight (5) to round the W tip and walk along the N beach to join the remainder of the walk as described after the 7.9km mark below.

» For the shorter route, bear R through the marsh towards the National Trust sign/pillar prominent on the sand dune above. Follow the faint path parallel to the dunes, initially veering away from the Hut. After 900m, at the end of the dunes, turn R towards the Hut along the small path through the vegetation. After a further 200m, just below the Hut, cross a creek bed and then climb up the steps. Take the grass path past the low-rise storage area into the higher dunes and look at for the path down to the beach on L.

» At beach turn E and walk along the sand and shingle (this meets the full circumnavigation route coming from the west tip), continuing along the beach for 4.4km to the island's E tip. Go round to return to the crossing points back to Burnham Overy Staithe (or swim S along Overy Creek).

LINDISFARNE

WILD NORTHUMBRIAN BEACHES AND ENIGMATIC RUINS ON A FULL COASTAL CIRCUIT OF SHIFTING SANDS AND TIDES

There are two ways onto this tidal island. You can follow tradition and walk barefoot across the glistening mud and sands of St Cuthbert's Way, the ancient pilgrim's path. Or you can drive over the causeway, which is submerged for a period either side of high tide. However you choose to arrive, the circumnavigation of Lindisfarne includes an unmarked route around the extensive and beautiful dunes of the western peninsula and the wilds of the North Shore. It then follows the well-trodden coastal path at the eastern end of the island past Lindisfarne Castle, the priory, and harbour. Short diversions inland are possible throughout the route to experience everything this spiritual isle has to offer.

Lindisfarne, or Holy Island, is located 1.6 kilometres off the north-east coast of England, close to the Scottish border and remains a significant pilgrimage site. It is also a designated National Nature Reserve and the extensive sand dunes and foreshore are protected. The island has a thriving village community but once away from the houses and the castle, it feels wild and remote.

The clockwise walk starts at the car park before the island's village, and heads back up the causeway towards the mainland. Polished grey mudflats glisten in the sunlight, the surface water reflecting the long, black marker poles of St Cuthbert's Way where refuges on tall stilts offer protection to those who have misjudged the tides. Departing from the main causeway at the far western end of the island, the route heads north into the salt marsh at the base of the dunes. Here, away from the traffic, you can drink in the peace and solitude and enjoy vistas of Berwick-upon-Tweed and the domed Cheviot.

TERRAIN: Beach, dunes, paths

STARTING POINT: Holy Island car park. Lat/Long 55.6759, -1.8021; GR NU 125 425

DISTANCE: 15.6km (ascent 255m)

TIME: 5 hours

OS MAP: OS Explorer 340

DIFFICULTY: 2

NAVIGATION: 3

ACCESS: 3 (4 via St Cuthbert's Way)

DON'T MISS:
- Enigmatic priory ruins at an ancient centre of Christianity
- A wild walk on the deserted North Shore
- Fantastic views of Bamburgh Castle and Farne Islands
- Walking barefoot across the sands on St Cuthbert's Way

SPECIAL NOTES: Causeway open 3 hours after high tide until 2 hours before next high tide. Tide tables giving safe crossing periods at www.northumberland.gov.uk/www2/ holyisland/holyisland.asp. Initial route to Snook Point may need to move slightly inland depending on tide.

GETTING THERE: Train to Berwick-upon-Tweed, then bus service (www.bordersbuses.co.uk). By road, leave the A1 at Beal following the signs to Holy Island. Pay car park before the village on the island. Or take St Cuthbert's Way, starting just S of causeway bridge over South Low.

FACILITIES: Wide range of facilities and toilets in the village.

LINDISFARNE

along the grass paths of the east coast, you pass agricultural land and the glistening water of the Lough, an inland lake, before catching sight of iconic Lindisfarne Castle. On the large pebble beach near Castle Point on the southwest tip, there are numerous stone cairns built by those who perhaps wanted to mark their visit to such an inspirational location.

Heading along the south coast, the cavernous tunnels of the limekilns offer an interesting diversion before you reach the castle itself. Originally built as a Tudor fort in 1550, the castle supported a small garrison until the middle of the 19th century, when the structure fell into disuse. In the early 20th century, architect Edwin Lutyens was commissioned to create a stately holiday home within its walls. Now owned by the National Trust, the castle draws visitors like a magnet. Slightly inland, the walled garden designed by Gertrude Jekyll provides welcome respite from the crowds, its summer colours vibrant and jewel-like.

Halfway along the south coast the pebbly harbour beach is fringed by a jumble of upturned boats, weather-proofed with thick tar roofs and tarpaulin. Deft hands at recycling, Lindisfarne's fishermen transformed the hulls of their old herring boats into storage sheds for nets and tools. They are still in use today.

The island's North Shore, a vast expanse of exposed, wind-blown sand, has been called one of the most stunning beaches in Britain yet few venture out here. At low tide, the North Sea seems very distant. Continuing east along this shore, a number of sandy paths wind through the marram-grass-topped dunes away from the rocks of Back Skerrs and Snipe Point where seals haul out, their haunting wails adding to the atmosphere. The varied coastal scenery of Coves Haven and Castle Head, which has crenellated formations, caves, and ledges, can be viewed from the two secluded coves backed by the soft dunes.

At the north-eastern tip a white obelisk, the navigational daymark of Emmanuel Head, overlooks the secluded sand beach of Keel Head. From here the views across to the Farne Islands and fairytale Bamburgh Castle are exhilarating. Turning south

The route then passes the ruined priory. Built on the site of the original monastery that was the centre of Christian teaching in Anglo-Saxon times, the priory is an important destination for modern pilgrims. The 7th-century monk and bishop, St Cuthbert, lived here before briefly moving to the small island (now St Cuthbert's Island) that sits close to the shore, later sailing to nearby Inner Farne for greater solitude. Marked by a large cross in its centre, the island can be visited at low tide. On the shore around St Cuthbert's Island, the rock pools are alive with crabs, sponges, anemones, starfish, pipefish, and gobies. You might even see the 15-spined stickleback, wrasse, or northern octopus in the deeper pools.

Walking north up the west coast, a number of short detours inland take you to the island's other main attractions, including the winery, and the inns and cafés that sell delicious sandwiches filled with locally caught crab. The route continues north along the top of the small cliffs of the Basin, where tiny, late-spring wallflowers sprout from every crevice and fill the air with their beautiful fragrance. The route returns to the causeway, past the poles that mark the end of the pilgrim's path. It may or may not surprise you that the incoming tide strands more motorists on the causeway than pilgrims walking across the sands.

Goswick Sands

Back Skerrs

Snipe Point

Castlehead Rocks

Keel Head

Snook Point

2

Primrose Bank

The Snook

Nessend · Sandham

3

4

Emmanuel Head

Beal Point

Refuge Box

fe Crossing nformation

Kiln (Ruin)

The Lough

Brides Hole

Sheldrake Pool

12

1

Holy Island Sands

Lindisfarne Castle

8

St Cuthbert's Isle

Priory (Ruin)

9

The Ouse

7 **6** **5**

10

11

Castle Point

Dolphin Stones

Long Ridge

Sandeel Beds

The Harbour

Fenham

Guile Point

Parton Stiel

Fenham Flats

Ross Back Sands

DIRECTIONS

» Leave the island's car park (1) and walk along the causeway, or the paths that run alongside it, back towards the mainland. After 3.4km, as the road sweeps L to cross the channel to the mainland, take the small path going N away from the causeway and walk along the base of the dunes. Continue ahead on the short grass into the dunes and reach the beach at Snook Point (2).

» Continue all the way along the beach of the North Shore until you reach the first of the rocks of Back Skerrs (3). Bear R into the rocks, then turn R into the dunes and go through the gap in the fence. Follow the dune path parallel to the beach around Snipe Point and continue past Keel Head.

» From the obelisk (4) at Emmanuel Head, continue on the grassy path parallel to the coast to reach the stone wall after 0.5km, then cross the stile and go through the kissing gate towards the castle. Reach the beach (5) then walk around Castle Point, keeping to R of the large, stone-arched limekilns (6) and go up the wooden stairs to join the main path.

» Pass to the R of Lindisfarne Castle (7), taking an optional trip to the Jekyll garden (8) and continue along the main track towards the village. After 600m, just before reaching the houses, turn L around The Ouse (9) bay and pass in front of the fishermen's sheds and boats. At the jetty, walk up onto the bank to the R of the brown shed and lifebuoy and follow

the grass track to the lookout tower – from here there are short diversions inland to visit the priory (10). Follow the wall down to the beach to pass in front of more fishermen's sheds and continue along the coast, or visit St Cuthbert's Island at low tide (11).

» After 400m, just beyond the last shed, find a faint path on R beside a wall and climb to the top of the bank. Continue parallel to the barbed-wire fence next to the houses. If you miss the path, continue along the beach to a bigger path up the bank, with a rope. Continue to the causeway and turn R back to the car park or follow St Cuthbert's Way (12) across the sands back to the mainland.

CHAPEL ISLAND

SHIFTING CHANNELS, FAST TIDES, AND SINKING SANDS ON AN EXHILARATING ROUTE ACROSS NOTORIOUS MORECAMBE BAY

After The Queen's Guide to the Sands, Ray, had looked me up and down a couple of times there was a certain point when he decided that I was good to go. Concerned about the water levels in the channel, he stopped short of commenting that I didn't possess the longest legs in the animal kingdom. As the cold rushing water from Coniston and Windermere passed above my belly button and almost took my legs from beneath me, I did for one moment wish that today he'd agreed to take only giants.

The walk starts at Canal Foot just outside Ulverston, goes through the channels of the River Leven, and crosses the main sands of Morecambe Bay to reach Chapel Island. The circumnavigation follows the sands of its foreshore. The use of a guide for this island is highly recommended. Each season, or after particularly bad weather, the location and depth of the channels may change. You can also join one of various walks to the island organised by different charities.

A tiny, uninhabited limestone outcrop in the middle of the Leven Estuary, Chapel Island is owned by the Cavendish Estate and sits about a mile offshore in sandy Morecambe Bay. Just 400 metres long and 100 metres wide, it is an impenetrable tangle of undergrowth and a popular destination for those who wish to enjoy the glorious sands that surround it. Of all the islands of Britain, this one probably attracts the most safety warnings owing to the notorious sinking sands and extremely quick tides of the bay.

I met up with Ray at Canal Foot and we started the route by negotiating slippery rocks to cross the smaller of the Leven's channels outside the Bay Horse. The inn was once a stopping place for the

---

TERRAIN: Soft sands and mud

STARTING POINT: Bay Horse Inn. Lat/Long 54.1894, -3.0536; GR SD 313 776

DISTANCE: 5.8km (ascent 53m)

TIME: 1 hour 45 mins

OS MAP: OS Explorer OL7

DIFFICULTY: 5 (1 with a guide)

NAVIGATION: 4 (1 with a guide)

ACCESS: 4

DON'T MISS:
- Crossing river channels and negotiating quicksand
- Ray's brown shrimp and catching flatfish with your feet
- The most southerly sighting of eider ducks
- Peaceful, sandy beaches with magnificent views

GETTING THERE: From Ulverston, a 4km walk or cycle ride along the Ulverston Canal towpath to Canal Foot. Limited parking at Canal Foot.

SPECIAL NOTES: Using the services of a guide for this walk is recommended (info@guideoversands.co.uk). No access to the island between 1 April and 31 July owing to nesting eider ducks.

FACILITIES: No facilities on the island. The Bay Horse at Canal Foot serves food. Nearby Ulverston has many facilities; the best tea and cake is at Gillam's.

stagecoaches that crossed the sands to Cartmel. The second, more challenging channel, has a deeper gully and much stronger currents that can sweep an adult off their feet even at low tide. The depth depends on the volume of rain that has fallen higher up in the mountains. Keeping a careful eye on the weather for the past week or so will give you a good indication of the water levels you are likely to encounter.

Once safely across the channels, the slippery sands open out, their smooth surface interrupted by thousands of worm casts and evidence of birds searching for rich pickings. Beware of sinking sands along this bank and around the island itself: the waters of many springs flow beneath the surface and create quicksand. Ray had the following advice: 'If you feel yourself sinking, don't stop, just keep moving'.

Turning south there are extensive views across to the seaside town of Morecambe, the nuclear plant at Heysham, and Blackpool Tower further on. After just over a mile you reach the rocks that form the approach to the north end of the island where you can climb up to explore the ruins, depending on the thickness of the undergrowth. Once the site of a 14th-century chapel built by monks from nearby Conishead Priory, these ruins are the remains of a folly built the early 1800s to romanticise the sea view from the priory.

As you walk anti-clockwise along the western shores of the island, enjoy the feel of the soft sands, their beautiful shapes sculpted by the tidal waters of the channel. On the tree-fringed island, oxeye daisies and pink campions bow their heads in the breeze, making this a peaceful destination for locals.

The southern end of the island, where the sands and rocks trap warm water, is the perfect place to stop to absorb the views – if the island's eider ducks are not in residence. These birds are the most southerly breeding eiders and, at the last count, almost 350 nests were found here. Gulls also nest on the shingle beach close by. Turning north, the steep cliffs of the east side come as something of a surprise. They rise almost vertically from the sands and form an impenetrable rock wall.

Returning to the mainland, the fabulous views are framed by the mountains of the South Lakes. In the foreground on Hode Hill there is a distinctive monument, modelled on the Eddystone Lighthouse and dedicated to a distinguished local naval officer. Walking back in the peace and solitude of the sands, you can't help feeling that parliament's rejection of George Stephenson's proposal to build a railway line from Cartmel to the Furness Peninsula was a real blessing. Chapel Island would have been turned into a halt and its raw natural beauty lost forever.

On the return crossing of the channel, Ray had more tricks up his sleeve. After talking about his life as a fisherman he offered to catch some flatfish – known locally as flukes – with his bare feet. Convinced he was trying to take my mind off being swept away by the tide, I foolishly challenged him. Within seconds he'd reached down into the water and was calmly holding a flapping fish in his hands. And there was another treat in store at Ray's shed – his own delicious, hand-picked brown shrimp for sale.

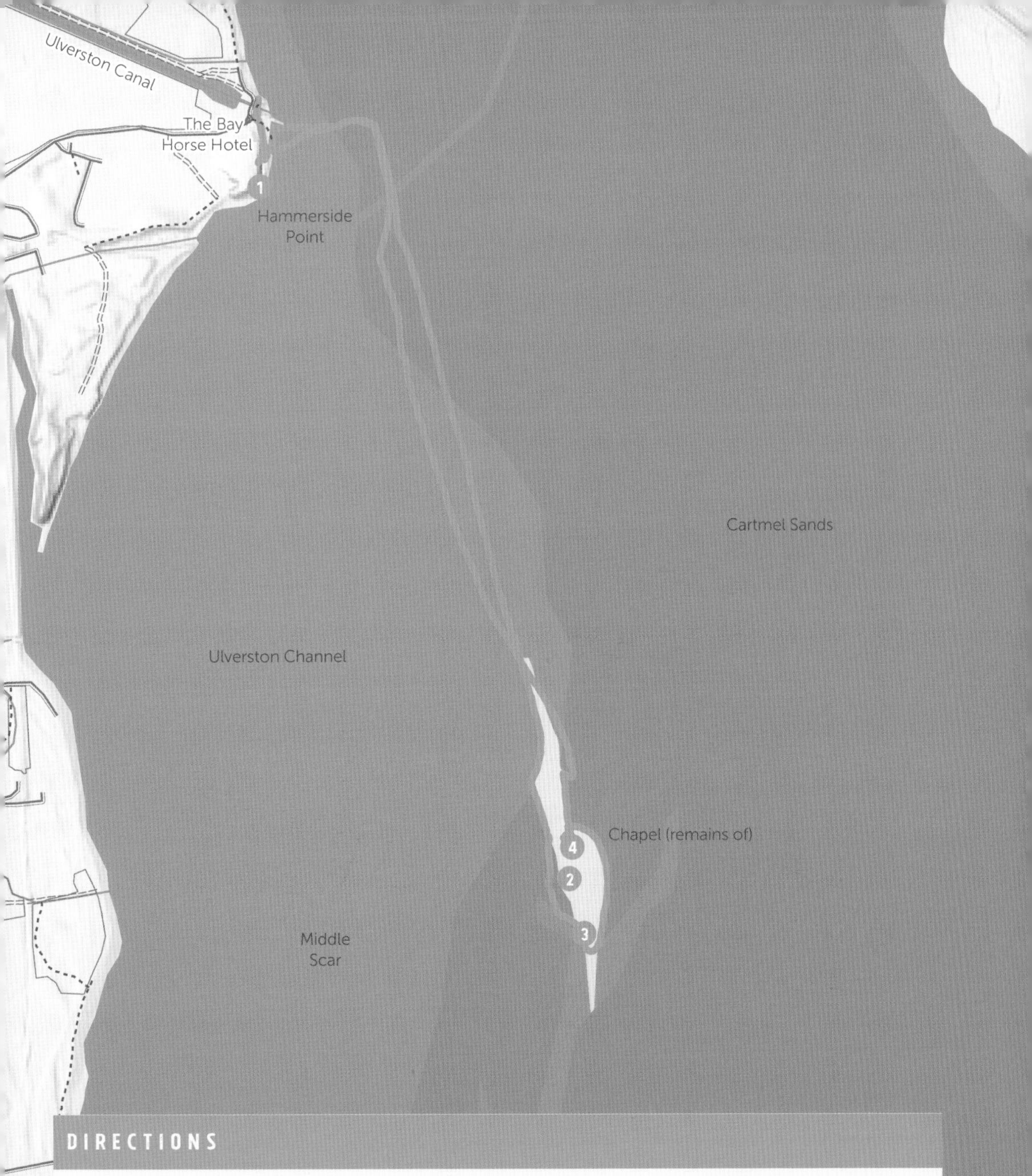

Ulverston Canal

The Bay
Horse Hotel

1

Hammerside
Point

Cartmel Sands

Ulverston Channel

Chapel (remains of)

4

2

Middle
Scar

3

DIRECTIONS

» Start at the car park of the Bay Horse inn (1) and walk down the bank to S of the jetty close to the last house on Hammerside Point. After crossing the channels of the River Leven, walk S along the sands. After 1km or so, cross a further small channel and after a further 1.1km reach the island.

» Walk along the beaches (2) of the W coast to reach the pools (3) at the southern tip. An exploration of the chapel ruins (4) is possible from the NE.

HILBRE

WAVE-SCULPTED CLIFFS WITH CAVES, ARCHES, AND GEOS TO EXPLORE ON AN EXHILARATING ESTUARY WALK TO A MINIATURE ARCHIPELAGO

I have walked to these islands twice now. Once, alone in the swirling mist, the thrill of crossing the vast sands of Liverpool Bay heightened by knowing the tide was creeping invisibly towards me. Then again on a hot, sunny August weekend amidst the happy exodus from the surrounding cities with the RNLI in attendance to shepherd the stragglers. Almost a rite of passage for the people of Merseyside, this crossing offers a unique inside into a natural world right on the doorstep of the metropolis.

Hilbre Island in the mouth of the Dee Estuary is part of a long rocky strand that, together with the small islands of Little Eye and Middle Eye, forms an archipelago. The route, which takes in all three very different islands, passes around the back of Little Eye, then over the top of Middle Eye, to reach Hilbre. There are plenty of opportunities to explore the wonderful geological features of the coastline and the eclectic mix of buildings on the uninhabited islands.

The route described avoids the sticky mud and softer sands around each island. A direct crossing from the mainland is not advised for this reason. The tides are very fast here and safe access is two hours either side of low tide. Although this time can be extended, neap tides cover the route only a couple of hours before high tide so always check conditions on the day with the RNLI on Dee Slipway.

Once safe passage is assured, setting off across the sands of the Dee Estuary from West Kirby is like stepping from one world into another. After just a few metres the bustle of the seaside town gives way to the calls of seabirds. As the route progresses, magnificent views of the English and Welsh coastlines unfurl, extending to Anglesey and the Irish Sea

---

TERRAIN: Sands and mud; footpath on island

STARTING POINT: Wirral Sailing Centre. Lat/Long 53.3715, -3.1903; GR SJ 209 867

DISTANCE: 8.3km (ascent 103m)

TIME: 2 hours (45 minutes to reach Hilbre Island)

OS MAP: OS Explorer 266

DIFFICULTY: 2

NAVIGATION: 4

ACCESS: 4

DON'T MISS:
- Exploring rock arches, caves, and sandstone geos
- Thrilling crossing of the vast tidal estuary
- Bird species from all over the world
- Being marooned and having the island to yourself

SPECIAL NOTES: Wear suitable shoes: there are sharp shells and weever fish under the sand.

GETTING THERE: By rail, West Kirby station and walk to Wirral Sailing Centre and the slipway. Car park on Dee Lane and free parking on the front.

FACILITIES: No food or drink on the island; compost toilets available. All food and accommodation facilities at West Kirby. West Kirby Tap, Grange Road, offers a great selection of real ales and ciders.

Just 100 metres or so further on, Hilbre is reached by a ramp that passes some beautifully sculpted, deep red sandstone cliffs – the Wirral's very own 'Ayers Rock'. Inland, the first building you encounter is the bird observatory, part of a national network of observatories and ringing stations. Further north along the main track, a small, grassy mound indicates the air-raid shelter where a generator once powered the decoy lights on Middle Eye. A little further on, the old Telegraph Station with large, semicircular windows was part of the chain of signal stations from Holyhead to Liverpool. The fastest recorded response time from Holyhead to a message sent from Liverpool was 23 seconds – faster than my current broadband service.

beyond – all in sharp contrast to the grey, industrial, inland landscapes of Deeside and Merseyside.

The Dee Estuary is home to a huge variety of wildlife, with every season bringing a different spectacle. The vast numbers of waders and wildfowl make this one of the ten most important sites in Europe for overwintering birds. In spring and summer, the relatively calm and shallow waters act as a nursery for the boisterous colonies of common, little, and sandwich terns that arrive from Africa and the Southern Hemisphere every year.

Crossing the sands the first stop is Little Eye. This tiny rock seems to wage a daily battle against erosion by the sea. The striated sandstone outcrop feels like a miniature Robinson Crusoe island, its golden sands topped by large ferns and its rock crevices blooming with wild flowers. After walking along the gooey mud and sand parallel to the shell-encrusted, treacherously slippery strand you reach Middle Eye. A grassy hump with a clear, bracken-lined path running through its centre, the island was once farmed and also used as part of the RAF's World War II decoy system to confuse enemy bombers heading for Liverpool. There is a rock arch to explore on this peaceful spot or you can sit and take in the stupendous views all around.

Even on the lowest ebb of a spring tide the northern tip of the island juts into the sea. A peaceful dip here is almost guaranteed: most would-be swimmers will still be waiting for the tide to reach them back on the mainland. Sitting on top of the low cliffs, the atmospheric ruins of the old lifeboat station are a reminder of times when the lifeboat men had to run from the mainland across the sands to respond to a shout. Close by, the Victorian tidal gauge set into the rock is a relic of the tidal monitoring system for the Irish Sea.

Although a full circumnavigation is not possible around the northern tip, the walk around the island's foreshore is not to be missed. There are plenty of opportunities to explore the cliffs, caves, stacks, wave-cut platforms, and small, sandy beaches of the west and east coasts.

On the west coast, different layers of rock are clearly visible in the overhanging cliffs, their bases adorned with colourful pink and orange wave-cut platforms. Towards the north end Lady's Cave, its floor littered with shells, is associated with a number of the island's legends. On the foreshore here there is a wide variety of seaweed, as well as rock pools and 'gutters' where gobies, plaice, dab, and flounder thrive. It is also the habitat of the honeycomb reef worm. This marine creature builds tubes from sand and shells to live in, and can build a whole reef – a rare sight in British waters. At low tide you'll see the huge colony of grey seals hauled out on Hoyle Bank. The walk along the foreshore of the east coast is similarly diverse and features small caves, deep inlets, and rock structures created by the erosive power of the sea.

There is so much to explore here that marooning yourself for the five or so hours of high tide is a pleasure. Take a large picnic, plenty of warm clothes, and binoculars to watch the wildlife – and to spot the next visitors making their way across the sands.

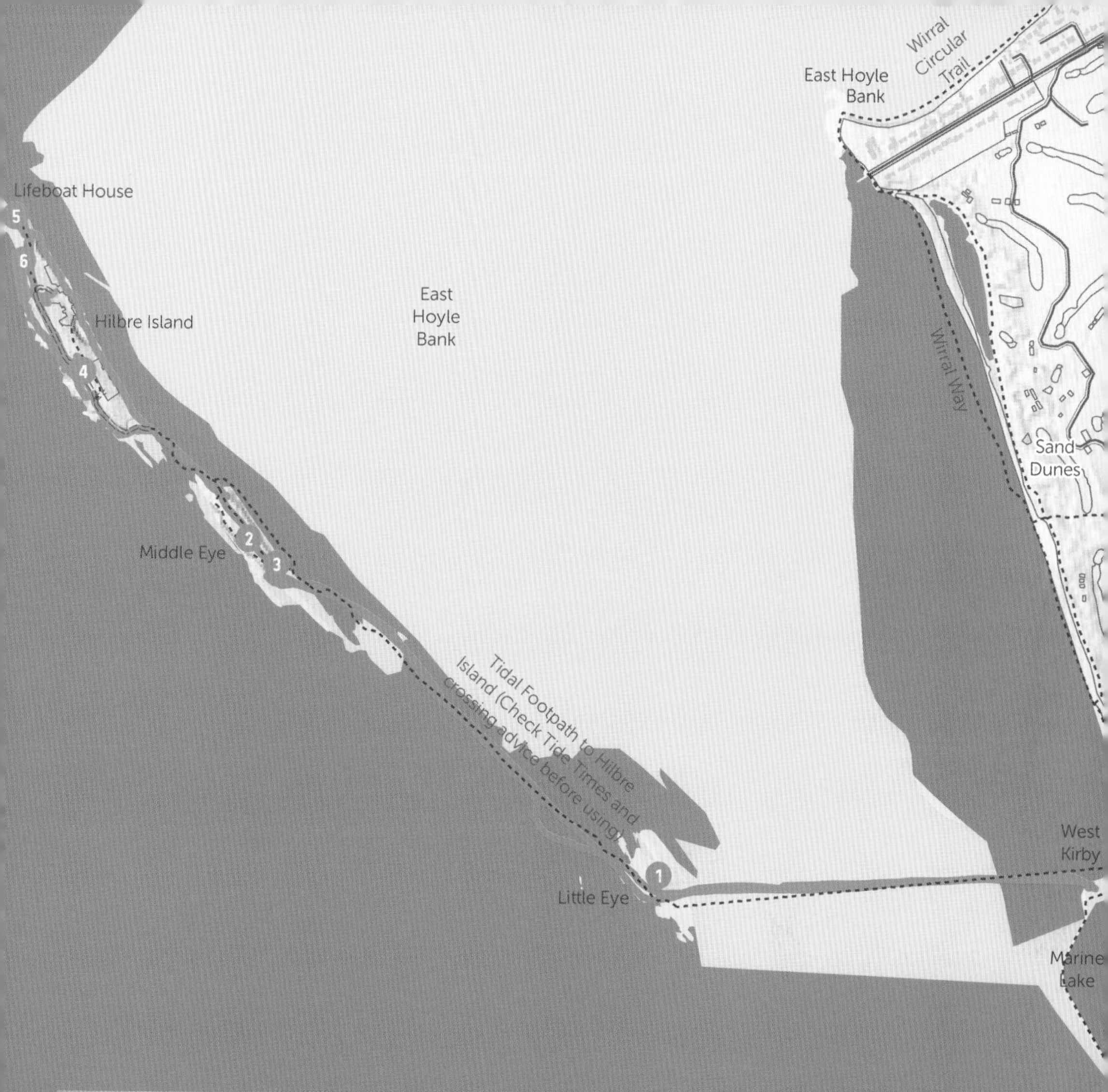

Wirral Circular Trail

East Hoyle Bank

Lifeboat House

5

6

Hilbre Island

East Hoyle Bank

4

Wirral Way

Sand Dunes

Middle Eye

2

3

Tidal Footpath to Hilbre Island (Check Tide Times and crossing advice before using)

West Kirby

Little Eye

1

Marine Lake

DIRECTIONS

» From the Dee Sailing Club car park, leave the slipway and walk 1km across the sands to reach the rocks of Little Eye (1). Walk around the back of Little Eye, keeping the island to the R, then walk to the E side of the rock strand to avoid the slippery rocks and the worst of the mud.

» After 1.6km reach Middle Eye (2) and the rock arch (3), then ascend the steps to traverse the island via the grass path before dropping back down to sand and rock. After a total of 3.3km reach Hilbre (4) and ascend the ramp to the L of the island. To explore the buildings follow the main island path to the old lifeboat station (5) at the N of the island.

» Follow the grass path down onto the rock ledges as far as Lady's Cave (6) to explore the W coast. For the E coast, drop down onto the foreshore close to the stone bridge before the lifeboat station. Follow the coast heading S to return to Middle Eye, then Little Eye, and retrace your steps back to West Kirby.

CHAPTER
22

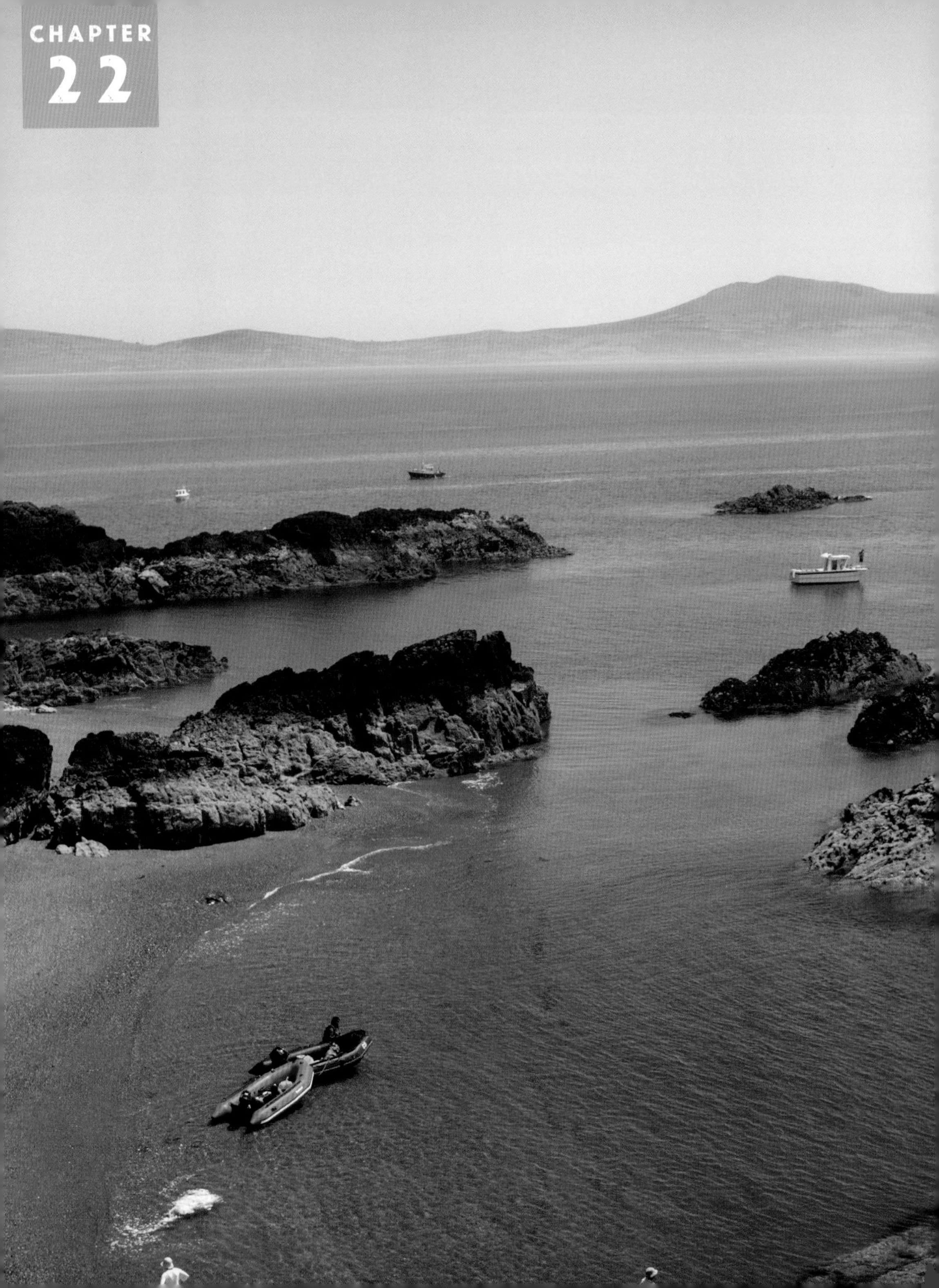

LLANDDWYN

A MAGICAL PLACE FOR LOVERS AND ADVENTURERS WITH MILES OF BEAUTIFUL BEACHES

This is a stunning island in all seasons. Follow glistening white-shell paths and enjoy summer dips in the clearest water at secluded, sandy coves. In winter, experience the thrill of the huge waves and fierce storms that lash Llanddwyn's shores.

Stunning beaches and views of majestic Snowdonia accompany the walk throughout. It starts along the well-marked 'Saint, Sand and Sea Trail', passing through tall pine forests and the magnificent coastal dune system of Newborough Warren before reaching the northern tip of Ynys Llanddwyn. Once on the island, the delightful shell paths are accessed via elaborately carved wooden gates decorated with swirling Celtic designs. Edged with sea holly and thrift, the route winds down to secluded sand and shingle coves, with short deviations inland to explore sites linked to the rich history and legends of the island.

Llanddwyn is a rocky peninsula in the south of Anglesey that juts out between the sandy expanses of Malltraeth Bay and Llanddwyn Bay. Although tidal, it remains attached to the mainland during all but the highest tides. The island's name reveals its association with St Dwynwen, the Welsh patron saint of lovers who retreated to the island, unable to marry the man she loved. Her Saint's day is 25th January, which Welsh speakers celebrate with the exchange of cards, flowers, and love-spoons – a traditional alternative to St Valentine's Day.

Starting at the northern tip of the island, the anti-clockwise route meanders down the west coast where there are plenty of secluded coves to explore as well as a freshwater well dedicated to St Dwynwen. This can be a little tricky to find but the romantically inclined may have the necessary deter-

---

TERRAIN: Steep sand dunes and easy rock paths; beach and boardwalks

STARTING POINT: Newborough Forest car park. Lat/Long 53.1444, -4.3849; GR SH 406 634

DISTANCE: 7km (ascent 154m)

TIME: 2 hours 30mins

OS MAP: OS Explorer 263

DIFFICULTY: 2

NAVIGATION: 1

ACCESS: 3

DON'T MISS:
- Incredible views of forest, beach, and mountains
- The romance of visiting on St Dwynwen's Day
- Discovering the secret divining well on the west coast
- Fabulous wild swims in several secluded coves

SPECIAL NOTES: Accessible at all but high tides. No access to beach at the side of the lighthouse in nesting season. No dogs allowed on beach May to September.

GETTING THERE: Off the A4080, 1km S of Newborough village.

FACILITIES: No facilities on the island. Seasonal snack vans and toilets in car park.

mination. Set high on the cliff, the tiny well's pure water cascades over the moss-covered rocks to a narrow, steep-sided bay below. A short scramble down from here, a small cave extends back into the cliff for a few metres, its walls displaying the vibrant reds and purples of the Cambrian rocks.

From the well, a short deviation inland leads to the 16th-century ruins of St Dwynwen's church on the spine of the island. This is the site of the 5th-century convent she founded and her body is said to be buried here. A Celtic and a plain cross, erected in her memory, can be seen on the skyline to the south.

Continuing along the coastal path, you reach Twr Mawr at the southwest tip of the island. The island's original lighthouse, it was modelled on the windmills of Anglesey and guided mariners through the treacherous Menai Strait. From this vantage point there are excellent views over the rocks of Porth Twr Bach, a colourful and chaotic mélange that includes lavas, quartz, shales, and limestones. To the west of the lighthouse, you can see and hear the noisy cormorant colonies offshore on white-capped Ynys yr Adar.

Around to the south-east tip, across the stone cob, the daymark marks the entrance to Pilot's Cove, site of the old stone lifeboat station and Pilots Cottages. Once home to the men who guided ships between Caernarfon Docks and the open sea – and also acted as lighthouse keepers and lifeboatmen – the cottages now house an interesting small museum and interpretation centre. Llanddwyn's geology is highly significant and the island is part of the UNESCO Global Geopark. Some of the oldest volcanic rocks in Wales are exposed on the island, their large pillow shapes formed when lava erupted from the seabed and cooled.

Beyond the museum and walking north up the east coast towards the end of the island, there are good beaches and secluded coves for swimming. Whether you choose to have a dip here or on the west coast will depend on the tides and prevailing conditions. One coast is generally protected, which means the water is clear and the pools are warm. There are also plenty of opportunities to snorkel for crab and lobster amongst the kelp beds and hope for a tasty lunch on the beach. Wild days open up the possibilities of high-adrenaline sports with the beaches around here presenting some of the best opportunities for kite surfing and board surfing. Whatever the weather, there is never a bad day on Llanddwyn.

Traeth
Penrhos

Traeth Llanddwyn

Llanddwyn Bay

12

2

Ffynnon Dafaden
(Spring) Cave

11

5 4 3

Church
(rem of)

Ynys yr Adar

10

7

6 9

8

DIRECTIONS

» From the coast end of the car park follow the blue markers of the 'Saint, Sand and Sea Trail' W along the gravel track through the trees and parallel to the beach. After 1km turn L to follow the track into the second car park then after a few metres turn R along the track for a short distance before descending the dunes onto the beach.

» Walk towards the strand of large, pillow-shaped rocks (1) that stretch from the mainland to the island and after 800m reach the steep steps at the N tip of the island. Follow the blue markers SW along the island's W coast.

» After 600m pass through the ornate gate and take the R fork or drop down onto the sandy beach to explore pools and rock inlets (2). At the end of the wooden walkway, almost parallel with the church ruins (3), turn towards the coast to locate St Dwynwen's spring-fed well (marked Ffynnon Dafaden) (4). Further south along the coast reach a sheltered gravel beach that is good for swimming and rock-pooling (5).

» Continue SW along the coast path to the old lighthouse (6), the view of the cormorants on Ynys yr Adar (7) and the geological wonders of Porth

Twr Bach (8). Continue around the S tip, then across the Cob to reach the old lifeboat building and an excellent beach for a swim (9).

» Walk N towards Pilots Cottages (10) then take the R fork to follow the coast NE through the dunes and along the E coast to reach two good swimming beaches (11, 12). Continue N along the small, sandy paths closest to the coast.

» Leave the island, pass the information board, and return to the rock strand to walk 1km back along the beach to the car park or return via the forest trail.

BARDSEY

CLIMB THE SUMMIT OF THIS ANCIENT HOLY ISLAND AND SEE DOLPHINS FROM ITS WILDLIFE-RICH SHORES

Visited by pilgrims as early as the 6th century, Bardsey is said to be the final resting place of 20,000 saints, while others claim Merlin of Arthurian legend is buried here. Bardsey's underground population may well outnumber those living on its surface as so many monks and missionaries travelled here over the centuries. Perhaps they created the atmosphere of peace and contemplation that persists today.

The coastal circuit of Bardsey is straightforward and includes an ascent of its 167-metre-high mountain, Mynydd Enlli. Incorporating the sites of many of the island's myths and legends, the route also passes evocative ruins, and there are good opportunities to spot dolphins and other wildlife along the way. It crosses the narrow isthmus to explore the deep inlets and gullies of the south before returning to the quay.

Bardsey lies just off the Llŷn Peninsula in North Wales. Its English name means 'Island of the Bards' and its Welsh name, Ynys Enlli, means 'The Island in the Currents'. Both give a sense of its rich cultural and natural heritage. Yet this ancient holy island is not only a National Nature Reserve but also a living, working landscape. A careful balancing act by its owners, the Bardsey Island Trust and the RSPB, has ensured that alongside tourism, some farming traditions are maintained within a healthy environment. As such, this is the only working island in Wales.

A visit here starts with boarding the island's boat on the mainland – which turns out to be quite an unusual affair. The craft is hauled onto the small, rocky cove of Porth Meudwy for embarkation then towed back into the sea by an aged tractor. The well-practised manoeuvre is executed perfectly by Colin Evans, a native of Bardsey, fount of all island

TERRAIN: Rugged hillwalking, easy grass paths

STARTING POINT: Bardsey Quay. Lat/Long 52.7544 -4.7936; GR SH 116 211

DISTANCE: 7.4km (ascent 233m)

TIME: 2 hours

OS MAP: OS Explorer 253

DIFFICULTY: 2

NAVIGATION: 3

ACCESS: 2

DON'T MISS:
- Soaking up the peace of the sacred sites
- Pods of Risso's dolphins offshore
- Climbing Mynydd Enlli summit for panoramic views
- Swimming off the sandy beach north of the jetty
- Seals and porpoises on the harbour beach

SPECIAL NOTES: Dogs are not permitted on the island.

GETTING THERE: Bardsey Island Boats (07971 769895) from Porth Meudwy: Sat Nav LL53 8DA; OS grid ref. SH163255. 10-minute walk to the boat. Follow signs from the car park.

FACILITIES: Tea and coffee at Ty Pellaf 11am to 1pm. Toilet in Plas-bach yard.

St Cadfan is thought to have established a monastery on Bardsey in the 6th century, and the island supported around 2,500 monks. Bardsey was deemed so holy that in the Middle Ages the Pope proclaimed that three pilgrimages to Ynys Enlli equalled one to Rome. St Mary's, which dates back to the 13th century, was dissolved by Henry VIII and today only the original bell tower remains. The Celtic cross amidst the ruins commemorates the many saints reputed to be buried here and the island is still a significant destination for pilgrims, marking the end point of the North Wales Pilgrim's Way.

For those who associate Bardsey with Avalon, the mythical isle where the wounded King Arthur was taken, and consider it a place of healing, the discovery of an aged apple tree proved significant. Avalon means 'place of apples' and it is believed that there was some sort of early greenhouse here where apples could grow, protected from the howling south-westerlies. A famous, gnarled old apple tree was discovered growing on the south-facing side of one of the island's houses, Plas-bach. Both the tree and its pink-striped, lemon-scented, unblemished fruit were pronounced unique. Today, only the original tree's roots survive and the apple is cultivated commercially.

knowledge and larger-than-life character. He will inform and entertain you for the whole journey through some of the most dangerous rip tides in Europe.

Arrival on the island is usually heralded by the eerie wails of a hundred or so seals jostling for position on their favourite beach next to the quay. Once the seals have settled down the peace is absolute – there are no cars, TVs, or mains electricity here. A short walk from the harbour, Ty Pellaf farm sells delicious island honey and has a small craft shop and café that operates on an honesty-box basis. Take a seat at one of the picnic tables and enjoy a cafetière of coffee, freshly brewed in the farmhouse kitchen.

Mynydd Enlli seems to rise up immediately outside the farmhouse door, its slopes bearing the traces of Bardsey's long history of habitation, including the remains of hut circles close to its ridge that date back more than 3,000 years. Its east cliffs are home to peregrines, razorbills, around 20,000 pairs of Manx shearwaters, and puffins. Stopping to observe the wildlife gives you a chance to catch your breath during the climb. Once at the summit ridge, there are amazing views across to the Llŷn Peninsula and the hills beyond, while the descent offers a bird's-eye view of the ruins of St Mary's Abbey below.

Bardsey Island is now just as famous for its wildlife and rugged scenery as it is for its legends. The Bardsey Bird and Field Observatory at Cristin, which has a small interpretation centre, reflects the island's position on the principal migration routes of several birds including the rare hoopoe. There are also wildlife hides on the north coast and on the isthmus where you can observe grey seals, porpoises, and even catch sight of the Risso's dolphins that visit the coastline.

Across the isthmus, Bardsey's southern peninsula is rugged, heavily indented, and well worth exploring. The clear water of its deep inlets magnifies the colourful rocks and seaweeds below.

If you have time to spare before the return journey and tides and currents permit, enjoy a swim off the crescent-shaped sand bay just north of the quay. If not, sit, relax and watch the antics of the seals and the manoeuvres of boat and tractor.

Penryhn Gogor

Tryn y Gorlech

5

Bae'r Nant

St·Mary's (remains of)

4

Mynydd Enlli

Plas-bach

10

9

Cristin

Ty Pellaf

3

Porth Solfach

2

6

1

Pen Cristin

8

Ogof Ysteffwl- Glas

Pen Dirban

7

Maen Du

DIRECTIONS

» From the slipway (1) turn R and walk along the grass track towards two stone pillars and gate posts, then along the main gravel track towards the houses and barn ahead. Go through two metal gates and head to the farm on R to reach the café (2) in the small outhouse.

» From the café take the small grass track uphill alongside the farm buildings. Pass through a gate and follow the path uphill through the bracken. Climb to the col (low point between ridges) where there is a stop sign to warn about the nesting birds on the E flank (3). At this point follow the skyline, climbing steeply though the gorse on a relatively clear path to reach the main ridge.

» Follow the ridge line to its end and then descend through rock, heather, and bracken. Towards the end of the descent bear SW to the Celtic cross of the chapel (4). At a T-junction turn R to meet the coast at Bae'r Nant by crossing the fence line and then a stile near the cliff edge.

» Take the small coastal path and cross a small stream and kissing gate before arriving at the wildlife hide (5) at Penrhyn Gogor. Then continue through the grazing land down the W side on the clear coastal path for approximately 1.5km.

» Cross the isthmus with its swimming beach (6) and bird hide on the sandy, crescent-shaped bay and follow the footpath through the middle. Pass through a gate to the lighthouse and make a circuit of the S of the island where there are deeper inlets to explore (7).

» Return to the harbour and observe the resident seal colony (8). To explore further inland, walk N along the main lane from the jetty to visit the bird observatory (9), toilets (10) and the apple tree roots at Plas Bach.

CEI BALLAST

SEEK ADVENTURE ON ONE OF BRITAIN'S NEWEST ISLANDS BUILT OF ROCKS FROM ACROSS THE GLOBE

Cei Ballast sits in almost compete secrecy in the northern upper reaches of the River Glaslyn, just a few hundred metres from bustling Porthmadog. Low-lying with good tree and shrub cover, this man-made island was formed around two hundred years ago from discarded ships' ballast.

The most interesting approach is to drop down onto the sands from the Cob, the stone embankment that spans the estuary and carries the steam trains of the Welsh Highland and Ffestiniog railways. Once on the sands, the short route to the island crosses a tidal stream before it heads into the salt marsh, samphire beds, and cockle-filled sands beyond. The colourful foreshore of Cei Ballast is a mix of chalk, red granite, brick, limestone, industrial slag, flint, and the occasional piece of pottery. There is no other foreshore quite like it in Britain.

In the 1800s Porthmadog was a trading and shipbuilding powerhouse. From its harbour, brigs, schooners, barquentines, and brigantines carried slate from the Ffestiniog quarries to all corners of the world. For the return trip, the ships took on coal, hardware, and grain, picking up local rocks as ballast to adjust their trim if needed. Once back in Porthmadog, the ballast was dumped on the sandbank east of the River Glaslyn and the island built up over time.

A little of the island's history is revealed on the circumnavigation. Along the west coast, the old posts of the jetty stand like a petrified forest. Sepia photos in Porthmadog's museum show the small mobile crane positioned here that transferred the ballast from the returning ships to small trucks. These were then manhandled along tracks and emptied. You can still see the ruins of the crane operator's house if the undergrowth isn't too dense.

TERRAIN: Tidal sands, rocky foreshore

STARTING POINT: Ffestiniog Railway car park, Harbour Station, Porthmadog LL49 9NF. Lat/Long 52.9244, -4.1267; GR SH 571 384

DISTANCE: 2.9km (ascent 16m)

TIME: 45 mins

OS MAP: OS Explorer OL18

DIFFICULTY: 2

NAVIGATION: 4

ACCESS: 3

DON'T MISS:
- Exploring rocks brought by ship from across the globe
- Diving into the deep, warm waters of the pool in the sandbanks
- Sampling locally brewed Purple Moose beer at the station

SPECIAL NOTES: Tidal stream below the Cob accessible 3 hours either side of low tide.

GETTING THERE: Train to Porthmadog station.

FACILITIES: Refreshments and toilets at Spooner's Grill, café, and bar on the railway platform; full facilities in Porthmadog.

Shouts of tradesmen, loadmasters, and the chatter of sailors once filled the river bank. Now the babble of the water and the halyards slapping on the masts of the gleaming white yachts in the marina opposite are the only sounds, along with the occasional whistle of a steam train in the distance.

The southern tip of the island has a superb tidal pool – an incredible place to swim when sun on the surrounding sandbanks has warmed the water. With views across to Harlech Castle and the distant peaks of Snowdonia, the island was, until fairly recently, a favourite picnic, swimming, and camping site for local people. Now overgrown with brambles and hawthorn, this estuary island is a haven for wildlife and the sound is of woodland birdsong, not the cries of seabirds.

Back on the Cob after your island adventure, somewhat dishevelled and spattered in estuarine mud, it's hard not to feel slightly smug. Among the crowds on the platforms observing steam trains or enjoying refreshments, few realise that this island even exists.

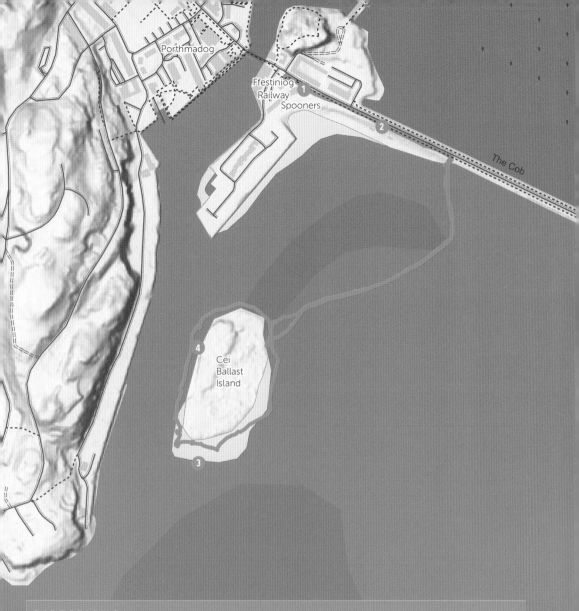

DIRECTIONS

» From the railway car park (1), walk along the marked footpath to the L of Spooners, then along the railings between the railway and the road towards the Cob (2). After 340m, at the end of the railings, turn R and cross the track to reach the wall of the Cob. Climb the low wall and drop down onto the stones.

» Wade across the Glaslyn Channel and walk towards the island, skirting L of the salt marsh to avoid further channels. At the island's foreshore continue around in a clockwise direction to reach the deep pools (3) at the S. Continue past the rotting wooden moorings and slate sidings (4) along the S and W side to the ash trees on the sheltered N tip. Return across the sands.

YNYS GIFFTAN

SALT MARSH AND VAST TIDAL SANDS WITH DEEP, SUN-WARMED POOLS – ALL FRAMED BY MAJESTIC MOUNTAINS AND FAIRYTALE TURRETS

Floating on my back in the deliciously warm pool in the middle of a remote estuary in North Wales, the last people I expected to see were two spear fishermen. Not the fearsome sort, just a father and son having an outdoor adventure catching fish and collecting samphire for their campfire.

Sitting at the head of the long Dwyryd Estuary, one of the most unspoilt places in Cardigan Bay, Ynys Gifftan is surrounded by vast tidal sands, salt marsh, and the mountains of Snowdonia. Its natural beauty is further enhanced by the ruined outline of Harlech Castle at the mouth of the estuary and the ornate spires and domes of Italianate Portmeirion just across the river.

Bequeathed to the current Lord Harlech's ancestors by Queen Anne in the early 18th century, the island has been uninhabited for well over ten years. The old stone farmhouse and outbuilding, which stand as a reminder that this island was once farmed, are almost hidden in a wilderness of lush green bracken, gorse, and elder. For explorers, tidal access to the island is straightforward and the delightful circular walk is on the sands and the bedrock of the foreshore.

The approach to the island is through salt marsh, a jigsaw of interconnected channels and sun-dried mud hollows. Wild flowers thrive here and the air is scented with their fragrance, while pollinating insects hum overhead. The area is also rich in wildlife and you may spot otters as well as seasonal wildfowl, egrets, and herons. It is possible to navigate around some of the larger water-filled channels on dry land, but not half so much fun as jumping in and squelching through the gloopy mud.

TERRAIN: Salt marsh, low-tide estuary sand

STARTING POINT: Talsarnau station. Lat/Long 52.9047, -4.0677; GR SH 610 361

DISTANCE: 4.5km (ascent 22m)

TIME: 1 hour

OS MAP: OS Explorer OL18

DIFFICULTY: 2

NAVIGATION: 3

ACCESS: 3

DON'T MISS:
- Secret swims in the deep, warm pools
- Foraging for samphire in the salt marsh
- Panoramic views of majestic Snowdonia mountains
- Heavenly picnic spots on the rocks

SPECIAL NOTES: Accessible 2 hours after high tide and up to 2.5 hours before the next high tide. Channels deeper after heavy rains. The incoming tide fills the channels closest to the mainland first, so even when the sands surrounding the island appear dry you can be cut off, unless you are happy to wade or swim back.

GETTING THERE: Take the A496 from Harlech, turning L at Talsarnau's pub, the Ship Aground, and follow signs to the station. Trains from Porthmadog and Harlech.

FACILITIES: None on the island; Ship Aground is friendly and serves food; more facilities in Penrhyndeudraeth.

Crossing the estuary sands to the island is short and straightforward. The looping watery channels arise from the smaller tributaries of the Afon Dwyryd, the mountain river. The depth of the channels, even at low tide, depends on the amount of recent rainfall in the mountains and can vary from negligible to knee-high. The sands are luxuriously deep and gentle on the feet except for the occasional sharp cockle shell. From the wide estuary there are uninterrupted views of Snowdonia, including Snowdon itself.

At the island's southern tip, deep, emerald-green pools are refreshed daily by the tide and heated by the summer sun to the temperature of bathwater. Their depths feel cooler. Floating, swimming, or diving into these remote pools from the rock ledges gives you a wonderful sense of freedom. Few are

aware that this slice of paradise exists and your only swimming companions are likely to be a shoal of grey mullet caught out by the tide.

On a sunny day the vast sands shimmer, creating a mirage effect. The tide appears to be coming in early while in the distance, walkers seem to hover on the air over the estuary. On such days, an atmosphere of other-worldliness seems to envelop the island. The pools continue at the foot of the bedrock around the western foreshore of the island and almost to the northern tip, where large oak trees flourish in the relative shelter and overhang shady pools. Salt marsh fringes the east coast and harbours an assortment of rusting agricultural tools and machinery.

About halfway down the east coast, the corrugated roof of an outbuilding appears above the trees, with the farmhouse just beyond. A narrow path through the bracken and nettles leads up to the buildings. The island hasn't been farmed for some years and the farmhouse is in need of complete renovation. The wind blows freely through unglazed windows that offer tantalising glimpses over neglected gardens to the sands beyond.

The island is currently up for rent and its new tenants will inevitably make changes, so don't hesitate to get your feet wet and discover what is still an enchanting wilderness.

Portmeirion

Ynys
Gifftan

3

2 1

Talsarnau

DIRECTIONS

» From Talsarnau railway station platform, turn L at the end of the car park, go through the gates and over the level crossing. Continue NW on the gravel track and after 330m pass through a gate, go over the dyke, and follow the derelict fence line ahead.

» At the first of the larger meanders in the creek, cross to L of the fence, then after a further 100m jump across the smaller creek.

» At the main channel follow its L bank to the coast. Depending on the position of the channels, there may be one (at low tide) to cross at the beach. Head 280m across the sands to the rocks at the S tip of Ynys Gifftan (1).

» Continue around the rocks and pools (2) to circumnavigate the island in a clockwise direction. At the N end a small channel is best navigated on the island side. About halfway down

the E coast the ruins of the farmhouse and outbuildings (3) can be accessed via a narrow path through rough vegetation.

» Cross back from the S tip to the mainland, keeping to the R side of the larger creek and retrace the route to the large, white buildings of the station.

CHAPTER 26

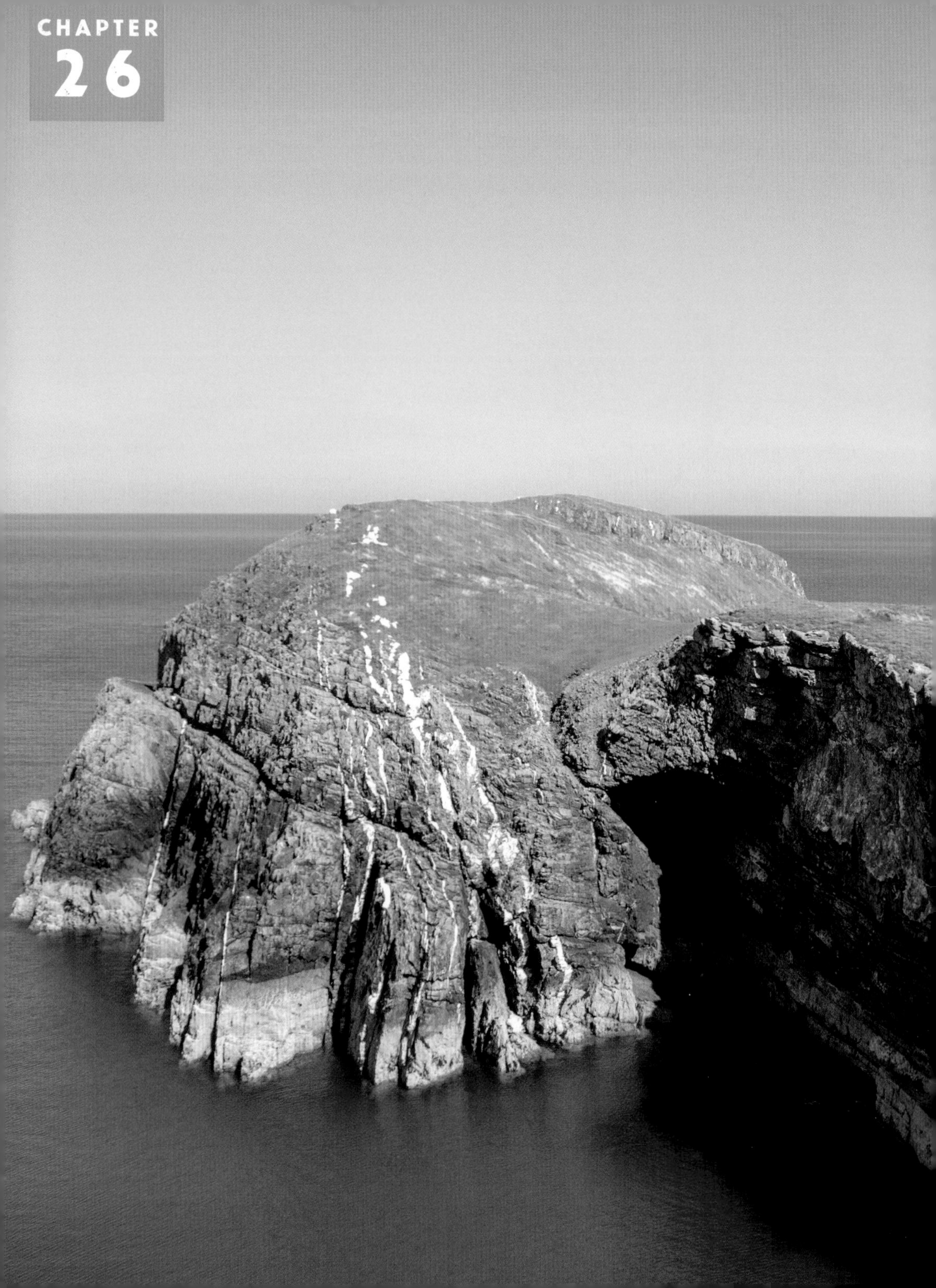

YNYS LOCHTYN

A ROCKY ADVENTURE WITH CLIFF AND SEA-CAVE SCRAMBLING TO SEE EUROPE'S LARGEST POD OF BOTTLENOSE DOLPHINS

Many walkers are content to stay on the section of Ceredigion Coast Path that snakes above the vertiginous cliffs between the charming seaside villages of Llangrannog and New Quay. They may stop to admire the dramatic and iconic headland of Ynys Lochtyn, but only from afar. For those with adventure in their veins, the expedition to this tempting wild island will not disappoint.

But getting to the island is not for the fainthearted. The only access from the headland is a precipitous path, often with loose stones underfoot, that drops down the sea cliffs. Once on the rocks below, the route then continues through a sea cave, onto a large ledge, then up a grassy path onto the island itself.

Small, wild and tidal, the island is a high, grass-topped plateau adjacent to the Ynys Lochtyn headland, from which it is cut off on all but the lowest tides. It is surrounded by steep cliffs that jut into Cardigan Bay – a setting that gives a thrilling sense of exposure. Up on the plateau, you can enjoy the whole sweep of Cardigan Bay, with views north as far as the craggy Llŷn Peninsula on clear days.

On the clifftop meadows of this beautiful section of heritage coastline, the grass is cropped short by the dainty teeth of Welsh ponies, and spring squill, thrift, and sea campion flourish. This is the favourite breeding and foraging ground of the rare chough as well as the peregrine falcons that swoop acrobatically overhead, searching the cliffs for prey. The cliffs display a variety of colour and shape, the exposed layers of shales, grits, and sandstones revealing their geological age. Little of their majesty can be seen from the coastal path, which makes the island a very special vantage point.

TERRAIN: Easy coastal path; steep, very uneven route down the cliffs; scrambling on the island

STARTING POINT: Car park at Llangrannog. Lat/Long 52.1599, -4.4718; GR SN 310 542

DISTANCE: 4km (ascent 237m)

TIME: 1 hour 30mins

OS MAP: OS Explorer 198

DIFFICULTY: 4

NAVIGATION: 4 (1 on the coast path)

ACCESS: 3

DON'T MISS:
- Spectacular cliffs only visible from the island
- Scrambling on rock ledges and exploring sea caves
- Watching the dolphins of Cardigan Bay

SPECIAL NOTES: Accessible 2 hours either side of low tide and best attempted in dry weather and on a calm day. The rocks at the base of the island are close to the sea even at low tide and can be very slippery.

GETTING THERE: At Brynhoffnant, about halfway between Aberaeron and Aberteifi on the A487, turn off onto the B4334 to Llangrannog.

FACILITIES: Cafés, inns, and toilets at Llangrannog.

After descending the cliffs to sea level, between the island and the headland, there are large and verdant rock pools to poke about in, sea caves to explore, and rock ledges to scramble around. You will have the beaches to the east and west of the peninsula to yourself, but beware of strong currents. The sound of the sea sucking at the base of the cliffs and gurgling through the caves increases the thrill of being in a place that feels much more the preserve of marine life than human.

After climbing up to the island's plateau, the northern tip is an excellent vantage point for bottlenose dolphins. There are around 200 of them in Cardigan Bay – Europe's largest population – and this stretch of coastline is the best place to see them. The last time I visited, the various wildlife-watching boats from New Quay were making a fruitless search far out to sea, while within almost touching distance of the island, the huge pod of dolphins swam undisturbed. The diving gannets overhead gave them away as they joined in with the feeding frenzy. As you wait for the dolphins to appear, porpoises and grey seals swim close to shore and the occasional basking shark, sunfish, whale, and even leatherback turtle could also make an appearance.

Apart from the wildlife, you might see a local fishermen hoping to catch bass, pollock, or mackerel, or there may be a couple of climbers testing themselves on some of the island's craggy routes – Lochtyn Syndrome, Fish Fingers, and Topple Blocks. But the chances are that you'll have this superb island adventure all to yourself.

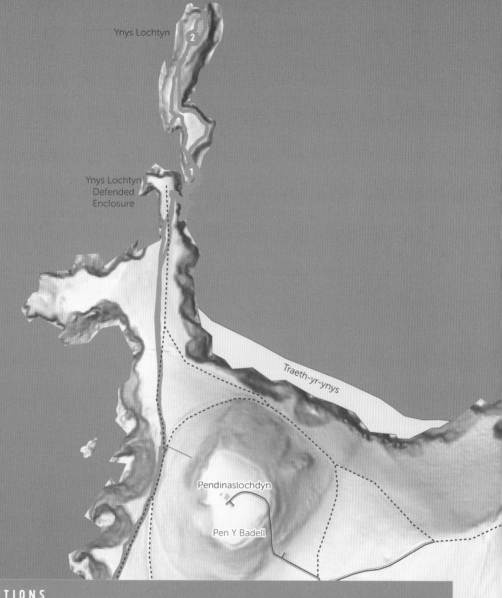

Ynys Lochtyn

2

1

Ynys Lochtyn
Defended
Enclosure

Traeth-yr-ynys

Pendinaslochdyn

Pen Y Badell

annog
ach

DIRECTIONS

» From the car park at Llangran-nog, turn R (NE) along the beach to climb the steps. Follow signs for Ceredigion Coast Path. After 880m turn L at the gate onto a bigger track to see the island ahead.

» On the approach to Ynys Lochtyn, leave the main path and follow the defined grass path N towards the island. Just before reaching the cliffs adjacent to the island look for the metal belay point on the E coast of the headland and after 10m (S), find a steep path leading down to the R.

Descend the cliffs on this path. It has some wide rock slabs but is steep with loose stones in some areas. Once at the base of the cliffs, walk through the sea cave (1) onto the ledges and ascend the steep, grassy path to the plateau (2) of the island. Return to Llangrannog via the same route.

RAMSEY

RIDE ACROSS SOME OF THE BEST WHITEWATER IN BRITAIN AND WALK THE HIGH CLIFFS OF THIS HAVEN FOR PORPOISE, SEALS, AND BIRDS

The anti-clockwise coastal circuit on grass and rock paths ascends Ramsey's three 'peaks' of which Carnllundain, at 136 metres, is the highest. The island has a very varied habitat: farmland in the north, heathland in the south, and some of the highest cliffs in Wales to the west. The views everywhere are spectacular.

Ramsey Island, immediately off St David's Head in Pembrokeshire, is just a short distance from St David's, Britain's smallest city. At just under a kilometre offshore, the island is a short but exciting boat ride across the notorious Ramsey Sound. Owned by the RSPB, Ramsey is famed for its wildlife and what it lacks in puffins it certainly makes up for in seals and other characterful species. The island is full of colour from May to September when bluebells, followed by pink thrift and purple heather, add a honeyed scent to the air.

Getting to Ramsey across the tidal flow known as 'The Bitches', a reef of jagged rocks that creates different tidal heights on either side, is an experience in itself. On rough days the big whirlpools, eddies, and spectacularly chaotic water make this stretch one of Britain's best whitewater play spots. On calmer days you can watch numerous porpoises feeding in the waters south of Ramsey Sound to the north of St David's Head.

Once on dry land the visit starts with an informative RSPB brief on the latest bird and seal sightings followed by a quick stop at the farmhouse for basic refreshments. The walk then heads out across flat grassland towards the first of the three heather-clad peaks, Carn Ysgubor. From the top, there are views east across to St David's Head and to the golden strip of Whitesands Bay. To the west, the jagged 'teeth' of the Bishops and Clerks skerries, and

---

TERRAIN: Easy grass paths rugged in places; 3 hill climbs

STARTING POINT: Ramsey's jetty. Lat/Long 51.8649, -5.3320; GR SM 707 237

DISTANCE: 7.4km (ascent 362m)

TIME: 2 hours

OS MAP: OS Explorer OL35

DIFFICULTY: 2

NAVIGATION: 2

ACCESS: 2

DON'T MISS:
- Braving 'The Bitches' – a maritime adventure
- Watching the porpoises in Ramsey Sound
- Seal pups enjoying their first swimming lesson
- Climbing the three peaks of Ramsey for stunning views

SPECIAL NOTES: The best time to see the seal pups is late August to November; the seabirds nest from springtime to early summer.

GETTING THERE: By boat from St Justinian's Lifeboat Station. Crossings at 10am and 12 noon, returning at 4pm (between 1 April or Easter, whichever is earlier, to 31 October) via Thousand Island Expeditions (01437 721721; www.thousandislands.co.uk).

FACILITIES: Teas, coffees, and snacks at the farmhouse.

South Bishop Lighthouse are visible. This stunning panorama is well worth the climb.

Descending to Aber Mawr, you reach one of the best places on the island to watch the largest breeding colony of Atlantic grey seals in Britain swim, sleep, and pup. Their numbers peak in late August through to November when up to a thousand come to the island to breed. An average of 600 pups are born here every year, their white, fluffy coats making them easy to spot. Initially, they spend little time in the water but soon loose their baby fur, learn to swim, and become independent. Towards the southern end of the cliffs above the beach is a small wooden observatory where wildlife researchers observe the colony. They are usually happy to answer questions but at certain times a 'Do Not Disturb' sign will be posted.

On the west coast of the island the seals are not the only draw for wildlife enthusiasts. From spring to early summer, the cliffs and caves are one of the best sites in Wales to see nesting choughs. Other birds breeding on these cliffs include ravens, peregrines, gulls, Manx shearwaters, razorbills, kittiwakes, shags, and guillemots. And one of the best places to observe them is around Ogof Glyma at the southern base of Carnllundain. Bottlenose and Risso's dolphins can also be spotted from many of the cliff tops and headlands along this coast. Inland, wheatears and little owls nest in the numerous stone walls and forage for insects in the maritime grass.

The heather, gorse, and coastal plants that flourish on the heathlands of the southern end of the island attract stonechats, meadow pipits, linnets, and skylarks. Surprisingly, this area is also a favourite haunt of red deer. The animals were transported from the mainland in a net suspended beneath an RAF helicopter in the 1970s and now thrive in this habitat. The deer have five Welsh mountain ponies for company, four of which are white. This should make them easy to see, but they still manage to elude many visitors.

Off Ramsey's dramatic southern tip lie three steep-sided islands: Ynys Gwelltog, Cantwr (both tidal) and Bery. Ynys Cantwr means Chanter's Island and it is said that St Justinian, a hermit who sought sanctuary and had a chapel on Ramsey, would send priests in need of punishment to the cave there. Tied to a large rock, they were obliged to chant their penance over a period of two high tides. Their survival was proof of God's forgiveness but in reality few lived to tell the tale, which St Justinian put down to their not having chanted zealously enough. At some point the monks rebelled against such an extreme regime and cut off St Justinian's head. Kittiwakes now nest in the cave and in the spring, bright blue squill frames the entrance.

If the wardens on Ramsey had one wish it would probably be for the return of puffins to the island. Eradicated by rats in the 1800s, they have not been spotted here since, despite the large and overcrowded colonies on neighbouring islands. The wardens have mounted 'Project Puffin' but the decoy birds and recorded calls have not lured any birds to date. After a day spent on the island, it seemed to me that the puffins were definitely missing out.

» Walk up the concrete steps from the jetty (1) and into the hut by the quay for the RSPB wardens' talk. Continue onto the island following signs to 'Trail and Shop'.

» From the farmhouse and shop (2) in Aberfelin Bay head N through the farm buildings and gate and follow the signs for 'North Route', crossing 800m of open grassland then passing through a gap in the stone wall. Go through the gate to start the climb to Carn Ysgubor (3), then retrace your steps to the base of the hill.

» Pass through a gate and stone wall and follow the grass path above the seal beach of Aber Mawr (4). Walk towards the wooden observatory through the gap in the wall and gate. Continue on the path to the top of the cliffs of Trwyn Garlic. Walk alongside the stone wall before turning R through a gap and continue on the grass path above the dramatic, steep cliffs. Looking back, you'll catch sight of the sea caves on the NW coast of the island.

» At the sign to Ogof Colomennod continue straight ahead to view the cave (5). Return to the sign and continue S on the coast path as it works its way uphill. As the grass path turns to rock, stone cairns start to mark the way.

» To climb Carnllundain (6) and the trig point, take the small path uphill to the L of the main path, then return to the main path.

» To reach the cairn at the top of the third hill (7) find the small path further S that bears L off the main island path. Return to the main path once more and continue on the coastal path, walking down past the seabird colonies of Ogof Glyma (8).

» At the large inlet of Porth Lleuog (9), turn L inland to take the short cut back to the farmhouse if time is running out. For the circumnavigation, keep to the path heading S along the coast to reach the SW point of Trwynmynachdy. Continue on the coast path around this small peninsula then turn R off the main path and walk uphill to Foel Fawr to reach the dramatic viewpoint (10) out across Ynys Gwelltog, Cantwr and Bery. Return to the main path and continue around the headland. At the junction, head straight ahead and continue N along the east coast on the well-defined path to the farmhouse and jetty.

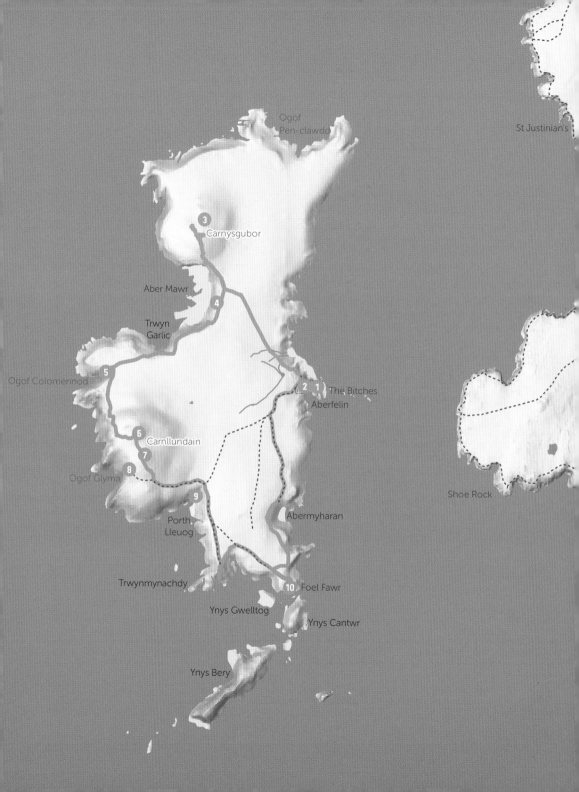

Ogof
Pen-clawdd

St Justinian's

③ Carnysgubor

Aber Mawr

④

Trwyn
Garlic

Ogof Colomennod

⑤

② ① The Bitches
Aberfelin

⑥
Carnllundain

⑦

⑧
Ogof Glyma

⑨

Shoe Rock

Porth
Lleuog

Abermyharan

Trwynmynachdy

⑩ Foel Fawr

Ynys Gwelltog

Ynys Cantwr

Ynys Bery

SKOMER

EXTRAORDINARY BIRDLIFE, WILD FLOWERS, AND DRAMATIC GEOLOGY – ALL CAREFULLY PROTECTED ON THIS UNSPOILT NATURE RESERVE

This is definitely the island for an all-nighter. The local residents are noisy, clumsy, and bring their seafood takeaways home. The wide-eyed visitors, weighed down with cameras, tripods, and blankets, stumble around in the dark. Welcome to one of Britain's greatest natural spectacles: the nightly return of thousands of Manx shearwaters. Back from a day's fishing, the birds feed chicks waiting expectantly in burrows for a tasty meal – and we stay up all night and watch them.

Skomer, only a kilometre off the coast of Pembrokeshire, is an island of exposed headlands, dramatic sea stacks, and sheltered bays that is famed for its extraordinary wildlife. It is the seasonal home to half the world's population of Manx shearwaters and the largest colony of Atlantic puffins in Southern Britain. It is the permanent home to the unique Skomer vole, plus other assorted creatures including three species of stick insect, glow-worm, and slow-worms. It boasts some of the most complete and untouched Iron Age remains in Europe and is a designated Ancient Monument.

Making the short hop from the mainland, the Dale Princess crosses the swirling waters of Jack's Sound, passing striking offshore rock formations and sheltered coves. You'll see diving gannets and rafts of puffins, as well as dolphins and porpoises. It is a tantalising taste of what's to come.

On disembarking at North Haven, take your time climbing up the steep steps: it is the best place on Skomer for close-up views of nesting guillemots and razorbills. Puffins also dig their burrows here, often showering waiting visitors with mud as they sculpt their earthy homes. The foreshore is also fabulous for exploring, as long as you seek guidance from the island's wardens and volunteers.

TERRAIN: Grass paths; beware of Manx shearwater and puffin burrows

STARTING POINT: Jetty, North Haven. Lat/Long 51.7377, -5.2816; GR SM 735 094

DISTANCE: 6.7km (ascent 188m)

TIME: 1 hour 30 mins

OS MAP: OS Explorer OL36

DIFFICULTY: 1

NAVIGATION: 2

ACCESS: 2

DON'T MISS:
- Staying overnight to experience the Manx shearwater spectacle after dark
- Seashore foraging with the wardens
- Springtime bluebell walks on the west coast
- Observing seal pups on the Garland Stone

SPECIAL NOTES: Keep strictly to the paths even when setting up camera tripods. No dogs permitted.

GETTING THERE: Boats daily (except Mon) Apr–Oct from Martin's Haven, weather permitting (01646 636600 for updates). Landing fee payable beforehand at Lockley Lodge, near the NT car park. No reservations: arrive 2–3 hours early in peak season. Pay on-board.

FACILITIES: No café on the island; toilets, water and self-catering accommodation at the farm in the centre. Buy provisions in Marloes or snacks at Lockley Lodge.

Dog whelks, blennies, and crabs thrive here as well as compass jellyfish, by-the-wind sailors, and keelworms.

At the top of the cliff, an easy path leads clockwise towards the southern tip of the island. In spring this route is lined with dense carpets of bluebells; in summer with ragged robin and sea campion. Passing South Stream Valley, where chattering birds hide in the scrub, there are dramatic views from Skomer's southern tip to the cormorant-studded sea stacks of the Mew Stone, and out to the distant islands of Skokholm and Grassholm.

Rounding the headland you reach The Wick, a spectacular deep inlet and the site of a ruined Iron Age village. On the dramatic cliff faces razorbills build single nests in crevices spaced well apart, while guillemots construct seabird cities that echo with their high pitched, kazoo-like calls. Away from the cliffs, however, the puffins are the main act. After a comical (to us) landing, they waddle proudly over the path to their burrows, beaks full of neat lines of sand eels for their young. Over 12,000 puffins nest in the grassy banks of Skomer's cliffs between April and July before overwintering in the Atlantic Ocean where they moult. During the winter months when they lose their wing feathers, they remain flightless and vulnerable to the severe storms of winter.

Between April and September, the stretch of coast to Skomer Head hosts the largest colony of Manx shearwaters in the world. The birds hunt far out to sea during the day, returning to the island at dusk to feed their chicks. After fledging, the remarkable young birds migrate to the coasts of Brazil and Argentina, remaining at sea for five years before returning to breed within a few metres of the burrow in which they were born.

On the north coast, seals haul out on the rocky skerries at the eastern end of the pyramidal islet of the Garland Stone. Offshore, gannets plunge into the racing tidal currents in search of fish before returning west to join another 30,000 breeding pairs on their white-tipped island home of Grassholm.

Opposite the Garland Stone, the path turns inland, passing small prehistoric burial cairns and a marshy area dotted in summer with yellow irises, before reaching Old Farm at the centre of the island. You may be lucky enough to see a Skomer vole running across the path – unless the short-eared owls that hunt close to the farmhouse got to it first.

On the way back to the boat in North Haven, the Harold Stone stands sentinel among the wild flowers. Some think it may be a Bronze Age monument marking a grave; for others, the stone's prominence on the skyline indicate its purpose as a marker, warning sailors of submerged rocks. A 19th-century limekiln near the farm is a reminder of the self-sufficiency of the last Skomer farmers who produced their own fertiliser and building mortar.

This is a fabulous island to visit during the day, but for the full wildlife experience, plan an overnight stay.

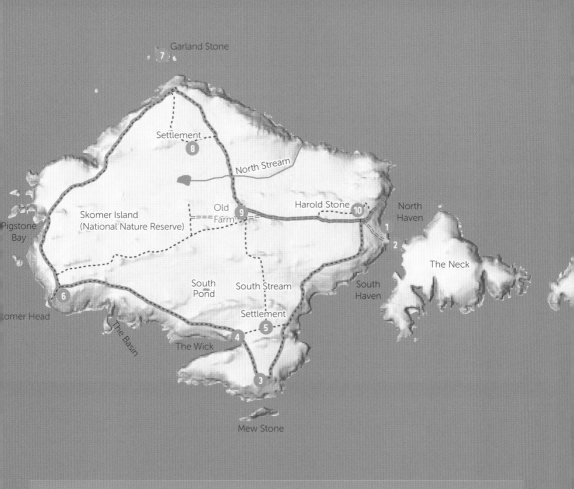

Garland Stone

7

Settlement

8

North Stream

Old
Farm

9

Harold Stone

10

North
Haven

Skomer Island
(National Nature Reserve)

Pigstone
Bay

1

2

The Neck

Skomer Head

6

The Basin

South
Pond

South Stream

South
Haven

Settlement

5

4

The Wick

3

Mew Stone

DIRECTIONS

» From the jetty (1), walk up the steps and steep track for an initial briefing by the wardens. Leave their hut and walk along the stone track past the island office and The Neck (2). After 250m, at a small crossroads in the bracken, turn L along the smaller path following signs to The Wick.

» Cross the small footbridge and V-shaped gully of South Stream. After 200m, turn L at the junction signed 'Wick Head, Skomer Head and The Farm' following signs to the Mew Stone.

» At the Mew Stone viewpoint (3) continue along the path and follow signs to The Wick. Just before The Wick (4) a roped walkway protects the bird burrows and the extensive rock strata of the cove come into view. Find the ruins of the Iron Age village slightly inland (5). Continue to follow signs to Skomer Head and the Garland Stone, passing The Basin cove on the way.

» Scramble onto the rocks of Skomer Head (6) for great views back to the Mew Stone, The Wick, and The Basin, and to watch the gannets dive. Retrace your steps back to the main path and continue north, following signs for the Garland Stone.

» Almost opposite the Garland Stone (7), turn R inland towards the farmhouse, passing ancient stone cairns (8). After 700m or so, a wooden walkway bypasses the boggy areas of North Stream.

» Walk through the Farm House complex (9) and leave it by the first path on L, following the sign to 'North Haven and Boat'. Pass the trig point on R and descend through the bracken, with views across to the industrial complex of Milford Haven. Pass Harold's Stone (10) and the limekiln close by as you return to the jetty.

WORM'S HEAD

A ROLLERCOASTER ROUTE ALONG THE ROCKY DRAGON'S SPINE OF ONE OF THE UK'S MOST EXHILARATING ISLANDS, FULL OF NATURAL WONDERS

More of an adventure than a walk, this route explores the many natural wonders of Worm's Head and starts from idyllic Rhossili village. Initially following the coast path above stunning Rhossili Bay, the route crosses the rocky tidal causeway and ascends the spine of the island to reach the spiral-shaped Outer Head. From a distance this looks to be the preserve of mountaineers but the short scramble up it makes for a spectacular finale.

Worm's Head marks the most westerly point of the Gower Peninsula, near Swansea. It was the first designated Area of Outstanding Natural Beauty (AONB) in the UK. The island is joined to the mainland by a rocky causeway and is divided into three parts, each accessed by clambering over low-lying rocky sections. The first section is the steep-sided, 30-metre-high, flat-topped Inner Head. Next is Middle Head, which is split into two by Devil's Bridge, a spectacular natural rock arch. To reach the rocky summit of the third section, Outer Head, requires a steeper but easy scramble.

The gentle beginning of the walk offers stupendous views north to Rhossili Bay, the winner of numerous accolades including the best beach in Wales, Europe and voted one of the top ten beaches of the world. No wonder almost 400 people attempted to break the world record here for the largest number of people skinny-dipping at one time.

Along the cliffs towards Worm's Head, the flatness of the terrain is noticeable. This was once the old beach, now lifted to a height of 60 metres. You will also pass the remains of an Iron Age fort to the right of the path, while over the stone wall on National Trust (NT) land, the medieval farming

---

TERRAIN: Scrambles on rocky foreshore, easy paths and steeper scrambles

STARTING POINT: Rhossili, NT car park. Lat/Long 51.5693, -4.2885; GR SS 415 881

DISTANCE: 7.8km (ascent 90m)

TIME: 2 hours

OS MAP: OS Explorer 164

DIFFICULTY: 4

NAVIGATION: 3

ACCESS: 3

DON'T MISS:
- Scrambling up vertiginous Outer Head
- Listening at the blowhole on Outer Head
- Exciting traverse of Devil's Bridge rock arch

SPECIAL NOTES: Safe crossing 2.5 hours before and after low tide. The top of Outer Head is off-limits between 1st March and 31st August owing to nesting seabirds.

GETTING THERE: Follow the B4247 to Rhossili car park. Regular bus services from Swansea to Rhossili. (Monday–Saturday, Sunday (summer service only). Buses 118/119 (NAT) and 114 (Sundays, First Cymru). Additional services connect quieter parts of Gower with the 118 and 116 (Swansea–North Gower service).

FACILITIES: Café, restaurant, and public toilets at Rhossili. The Bay Bistro is a personal favourite.

system of small field strips divided by banks is still visible. This area, called The Vile, is one of the UK's few surviving examples.

The route to the island leaves the coastal path and descends to the long and jagged causeway below the old Coastguard lookout at the western tip of the peninsula. A large board outside displays the safe crossing times and there is a siren to warn stragglers of the incoming tide.

The rocks of the causeway are deeply encrusted with barnacles and small mussels, the latter so numerous the rock surface takes on the look of rough tarmac. Close to the north shore a two-metre-long anchor among the rocks is from a ship that foundered here, carrying a cargo of coal. On the path down from the lookout, you might still see small pieces of coal that were dropped when locals salvaged the fuel. If time permits, delve into the rock pools along the causeway to discover hermit crabs, snakelocks anemone, coralline weed, and blennies.

Stepping onto the island, you notice a bell on the shore for summoning the coastguard. It is a gentle reminder that many do get cut off by the tide. The route then ascends to the ridge, Inner Head, from which there are fabulous views north

to Rhossili Beach and south-west to Lundy Island in the Bristol Channel. The south side of Inner Head is flat with dense, lush grass that would make a comfortable wild-camping spot.

The route then crosses to Low Neck, a landscape of jagged, upended rock layers arranged row after row with deep chasms in between. It leaves you in no doubt as to the massive upheavals that formed these strata. They are easy to clamber across with care.

The traverse to Middle Neck is via the airy crossing of Devil's Bridge, the remains of a collapsed sea cave. To the south, the rocky shore has been completely flattened by the sea to create a wave-cut platform. To the west, there are tremendous views of the steep cliff walls of Outer Head. Towards the end of Middle Neck, to the right of the path, a truncated cave offers a window through to the unrelenting north wall of the Worm.

Stepping onto the final section, Outer Head, the NT sign warns that access is prohibited during nesting season. The route then passes through a prehistoric shell midden and a short distance further on, up on the sloping bank to your right, a narrow band of exposed limestone can be seen. Climb up and listen for a whooshing sound through the narrow fissure; it emanates from the sea cave below. In really rough weather this becomes a blowhole and emits a towering spout of spray. In

calm conditions and on very low tides, it is possible to kayak into the cave between swells.

A rough scramble will take you to the rock outcrop at very end of the Worm, a raw and elemental place with waves crashing on the rocks below. The aptly named scrambled-egg lichen – a threatened species in the UK – that coats the rocks at Outer Head is testament to the special significance of this place for plants and wildlife. It is also one of the top places in Wales to see seabirds including kitti-wakes, razorbills, guillemots, fulmars (and sometimes puffins), storm petrels, Manx shearwaters, and eiders depending on the season. If you are a climber and well equipped, it is possible to scramble down the cliff at the western tip to explore the caves beneath. A small treasure trove of prehistoric bones and ancient stone tools has been found there.

Heading back to the whitewashed cottages and cafés of Rhossili it is hard not to deny that this is one of Britain's most visually impressive landscapes on a route stacked with adventure.

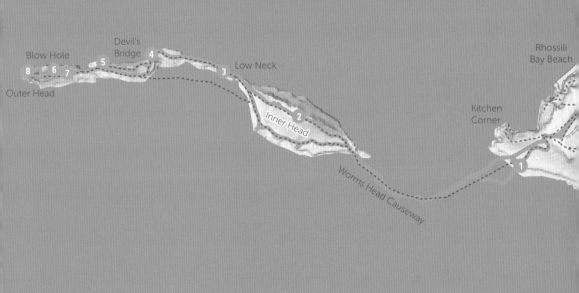

Blow Hole
Devil's Bridge
Low Neck
Outer Head
Rhossili Bay Beach
Kitchen Corner
Inner Head
Worms Head Causeway

8 6 7 5 4 3 2 1

DIRECTIONS

» From the car park turn L (W), head through the hamlet of Rhossili, then follow the coast path for 1.2km to the coastguard station. Walk downhill past the sign with details of safe crossing times to the island. Drop down onto the beach at the lifebuoy post and find a route through the rocks and pools to the starting point of the causeway (1). Keep to the N side of the causeway to cross over to the island.

» Once on the island you can follow an easy path along the S coast or a steep path that ascends Inner Head (2) for a short but thrilling ridge walk. Descend to Low Neck (3) and scramble across the top edges of the folded rocks for a short section before reaching the grass and rock path that crosses Devil's Bridge (4).

» Take the path immediately after Devil's Bridge to keep to the spine of the island (or follow the easier S coast path). Immediately before the sign for

Outer Head there is a rock window to the R (5).

» Just before reaching the tip of Outer Head (6) find the fissure of the blowhole (7) to the N of the path and the cave beneath, which is only accessible from the coast. There is an easy rocky scramble to the R to reach a small plateau, then another shorter but steeper rock scramble takes you to the summit of Outer Head (8).

SULLY

CROSS THE SECOND HIGHEST TIDAL RANGE IN THE WORLD TO DISCOVER A HIDDEN BEAUTY JUST A SHORT DISTANCE FROM CARDIFF

WARNING! WARNING! Dangerous tides. Many people have been drowned attempting to visit or return from Sully Island. The causeway is a death trap. Please take great care'. This was one of several stern signs on the approach to Sully, which is just 400 metres from the mainland. Even so, it is surprising how many people get themselves into trouble on the sometimes slippery but otherwise straightforward causeway crossing.

Uninhabited and just 450 metres long, Sully is popular with people staying locally who enjoy exploring the rock pools of the causeway or visiting the wreck of a Victorian ship. The island was once a haven for pirates, including Alfredo de Marisco, known as the 'Night Hawk', and a smugglers' tunnel was reputed to run from the island to the Captain's Wife pub. Now a Site of Special Scientific Interest,

Sully is a place to experience the vastness and power of the Bristol Channel. The circular walk follows the rocky foreshore of the north and west coasts before continuing on a grass path along the cliffs.

Given the number of visitors cut off by the tides, the RNLI installed a traffic-light system at the head of the causeway. Green, amber, and red lights indicate when it is safe, when time is running out, and when it is unsafe to attempt the crossing. The causeway itself is a wide expanse of rocks speckled with shallow rock pools that are brimming with seaweeds and shells. Once on the island's north coast there are views west to Barry Island, north to the striking orange cliffs of mainland Swanbridge, and east to the grey and cream cliffs of Lavernock Point.

TERRAIN: Rock causeway (can be slippery); rocky foreshore; and grass paths

STARTING POINT: Car park of the Captain's Wife pub. Lat/Long 51.4003, -3.1977; GR ST 168 675

DISTANCE: 2.3km (ascent 42m)

TIME: 45 mins

OS MAP: OS Explorer 151

DIFFICULTY: 2

NAVIGATION: 3

ACCESS: 3

DON'T MISS:
- Seabed walks on an island with a huge tidal range
- Fabulous sculptures and rock layers in the cliffs
- Exploring the rock pools of the causeway
- Magnificent views of the Bristol Channel islands

GETTING THERE: From Sully village on the B4267, between Penarth and Barry, head towards Swanbridge and the Captain's Wife.

SPECIAL NOTES: Generally safe to cross 3 hours before and after low water. See board with traffic-light system at start of walk for further information on safe passage. Very fast incoming tide so if at all unsure, stay on the island and sit out the high tide.

FACILITIES: No facilities on the island; good snacks and meals available in the pub.

Once on the island's foreshore and walking clockwise the black wooden ribs of a boat hull partly submerged in the sand continue to intrigue local people. Although its origins are widely speculated the remains are likely to be those of a ketch carrying coal, a smack carrying stone, a barge carrying sand and gravel, or one of the iconic Bristol Channel Pilot Cutters that guided ships through the dangerous and congested waters.

The geology of the foreshore on the north coast is fascinating. Striking deposits of rocks made of angular fragments cemented together by mineral cement sit on top of a limestone bed. The layered cliffs, again with their distinctive layers exposed, make a colourful backdrop for the walk along the foreshore.

Towards the north-east of the island a small plaque commemorates Burt Peterson 'who fished this island for more than 50 years, man and boy'. With plentiful stocks of cod, whiting, dogfish, eel, and bass, these waters remain a firm favourite with fishermen who perch on the precarious stone platforms around the island.

On the south coast the beauty of the overhanging red and cream sandstone that overlays ancient grey limestone is made for a geology field trip. There are expansive views across to Exmoor and Brean Down in Somerset, while in the foreground are the distinctive shapes of two other islandeering destinations in the Bristol Channel – Flat Holm and Steep Holm.

Walking around to the west coast, again you'll pass a fabulous mix of layered rocks before you return to the causeway. As you leave, look back over your shoulder at the island's 'welcome' sign: 'Warning, you are risking your life by visiting this island, avoid being caught on the way'. It's a useful reminder to look left and right for the incoming tide.

Beach Road

Captain's Wife

St Mary's Well Bay Road

Sully Sound

1

Swanbridge Bay

2

West Point

Sully Island

3

East Point

DIRECTIONS

» Exit the Captain's Wife car park and turn immediately L to cross the causeway (1). After 500m arrive at the island and walk clockwise on the foreshore to pass the decaying ship's hull (2). After a further 400m, go round the northeast headland and walk up the slabs of rocks to find the footpath that leads to the island's scrubby interior.

» Continue on the rough path, which may be overgrown later in the season, and walk parallel to the E coast to the 'high' point (3) at the SE corner. Continue along the top of the cliffs of the S coast, where it is possible to venture down to explore the colourful rocks and ledges.

» Drop down to the foreshore on the W coast of the island to complete the circumnavigation and return across the causeway.

FLAT HOLM

BOISTEROUS WILDLIFE, VICTORIAN GUN EMPLACEMENTS, AND A REMOTE BAR ON AN ISLAND THAT MADE COMMUNICATIONS HISTORY

Setting off from Mermaid Quay the vast lock gates of the Cardiff Bay Barrage close far above your head and there is a certain apprehension at leaving the calm lagoon to enter the treacherous brown waters of the Bristol Channel. Soon the throttles of the small RIB open up and the next group of visitors hurtles towards the speck of rock in the distance that gives the island its name.

From a distance, there are few landmarks apart from the white lighthouse but once on land, the short, circular walk reveals a striking shoreline with rock outcrops, caves, and rock beaches. There are also plenty of opportunities to deviate inland and explore the many intriguing historic sites along the way.

Flat Holm is a limestone island lying in the treacherous currents of the Bristol Channel, approx-imately four kilometres off the coast of Wales. Its gentle, grassy slope rises from the exposed rocky shore of the west to the more sheltered easterly cliffs. The interior is open, flat, and windswept. Managed by Cardiff Council it is a significant nature reserve. Yet it is not only natural forces that have shaped the island's character. Augustinian monks, a radio genius, Victorian gunners, and cholera sufferers have occupied it over the last 800 years and all made their mark.

The walk starts with a short orientation talk by the wardens at the old Barracks, once the quarters of the six gunners stationed here as part of the Victorian strategic coastal defence system. The building is surrounded by the extremely rare purple-headed wild leek, standing to attention at 1.5 metres tall. Just touching this protected species could incur a fine of £1,000. Close-by, the impressive tiled water

---

TERRAIN: Easy grass paths; some free-range walking

STARTING POINT: Mermaid Quay, Cardiff Bay. Lat/Long 51.463040, -3.164097; GR ST 192 744

DISTANCE: 2.1km (ascent 44m)

TIME: 45 mins

OS MAP: OS Explorer 153

DIFFICULTY: 2

NAVIGATION: 2

ACCESS: 2 (steep steps from landing quay)

DON'T MISS:
- Super-fast, exhilarating RIB ride to the island
- Exploring rock arches and 'fossilised' beach features
- The rare wild leek (June to September)
- Refreshments at the island pub with the largest beer garden in Wales

SPECIAL NOTES: Small entry fee is collected by the warden on the island.

GETTING THERE: By RIB operated by two companies from Mermaid Quay CF10 5BZ. Bay Island Voyages run daily 2–2.5 hour excursions www.bayislandvoyages.co.uk and Cardiff Sea Safaris run a more limited service on specific dates that allows 10–12 hours on the island www.cardiffseasafaris.co.uk.

FACILITIES: Drinks, limited selection of snacks, and toilets at the island's Gull and Leek pub.

catchment area and underground storage tank is testament to the ingenuity of the Victorians who tamed this island to meet their needs.

Walking clockwise from the Barracks to the working lighthouse on the south east point, you reach the Lighthouse Battery. Here, the Moncrieff pit housed a platform-mounted cannon that, once fired, could be lowered back down below the horizon line. The tunnels and storerooms of the battery are all fascinating to explore. Slightly further west, Swimmers Bridge passes over Victorian Trench, a ravine dug as the last line of defence for the batteries. From here there are wonderful views across to Steep Holm, and to Brean Down and Weston-super-Mare beyond.

The island's principal gull colony breeds in the south-west of the island so this area may be out of bounds during the early summer months, although wardens can advise on alternative routes. These bold, urban scavengers pick up their meals from Cardiff and litter the island with plastic wrappers, chicken bones, and burgers. They take flight if you walk anywhere near, not only screeching menacingly but also swooping and dive-bombing from behind.

After the noisy gull encounter the walk continues down through the scrub to the rocky shoreline near North West Point. Here the impres-

sive wave-cut platform is indented with large, fossilised 'ripple marks' and the views open up in all directions. With Steep Holm to the south and Sully Island to the northwest Flat Holm completes the set of Carboniferous stepping stones between the coastlines of England and Wales.

Just inland from the fossil beach there is a cluster of dilapidated buildings with a grim history. This is the site of the isolation hospital where ships would drop off crew or passengers suspected of carrying cholera to stop it spreading to the ports of the mainland. The last patient to die here was the victim of bubonic plague. At its peak the hospital had 16 beds, its own laundry, and even its own crematorium – a sight that must have been somewhat discouraging for new patients arriving. The building was condemned in 1935 but subsequently repurposed as a NAAFI store and cinema by the 350 soldiers stationed on the island during World War II. Near the buildings, a silver plaque commemorates the delivery of the first-ever wireless transmission across 4.3 kilometres of open water from Flat Holm to Lavernock Point on the south coast of Wales. It was sent by the pioneering radio engineer Marconi and his message read 'Are you ready'?

A little further to the north, the farmhouse is the island's hub. Once a thriving farm that sent high-

quality lamb to the Cardiff markets it was, for a short while, a hotel with a bar and skittle alley. Today the high levels of lead in the soil prohibit livestock and food crops and the farm buildings provide accommodation for the warden and visitors alike.

At the northern tip of the island, Castle Rock is the best place to see the breeding pair of great black-backed gulls – the largest members of the gull family with an impressive wingspan of 1.7 metres. From here on a clear day there are views to the M4 suspension bridge and at night-time lights are strung like arteries along the long arms of the Bristol Channel with the cities and towns appearing as the brighter nodes.

If your visit coincides with a low tide and if the nesting birds have left the island, it is possible to descend via the jetties to the landing beach. The natural arch below Castle Rock is well worth exploring for a completely different perspective on Flat Holm. From here it is also possible to walk around the whole island at the base of the cliffs. You will need precise knowledge of the tide times and an appreciation of the danger posed by a tidal range of 15 metres. For the adventurous, this is a great opportunity to explore the various small caves and rock arches the island has to offer.

Continuing on the island's plateau along the steep cliffs of the east coast, you can hear the harsh shrills of peregrines above the din of the seagull colonies. You may even see the falcons swooping acrobatically on the thermals. The route then returns past the Foghorn Station to the Barracks building where the other visitors who have been on a free warden-led tour gather to compare notes. Some report slow-worm sightings; others have caught glimpses of the elusive, feral Soay sheep.

The best way to round off your visit is to take refreshment at Wales' most southerly inn, the aptly name Gull and Leek that also boasts the 'largest beer garden in Wales'. Suitably fortified, the thrilling RIB ride back awaits.

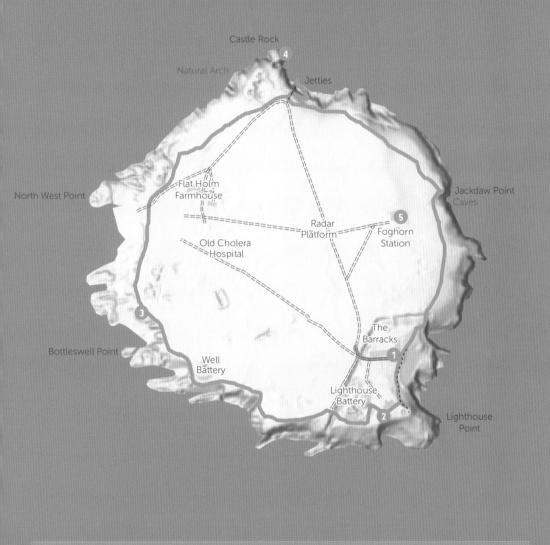

Castle Rock

4

Natural Arch

Jetties

North West Point

Flat Holm
Farmhouse

Jackdaw Point
Caves

5

Radar
Platform

Foghorn
Station

Old Cholera
Hospital

3

The
Barracks

1

Bottleswell Point

Well
Battery

Lighthouse
Battery

2

Lighthouse
Point

DIRECTIONS

» Start at the Barracks (1) and follow the coast path to the lighthouse and battery complex (2). After 200m cross the deep defensive ditch via Swimmer's Bridge and take the L fork through the scrub and along the coast to the observation post and Nissen huts.

» Turn N and after 250m pass the wave-cut platforms and fossilised ripples (3) that start almost opposite the isolation hospital. Continue past the farmhouse on R and head L towards an isolated set of steps and cross the helipad. After 400m pass Castle Rock (4) and the jetty and follow the path to the R of Halfway

House and uphill. Keep to the L of the fence line of John's Plot and head towards the Foghorn Station (5).

» Pass through the kissing gate, cross a small concrete bridge over the old defensive ditch, then take the steps around the back of the toilet block to return to the Barracks.

HOLY ISLAND (ARRAN)

A TIBETAN BUDDHIST VISION REALISED ON AN UNSPOILT ISLAND IN THE FIRTH OF CLYDE WHERE PEOPLE LIVE IN HARMONY WITH NATURE

You don't have to travel to Tibet to visit a remote Buddhist monastery – there is one just off the west coast of Scotland. Enjoy a day's walk round Holy Isle in Lamlash Bay where a Buddhist community thrives in a landscape of towering peaks, tranquil gardens, and wild shores.

After the short ferry trip from Lamlash on nearby Arran, you arrive at the pier to a welcome by a member of the community. Among the large, white stupas and multi-coloured prayer flags you'll get a short but fascinating introduction to their lives and the natural features of the island. The first half of the walk is through wood and moorland on the steep, rough path over Mullach Beag and Mullach Mòr, the highest point on the island. The second half is via the gentler coastal path, passing sacred caves, Buddhist rock paintings, fruit-filled orchards, and flourishing vegetable gardens.

Holy Isle is only three kilometres long but rises steeply to 300 metres in the centre. This place, where all life is sacred, sits in a marine conservation zone and its precipitous east coast is maintained as a wildlife sanctuary. With a history as a sacred site that goes back centuries, the island has a spring and holy well, a monk's cave, and was the site of an early monastery. The Samye Ling Buddhist Community now owns the island and operates two retreat centres in the north and south. The remainder is treated as a nature reserve and is freely grazed by Eriskay ponies, Saanen goats and Soay sheep. Overhead, peregrines soar along the cliff edges and eider ducks nest undisturbed on the shores.

The island is open to Buddhists and non-Buddhists alike – as long as everyone respects the Five Golden Rules of Buddhism. Rule one is to 'refrain from taking any life'. Yet by the time I had climbed

TERRAIN: Steep climbs on rugged paths; easy path along the west coast

STARTING POINT: Holy Isle jetty. Lat/Long 55.5335, -5.0886; GR NS 052 310

DISTANCE: 8.7km (ascent 423m)

TIME: 2 hours 30 mins

OS MAP: OS Explorer 153

DIFFICULTY: 2

NAVIGATION: 2

ACCESS: 2 (steep steps from landing quay)

DON'T MISS:
- Colourful Buddhist rock art along the west coast
- Wandering through peaceful organic vegetable and flower gardens
- Runic signs on the walls of a holy hermit's cave
- Views from Mullach Mòr's summit to Goat Fell, Arran

SPECIAL NOTES: No dogs allowed. All visitors are asked to observe the five rules of Buddhism during their visit.

GETTING THERE: Regular private boat service from Lamlash Pier, weather and tide permitting (Holy Isle Ferry 01770 700463/07970 771960). There is a regular bus service to Lamlash from Arran's ferry terminal at Brodick www.spt.co.uk/timetable/arran/.

FACILITIES: Complimentary tea and coffee in the information centre on the island; soup and delicious cakes in the Old Pier Café next to Lamlash Pier.

through the rough moorland and reached the top of Mullach Mòr, the midges were really trying my patience. Silhouetted on the skyline, I jumped up and down, hands slapping wildly. I feared I would be branded a rule-breaker and escorted off the island. When I tried to sit serenely and soak up the views of Goat Fell over on Arran, the island started to feel more like Tibet.

There are two key settlements on the island. The first, the Centre for World Peace and Health in the north, holds courses and retreats in the former farmhouse that has been sympathetically and sustainably restored. The second, the Inner Light Retreat, lies to the south. Closed to the public, it is reserved for those undertaking long-term retreats. Biodynamically grown plants and seeds are offered for sale on a table outside. There are also more extreme forms of solitary retreat in the form of small hermit-like cells that can be seen half-buried in the hillside on the way down from Mullach Mor. Close by, the small wooden chalet is the island home of the founder, Lama Yeshe Rinpoche.

Along the west coast, the rocks are adorned with large and colourful rock paintings that depict different Tibetan Buddhist deities and teachers within the Karma Kagyu lineage. Each is vibrantly coloured and some of them almost appear in 3-D. There you'll also find the ancient healing well, but be aware that the water isn't safe to drink.

Further north on the west coast, the cave was once the home of St Molaise. This relatively well-appointed retreat has a fireplace, fresh water supply, drainage, and a large stone dining table and stone seats. The roof and sides of the cave are covered with runic inscriptions – possibly made by sailors from a Viking fleet that sheltered between Arran and Holy Isle before the Battle of Largs.

Back at the Peace Centre the sheer abundance of produce in the organic gardens is inspiring. Supplying the vegetables and fruit for residents and guests, the plots are enchantingly decorated with rustic furniture and hand-painted plaques inscribed with the wise words of Buddha. Follow the winding paths through a profusion of vegetables, fruit, and flowers and take time out to soak up the atmosphere of this magical place, which is peacefully and lovingly tended by the community and volunteers.

The walk ends at the information centre and shop – a historic little building just south of the jetty that looks like a boathouse. Here, before catching the boat back to Arran, you will be offered tea and coffee in exchange for a small donation.

In this beguiling free and wild place a small Buddhist community lives in complete harmony with its natural surroundings. Although only ten minutes from the mainland, it seems light years away.

Let us be grateful
to people who
make us happy,
they are the charming
gardeners who make us
Blossom ~ Marcel Proust

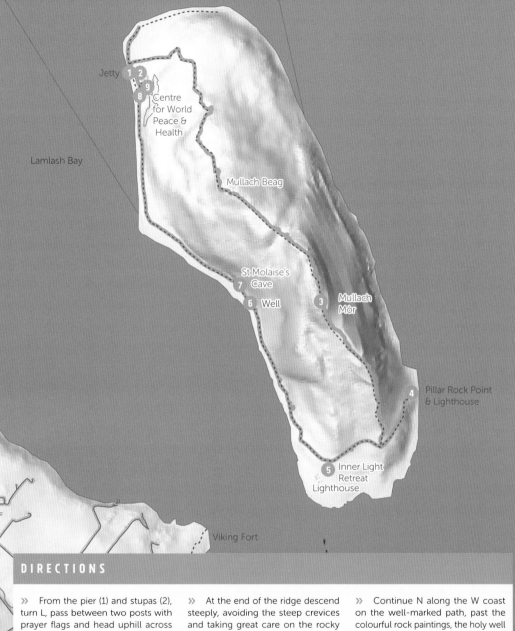

Jetty

Centre
for World
Peace &
Health

Lamlash Bay

Mullach Beag

St Molaise's
Cave

Well

Mullach
Mòr

Pillar Rock Point
& Lighthouse

Inner Light
Retreat
Lighthouse

Viking Fort

DIRECTIONS

» From the pier (1) and stupas (2), turn L, pass between two posts with prayer flags and head uphill across the field to the stile. Follow all signs 'To the Top' through gorse and trees to Mullach Beag, then hike over the saddle and up to Mullach Mòr (3).

» At the end of the ridge descend steeply, avoiding the steep crevices and taking great care on the rocky slabs, to meet the lower path. Turn L to visit Pillar Rock Lighthouse (4) where there are wonderful views over the E coast nature reserve. Retrace your steps and carry on towards the other lighthouse and the Inner Light Retreat (5) on the W coast.

» Continue N along the W coast on the well-marked path, past the colourful rock paintings, the holy well (6) and St Molaise's Cave (7), to reach the information centre (8) and organic vegetable garden (9). The north point can be explored by continuing on past the jetty and through the bushes.

DAVAAR

AN ISLAND OF ARTFUL DECEPTION, FREE-RANGE WALKING AND CAVE EXPLORATION

Walking unsteadily among the smooth boulders of the southern foreshore, I began to wonder if I'd missed the Crucifixion Cave. Like a bat searching for a new roost, I'd stuck my head into a number of grottoes along the cliffs with no result. Then I found it and saw a vibrantly coloured, life-sized masterpiece painted on the cave wall. The assortment of offerings placed beneath this stunning depiction of Christ's Crucifixion clearly demonstrated its continuing significance for pilgrims. For the adventurer, however, the cave makes a spirited wild-camping spot, the sea lapping well away from its dry entrance.

The free-range clockwise walk around a rugged island starts with a 30-minute tidal crossing of a sand and pebble causeway, the Doirlinn, followed by a steep ascent above the lighthouse to the precipitous east coast. The views north-east to the Isle of Arran and south-east to Ailsa Craig with the Ayrshire coast beyond, are breathtaking. A further climb to the trig point reveals equally fine views of Campbeltown and its busy harbour before a descent and a rough foreshore walk across the rounded cobbles and boulders to explore several sea caves.

Davaar, in Argyll and Bute, lies off the east coast of Kintyre and sits at the head of Campbeltown Loch. Sheep crop the grass on the exposed summit and there are also wild goats and mink. The lighthouse, at the island's northern tip, is permanently occupied by a caretaker and the adjoining buildings are operated as holiday lets. You can stay in the square, cream-painted building known as The Lookout, which stands on a small knoll close by. It was built during World War II as a base for the naval crews who installed anti-submarine nets to protect Campbeltown.

TERRAIN: Shingle causeway, animal tracks and over smooth rocks

STARTING POINT: Lay-by near Doirlinn. Lat/Long 55.4169, -5.5639; GR NR 745 1940

DISTANCE: 7.4km (ascent 437m)

TIME: 2 hours (plus time to explore the caves)

OS MAP: OS Explorer 356

DIFFICULTY: 2 (4 for caves)

NAVIGATION: 3

ACCESS: 3

DON'T MISS:
- Victorian sacred art in the Crucifixion Cave
- Foraging for cockles and winkles along the causeway
- Far-reaching views of outlying isles and Northern Ireland
- Looking out for whales, dolphins and basking sharks from the east coast

SPECIAL NOTES: Tide times are listed in the tourist information centre, the Pier, Campbeltown. The causeway is accessible about 3 hours either side of low tide.

GETTING THERE: Head E from the CalMac ferry terminal on the minor road, reaching the lay-by after 3km.

FACILITIES: All facilities in nearby Campbeltown.

Although Davaar is sparsely populated, its waters support an abundance of life. On calm summer days you can spot basking sharks, dolphins, and whales from the northern tip and watch gannets from the large colony on Ailsa Craig swoop and dive for their prey off the causeway; a good spot to forage for cockles and winkles.

The main attractions for most visitors are the seven accessible sea caves on Davaar's south coast, particularly Crucifixion Cave. In 1887 local fishermen discovered a painting that seemed to have appeared overnight, and frenzied speculation ensued. Locals believed the painting was a miracle sent from God but the mystery artist was Archibald MacKinnon, a local art teacher 'guided' to paint the scene. He didn't reveal his secret for 47 years and was subsequently banished from Campbeltown, but managed to go back and retouch his artwork. The painting had one more mystery up its sleeve when Che Guevara was painted over Christ's face by an unknown artist in 2006 but the original painting has since been restored.

Nearby Campbeltown is a gem and the Mull of Kintyre lies a little further south. Both warrant spending extra time in the area. The Kintyre Peninsula is also a great jumping-off point for other island adventures with ferries to Colonsay, Islay, Jura, Gigha, and Arran all close by.

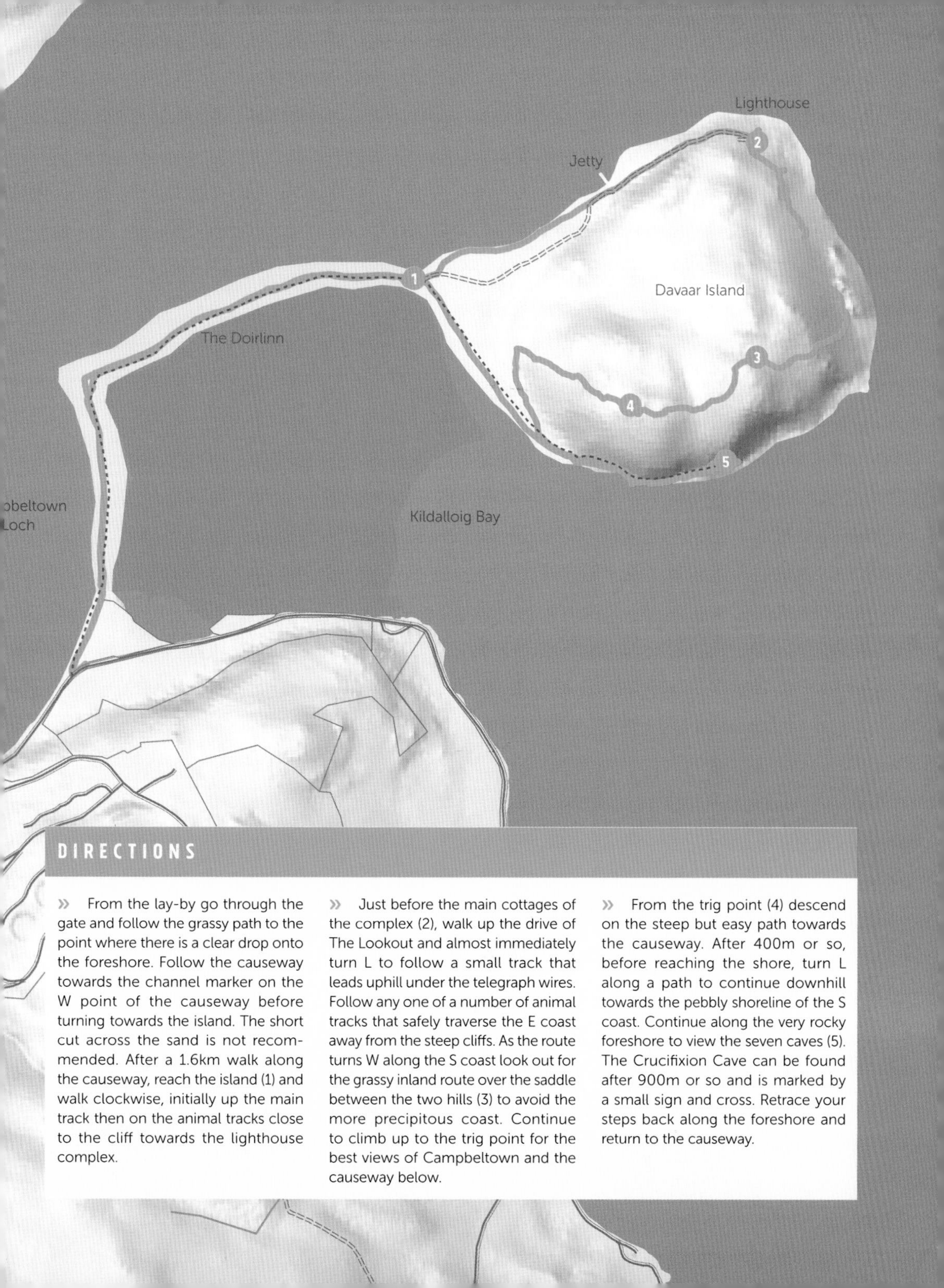

Lighthouse

Jetty

2

Davaar Island

1

The Doirlinn

3

4

5

beltown
Loch

Kildalloig Bay

DIRECTIONS

» From the lay-by go through the gate and follow the grassy path to the point where there is a clear drop onto the foreshore. Follow the causeway towards the channel marker on the W point of the causeway before turning towards the island. The short cut across the sand is not recommended. After a 1.6km walk along the causeway, reach the island (1) and walk clockwise, initially up the main track then on the animal tracks close to the cliff towards the lighthouse complex.

» Just before the main cottages of the complex (2), walk up the drive of The Lookout and almost immediately turn L to follow a small track that leads uphill under the telegraph wires. Follow any one of a number of animal tracks that safely traverse the E coast away from the steep cliffs. As the route turns W along the S coast look out for the grassy inland route over the saddle between the two hills (3) to avoid the more precipitous coast. Continue to climb up to the trig point for the best views of Campbeltown and the causeway below.

» From the trig point (4) descend on the steep but easy path towards the causeway. After 400m or so, before reaching the shore, turn L along a path to continue downhill towards the pebbly shoreline of the S coast. Continue along the very rocky foreshore to view the seven caves (5). The Crucifixion Cave can be found after 900m or so and is marked by a small sign and cross. Retrace your steps back along the foreshore and return to the causeway.

ORONSAY

BEAUTIFUL TIDAL CROSSING TO A WILDLIFE ISLAND ONCE THE PARTY CAPITAL FOR ANCIENT MAN. A WILD FORESHORE WALK

I have often heard the corncrake, one of Britain's rarest birds, but had never actually seen one until I visited this island for the second time. Two of them walked nonchalantly in the short grass ahead of me, a fair distance away from the RSPB-managed habitat on the other side of the island. They had clearly given the birdwatchers the slip. But even if you don't encounter corncrakes you're almost sure to encounter the wardens. They swell the island's ranks to six or so in the summer and work extremely hard to manage the land for conservation purposes. Other than that your only other company is likely to be grey seals, a chough or two, and a handful of rare plants.

After a fabulous low-tide crossing of The Strand, the route follows the main island track to the Priory and Oronsay Farm before an easy free-range section along the coast. There are magnificent views of the peaks of Islay and Jura for most of the walk, which takes in a secluded bothy and the stunning, deserted white-sand beaches on the south and east coasts that make such idyllic swimming spots.

Oronsay is a tidal island that sits just off the south coast of Colonsay in the Inner Hebrides. Some 6,000 years ago, this wild and rugged place was the site of human settlement and excavation of shell middens on the island have yielded valuable information about their diet.

Good planning is essential before embarking on a visit to the island as not all low tides are equal – on neap lows The Strand may not be passable at all. For sound advice on crossing times visit the post office on Colonsay where Keith, the friendly and knowledgeable postmaster, displays a handwritten log of days and times that are safe for the post van to cross.

TERRAIN: Tidal crossing; island tracks; free-range walk on open ground

STARTING POINT: Track head on Oronsay. Lat/Long 56.0282, -6.2280; GR NR 367 898

DISTANCE: 14.3km (ascent 208m)

TIME: 3 hours 30 mins

OS MAP: OS Explorer 354

DIFFICULTY: 2

NAVIGATION: 3

ACCESS: 3

DON'T MISS:
- Secret swims off deserted white-sand beaches
- Exciting crossing over sands still wet from the last tide
- Stunning views of the Paps of Jura and Islay
- Trying to spot the elusive corncrake

SPECIAL NOTES: Access may not be possible on neap low tides, consult Oronsay Post Office (01951 200323) for advice. Full route not possible during bird breeding season April-end July, seek advice from RSPB warden (01951 200367).

GETTING THERE: CalMac ferry to Colonsay from Oban www.calmac.co.uk. From the B8086 at Scalasaig, pass the Hotel and after 1.3km turn L onto the B8085 to reach the head of the causeway at the road end.

FACILITIES: None on the island; hotel, café, general store, and post office in Scalasaig, Colonsay.

Even on the lowest tide The Strand is rarely dry and I made my first crossing by mountain bike to gain more time on the island. It was the one and only time that I saw small fish swim between the spokes of the wheels and the disc brakes have never been the same since. The second time I crossed in the company of a father and his young daughter. Resplendent in a bright pink waterproof all-in-one, she was looking for mermaids while he carried a professional camera and hoped to see the rare and beautiful white orchid known as Irish Lady's-tresses.

Once on the island the main island track leads to the priory, initially through the rock gardens of the foreshore and then across the moorland at the base of Beinn Oronsay, the island's high point and home to two pairs of choughs. The well-preserved Augustinian priory ruins are thought to be on the same site as an earlier Celtic monastery and probably date from the middle of 14th century. There is an amazing set of carved gravestones and the beautiful Celtic Oronsay Cross, possibly carved on Iona, which is one of the best examples of its kind.

From the priory the anti-clockwise route continues towards Oronsay Farm then south along tracks through the corncrake habitat and on to the coast. Outside nesting season it is possible to visit the nearby tidal island, Dubh Eilean. Numerous gull and terns colonise the rocky strands here during the summer months, while barnacle geese flock here in the winter. From May onwards, the machair is covered with wild flowers that sparkle like gems against the white sands of the beach.

On the way down to the southern tip of the island the route passes a sweeping crescent bay watched over by a tiny bothy. Glancing through the window, I was struck by the care and attention given to the interior, which was beautifully decorated with wall hangings and items found on the beach. Fish boxes served as furniture and ropes, buoys, and even coconuts had been fashioned into unique and quirky ornaments.

The skerries at the southern tip of the island are home to several seal colonies and Eilean nan Ròn (Seal Island) is a designated nature reserve. In the autumn over 1,000 grey seals may be found here, all noisily pupping and fishing in a scene worthy of a voiceover from David Attenborough himself.

Turning north-east to follow the east coast, there are postcard-perfect views to the Paps of Jura and the mountains of Islay. Clouds pass, then mists obscure the peaks and the brooding blue

vistas seem to change with every moment. Look out for the corncrakes here if you didn't spot any by the priory. September, when the young are out foraging before they fly to Africa, is a good month to see these elusive birds.

At intervals along the east coast are the celebrated shell middens – mounds of kitchen waste left by early man. It is thought that Oronsay was once the heart and soul of parties thrown by the hunter-gatherers with much feasting, matchmaking, and gossip, although the menu seemed fairly monotonous: limpets, limpets, and more limpets.

Before arriving at Seal Cottage on the east coast, stop at Tràigh Uamha Seilbhe, a gorgeous protected beach and the perfect place for a secret swim. Around this isolated, tiny cottage overlooking the sands, Highland cattle graze while the whiskered faces of grey seals bob in the water below, watching carefully from a safe distance.

On the way back to The Strand, stop at the spring near Seal Cottage and drink cold, clear water

from the metal cup provided. This is the only source of water on the island and perhaps explains, along with the abundance of shellfish, why Mesolithic peoples settled here. A single visit for the duration of one low tide will not be enough to explore everything that drew them to this peaceful and special place.

The Strand

Beinn Eibhne

① (1)

② Beinn Oronsay

Leaba Mhor

③ Priory

④

Port na Luinge

Dubh Eilean

⑤

Spring ⑨ Seal Cottage

⑦

⑥

⑧

Mesolithic
Shell Mounds

Tràigh Uamha Seilbhe

Port na Blàthach

Eilean
Ghaoideamal

Eilean nan Ròn

DIRECTIONS

» At the S end of B8085 follow the tyre marks to cross The Strand and, after 2.3km, take the shingle track between two posts and a standing stone to R (1) onto the island. Follow the track through the rocky foreshore, over moorland at the base of Beinn Oronsay (2), and through farmland to the priory (3).

» Take the track through the gate to L of the main house towards Oronsay Farm. Just before reaching the RSPB office turn L, opposite the house, go through the gate and along the grass track through the managed corncrake habitat (4). After 200m turn L through a gate and continue towards the shore, walking alongside the stream.

» Go through the metal gate and onto the beach. Turn R to access the tidal islet of Dubh Eilean (5) or continue S to the white bothy (6) at the end of the long beach. Go through the gate in the stone wall, turn R parallel to the stone wall, and continue over the open ground and machair, keeping to the coast.

» At the S tip continue around the low rock terraces of Port na Blàthach then rejoin the grass island track between the head of the inlet and a raised pebble 'beach' to the L. After about 1.9km, pass through the remains of a stone boundary wall.

» Continue, past the shell mounds (7) to Tràigh Uamha Seilbhe (8). From Seal Cottage (9) take the L fork and continue NW through a metal gate, towards the main island track. Turn R at the metal gate in the stone wall and continue along the main island track, retracing your steps back to the causeway.

LUING

JAGGED TOWERS OF SLATE, FORESHORE WALKING AND INCREDIBLE SUNSETS FRAMED BY THE ISLES TO THE WEST

Nestled in the Firth of Lorn and just 24 kilometres south of Oban, Luing is a short ferry crossing from the Isle of Seil – itself connected to the mainland by the much-photographed Bridge over the Atlantic. The island was the centre of a once-thriving slate industry and the surreal landscape of fractured cliff walls in the north is thrilling to explore. The most southerly of the so-called Slate Islands of the Inner Hebrides, it is a place of peaceful pastureland grazed by distinctive red Luing cattle, and unspoilt foreshore. From its western coast there are incredible sunset views to the neighbouring isles.

Starting in the north, the clockwise route follows the main island lane south towards Ardinamir Bay. A good track along the rural east coast of Luing then takes you to the harbourside hamlet of Toberonochy before embarking on a gentle, free-range section around the remote foreshore of the southern part of the island. From the higher path along the west coast, on a clear day there are views over the Sound of Luing to Mull, Scarba, Fladda, and the Garvellachs with Colonsay, Islay, and Jura visible in the far distance. Arriving at the main village, Cullipool, stop off at the welcoming community café and island bakery before exploring the immense slate quarries and workings that stretch throughout the northern end of the island.

Just before Toberonochy, take time to look at the ruins of 12th-century Kilchattan Chapel. The stones on the north and south sides of the ruins feature incisions and the outline of Hebridean galleys, and you'll notice the gravestone of a highly opinionated and intolerant man, Alexander Campbell. This fervent Covenanter (Presbyterian) erected a number of stones with hand-carved inscriptions threaten-

---

TERRAIN: Foreshore of grass, sand, easy rocks and some boggy areas; minor island roads and good tracks

STARTING POINT: Cuan Ferry jetty. Lat/Long: 56.2663, -5.6332; GR NM 751 141

DISTANCE: 24km (ascent 430m)

TIME: 6 hours

OS MAP: OS Explorer 359

DIFFICULTY: 2

NAVIGATION: 3

ACCESS: 2

DON'T MISS:
- Stone skimming on the slate beaches
- Exploring the disued quarries north of Cullipool
- Home baking, local seafood, and views from the Atlantic Centre

SPECIAL NOTES: Path is eroded N of Cullipool so rock hopping across the beach head is necessary. Best attempted on lower tides. The walk can be done over 2

days, split into a S and N loop and using the link road between Toberonochy and Black Mill Bay.

GETTING THERE: From Oban drive S on A816, turn R onto B844 over to Seil, then L on B8003 to reach the small village of North Cuan on the Sound of Cuan and the CalMac ferry crossing to Luing. www.calmac.co.uk.

FACILITIES: Luing Store, on road S of Cullipool; food and toilets at the Atlantic Centre; Luing Bakery in Cullipool.

ing divine retribution against anyone who dared to remove them. On his death he left a testimony that denounced virtually everything and everyone including King George III, dancing schools, 'women that wear Babylonish garments', the low country, steamships, men's whiskers, Quakers, Tabernacle folk, Roman Catholics, and all sectarians.

Southeast of the chapel lies the village of Toberonochy, its white former quarriers' cottages set round an attractive green. There are lobster pots stacked around the lovely sheltered harbour and a slate beach. From Toberonochy, the foreshore section of the walk around the south of the island is gentle and at times marshy, passing through grassland interspersed with dark, peaty pools. Notice the bright green grass mounds that top many of the natural ridges of the landscape. These are otter spraint sites – territorial markers built up from dung and possibly hundreds of years old.

After accessing the exposed southern tip of the island through a gap in the rocks, the grassy route up the west coast then hugs the base of low inland cliffs that resemble a raised beach. There are great views across the Sound of Luing to Scarba and you might even hear the roar of the world's third largest whirlpool, the mighty Corryvreckan between Scarba and Jura, if the tides are just right. Further north along the west coast Blackmill Bay, once the main entry and exit point for people, livestock and goods to Luing, is one of the island's main east-west crossing points. From Blackmill Bay, the route continues north and slightly inland on well-defined farm tracks. Lobster fishing is an important source of income on Luing and between Eilean Loisgte and Fraoch Eilean you'll see one of the largest lobster ponds in Scotland.

Continuing up the west coast, almost to the northern tip, the main village of Cullipool is the destination for most visitors. The Atlantic Islands Centre serves locally sourced food and there are displays describing the island's wildlife, culture, and history. It's a great place to sit and enjoy the views.

Just north of the village the disused quarries are an impressive legacy of the slate industry. More than 150 men were employed here, at one point producing an annual total of 2.8 million slates. These were destined for homes and high-profile structures such as Iona Cathedral. Large heaps of spoil and steep undercut cliffs line the route taken many years ago by the quarriers.

Across the sound, there are views south-west to Fladda and its lighthouse, and west to the cliffs of Belnahua – another slate island with a deep quarry pool at its centre. To the north, the whitewashed slate-roofed cottages on Seil and the tiny island of Easdale shine out against the grey backdrop of steep, jagged quarry cliffs. As you prepare to leave, the grey slate of the beaches immediately before the jetty is another reminder of the natural resource that quite literally shaped this island. It's a great place for stone skimming, too.

DIRECTIONS

» From the jetty (1) walk uphill on the minor road past several houses as it heads S onto the moorland. After 2.6km, at the top of the hill just before a cattle grid, turn L onto a good track. After 250m go through the gate to R of the sheepfold and continue on the track through further enclosures and gates.

» After 350m turn L at the island lane, past a fort above the lane on L. After 50m or so turn R onto the track, just ahead of the wooden fence of the house at Ardinamir (2), and then take the R fork uphill.

» Continue on the track for 2 km and pass the ruins of an old farmhouse on L to see the hamlet of Toberonochy ahead. Pass Lochan Iliter, a farmyard, then at the island's main road turn L towards the chapel ruins (3). Continue downhill into Toberonochy (4) past the jetty and along the small lane for 240m. At the last white house continue on the grass track that runs parallel to the foreshore alongside a row of conifers. Go over a stile and continue along the foreshore.

» Cross a stone wall and then after 1.3km, at the fence line, walk inland for 100m or so to the gate. Continue parallel to the foreshore keeping 100m or so inland, passing below the pine forest and hugging the base of the rocks to avoid boggy areas. Climb up to the 10m contour marked on the map and continue at that height towards the SW tip of the island.

» Pass through a gap in the rocks (5) and then head down to the foreshore of the SW tip and follow the faint path along the shoreline keeping the rock bluffs to your R. After 1.2km pass through a gate in the fence line and then another after a further 1.3km.

» Continue along the faint path along the foreshore, across the black sands of Camas nan Gall (6) to see two cave entrances in the rocks inland. After 700m reach the first house of Black Mill Bay (7) and continue inland along the track. Turn L just before the cattle grid along the drive to Ardlarach House (8). At the top of the drive, before the farmyard, turn L through the gate and along the track at the back of the bungalows, then walk uphill into the trees.

» Pass through the smaller gate and turn R to walk parallel to the tree line to reach a gate after 150m or so. Follow the grass track initially uphill and then drop down

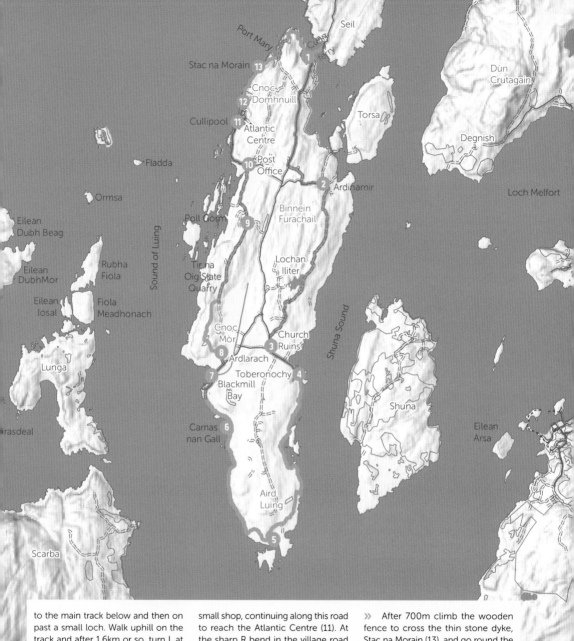

Port Mary
Seil
Stac na Morain **13**
Cnoc
Domhnuill
12
Cullipool **11**
Atlantic
Centre
10
Post
Office
Ardinamir
2
Torsa
Dùn
Crutagain
Degnish
Loch Melfort

Eilean
Dubh Beag
Ormsa
Poll Gorm
Binnein
Furachail
9

Eilean
DubhMor
Rubha
Fiola
Tir na
Oig State
Quarry
Lochan
Iliter

Eilean
losal
Fiola
Meadhonach

Cnoc
Mòr
8
Church
Ruins
3
Ardlarach
Lunga
7
Toberonochy
4
Blackmill
Bay

rasdeal
Camas
nan Gall
6

Shuna Sound
Shuna
Eilean
Arsa

Aird
Luing

5

Scarba

Gulf of
ryvreckan

to the main track below and then on past a small loch. Walk uphill on the track and after 1.6km or so, turn L at the stone barn (9) taking the track downhill. After 400m turn R on the track towards the first of Cullipool's houses.

»   On reaching the main island road turn L to pass the post office (10) and

small shop, continuing along this road to reach the Atlantic Centre (11). At the sharp R bend in the village road head straight over to the stone track leading towards the quarries (12) and continue N. Follow the track to where it has been washed away and drop down onto the rocks of the shoreline to bypass the rock fall. Rejoin the path along the shoreline.

»   After 700m climb the wooden fence to cross the thin stone dyke, Stac na Morain (13), and go round the small bay of Port Mary. Follow the path through the old quarry workings and past a water-filled excavation site at the N tip of the island. Continue round on the clear path to return to the ferry jetty.

CHAPTER 36

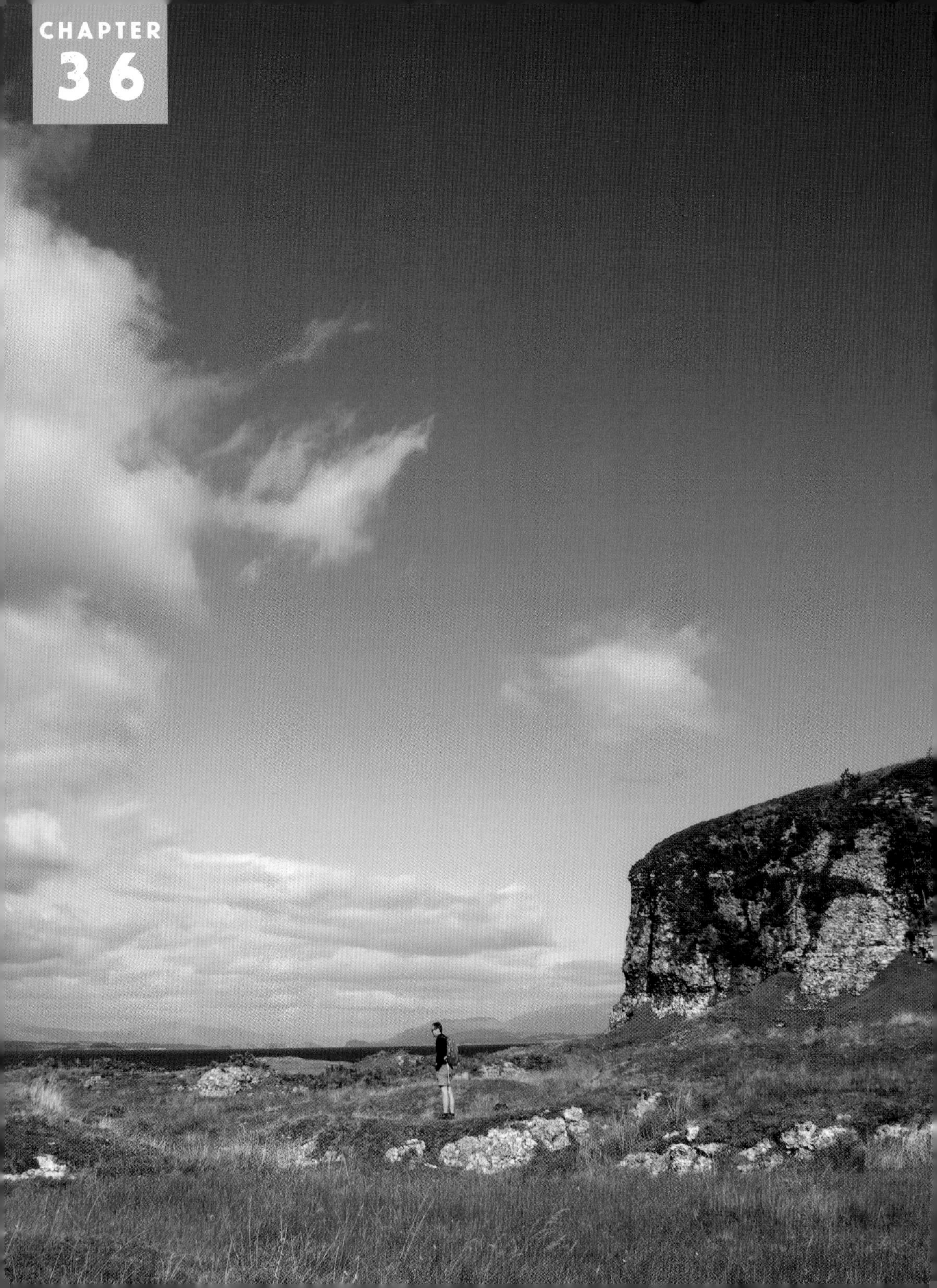

KERRERA

VISIT CAVES, HIDDEN BAYS, AND A RUINED STRONGHOLD ON THIS FREE-RANGE ROUTE. AND FOR CAKE, JUST FOLLOW THE TEAPOTS

Sheltering the bustling harbour of Oban, just a few hundred metres over the water, Kerrera is a hilly island with a terraced coastline. The effects of changing sea levels are evident in the ancient cliffline above dry raised beaches, which makes a perfect walking platform. The land is farmed, tourism is a principal source of income, and there is a busy marina in the north. Yet the island remains peaceful and unspoilt with romantic castle ruins and a single but exceptional tearoom in the south.

From the jetty, the clockwise route follows a stone track to the café and Gylen Castle with an easy grass path beyond to Barnabuck. The rest of the west coast route is free-range through pasture, some of it boggy, and passes caves, beaches, and rock gardens on the low plateau between the old cliffs and the coast. Depending on the season,

there may be some bushwhacking through bracken around the northern tip of the island at the base of Hutcheson's Monument before the route continues past the farm at Ardentrive, then along the east coast on the return leg.

Most visitors avoid the free-range elements by sticking to the marked south circuit or the easy track to Hutcheson's Monument in the north. The island map at the jetty displays both routes but for the adventurous, there is so much more to explore.

Arrival on Kerrera is via a mini-CalMac ferry, which can be crowded when a small sewage truck has to fit on-board. I watched the skipper remove the bad-weather shelter so the truck could squeeze on: the ingenuity of island logistics never ceases to amaze. Minutes later, I was walking parallel with Kerrera Sound on one of the island's main tracks and soon reached Horseshoe Bay, where Alexander

---

TERRAIN: Easy tracks; free-range walk on grassy raised beaches with some boggy areas; beach crossings

STARTING POINT: Kerrera ferry jetty. Lat/Long 56.4002, -5.5179; NM 830 2868

DISTANCE: 21.6km (ascent 456m)

TIME: 7 hours

OS MAP: OS Explorer 359

DIFFICULTY: 2

NAVIGATION: 3

ACCESS: 2

DON'T MISS:
- Atmospheric ruins of Gylen Castle
- Exploring raised beaches and caves of the north coast
- Fine views of Oban from lofty Hutcheson's Monument
- Watching otters on Slatrach Bay

SPECIAL NOTES: To avoid going through thick bracken on N section, from Oitir Mhor turn R on the main track to Ardentrive Farm.

GETTING THERE: CalMac ferry on Gallanach Road, just south of Oban; also ferry service to N of Kerrera from the North Pier in Oban.

FACILITIES: The Kerrera Tea Garden near Gylen Castle for snacks including delicious rhubarb cake, toilets, and bunkhouse accommodation.

II died. The king's fleet in Oban Bay was just about to set sail to take back control of the Hebrides from the Norwegians when he was taken ill and brought ashore. More recently, the bay was the site of packing sheds for the succulent lobsters from nearby Luing.

The track, lined with wild roses, meadowsweet and honeysuckle, continues along the east shores past the island's houses and a row of cottages. Until 2016, one of the cottages was a parrot sanctuary. Just beyond, a teapot-topped wooden post lures you on with a sign announcing that you're 'Halfway there'. This is the first call to the Kerrera Tea Garden, followed by 'Nearly there, next stop cake', and then – just over the brow of the hill – 'It's all downhill from here'. Serving the only refreshments on the island, it is a destination in itself. On a warm day you can sit outside in the vibrant cottage garden, pour tea from an eccentric pot, and choose from a range of delicious home-made cakes.

After the obligatory cake stop, the imposing ruins of Gylen Castle provide a stark contrast to the joyful atmosphere of the tearoom. Commanding the once-busy shipping lane through the Sound of Kerrera, the castle perches on its own promontory with sheer cliffs on three sides. The last Royalist inhabitants of this stronghold who were besieged by Covenanters, surrendered when drinking water ran out and were promptly slain. As you scale the spiral staircase of the moss-tinted ruin up to the old kitchen and imagine what life must have been like here, the atmosphere draws you in.

Brought back to the here and now by the abrupt calls of ravens, make sure you stop on the way out of the castle to explore an interesting rock passageway and markings below. From the castle promontory there are also spectacular views to Seil, Colonsay, the high peak of Scarba, and beyond to Jura in the south.

After working your way west along the raised beach of Port a' Chaisteil on the south coast, you reach the house at Ardmore selling handmade scented candles and soap out of the back of an old Isuzu Trooper. Put your money in the honesty box if you can choose between the tens of different fragrances and designs on offer. From the house there is a short climb and the views from the west coast open out to the mountains of Mull. The route then drops down to Barr-nam-boc Bay, its small jetty once the main entry point for cattle shipped from Mull to mainland Scotland.

From Barr-nam-boc Bay to Slatrach Bay, the free-range route follows animal tracks along the base of the cliffs on the grass plateau. Of the three cliff caves, the most impressive is at Uamh Rubha na Lice in a setting that feels like Hobbit country. At Slatrach Bay and towards the salmon farm it is possible to see otters and the many seals that enjoy pilfering the fish.

The north tip of the island is wild and rugged. Ploughing through bracken, the views to Lismore and the sight of the CalMac ferries gliding to Mull and the Outer Hebrides are rewarding. A short deviation uphill takes you to Hutcheson's Monument, named after the founder of a steamship fleet that later became Caledonian MacBrayne ferry services. From here there are fabulous views of Oban. The route then skirts the busy marina and farmyard of Ardentrive where pigs, cattle, guinea fowl, ducks, chickens, and peacocks roam.

The unmarked route back alongside Kerrera Sound to the jetty crosses marsh, shrub and pastureland, then climbs over Ellery Hill before passing through the old chapel back to the ferry.

Kerrera is only a short hop from Oban, the gateway to the islands of the Hebrides, yet visitor numbers remain surprisingly low and most keep to the shorter routes. This is good news for islandeers venturing off the beaten track.

DIRECTIONS

» From the jetty (1), keep to the track along the shoreline, passing Horseshoe Bay, and follow signs to the Castle and Tea Gardens. After 4km and a short descent arrive at the tearooms and bunkhouse (2).

» Retrace your steps for 100m to follow signs, past the toilet (3), and ascend to Gylen Castle (4) via clear paths. Leaving the castle, look to L across the bay and head for the gap in the dyke, by crossing the pebble beach at Port a' Chaisteil. Continue on the animal track at the base of the short cliff towards the telegraph poles ahead. After 600m, pass through an old fence to reach the main track just beyond.

» Turn L, cross a small ford and head uphill. Pass to the L of the house and follow the 'Ferry' sign, crossing over the stream and continuing uphill. After 1.5km, just before the stone cottage at Barnabuck, take the track to L towards the beach (or continue on the track through the cottage buildings for the quick route back to the ferry).

» After 200m or so, follow the animal track to the R towards the yellow cable marker and the head of the beach, then continue along the foreshore of Barr-nam-boc Bay. After 1.2km pass Uamh Fhliuch, the first cave, and after 150m or so reach the second, Uamh nan Calman. Reach Uamh Rubha na Lice (5) on the headland then find the animal tracks through the rock gardens.

» Cross a fence line and after a further 400m pass the corner of the ruined sheepfolds followed by building remains 600m beyond. Walk across the head of the pebbly bay towards the cable markers. Pass through gate and fence and after 200m cross a small stream and reach the ruined fisherman's cottage on Slatrach Bay (6). At the end of the beach walk on the grass to L side of the fence line, crossing it on the wall close to the coast.

» At Rubha Redegich, follow the sheep tracks to climb onto the plateau and then drop down to the foreshore of Oitir Mhor. Continue around the bay then turn L on the main track. After 600m, pass the house and just beyond the telephone wires turn L along the stone wall towards the beach. Cross the stream after 200m and find one of the many animal trails round Rubh' Ard an Duine.

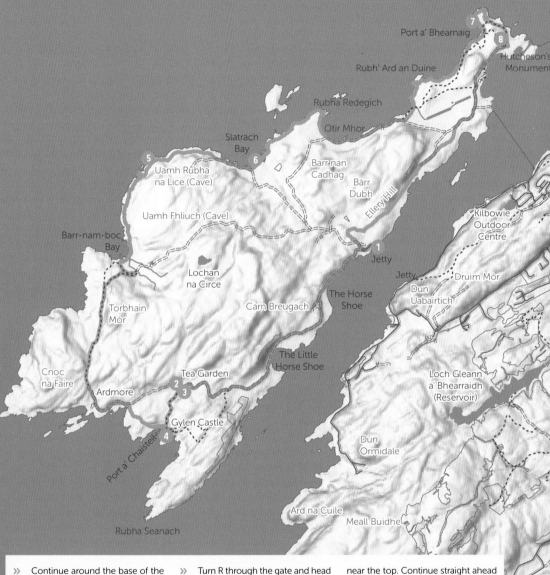

Port a' Bhearnaig

7

8

Hutcheson's
Monument

Rubh' Ard an Duine

Rubha Redegich

Otir Mhor

Slatrach
Bay

5

6

Uamh Rùbha
na Lice (Cave)

Barr nan
Cadhag

Bàrr
Dubh

Ellery Hill

Kilbowie
Outdoor
Centre

Uamh Fhliuch (Cave)

Barr-nam-boc
Bay

1

Jetty

Lochan
na Circe

Jetty

Druim Mòr

Dun
Uabairtich

Carn Breugach

The Horse
Shoe

Torbhain
Mòr

The Little
Horse Shoe

Loch Gleann
a' Bhearraidh
(Reservoir)

Cnoc
na Faire

Tea Garden

3

Ardmore

2

Gylen Castle

4

Port a' Chaistell

Dùn
Ormidale

Rubha Seanach

Ard na Cuile

Meall Buidhe

Carn
Breagach

» Continue around the base of the cliffs, via animal tracks, and across the beach of Port a Bhearnaig to go round the NW tip at Rubh' a' Bhearnaig and through the rock gardens (7). Continue around the N coast on clear grass paths through the bracken. After the metal gate take the small track uphill to reach Hutcheson's Monument (8) and return by the same route. Continue on the easy track around the marina.

» Turn R through the gate and head uphill through Ardentrive Farm, exiting the farm complex through the gate. Leave the path and walk 200m diagonally L across the open land towards the gate in the fence line underneath the telephone wires. Follow the telephone lines uphill, crossing various gates and fence lines and keeping Ellery Hill to your R. Follow the R-hand line of poles to a grass track uphill through bracken and through a gate

near the top. Continue straight ahead on the grass track until it curves to R and crosses a small brook. Go through the gate, keep straight ahead and after 100m or so take the grass track to L that rises slightly then descends down towards the old chapel and house. Turn L on the island's main track back to the jetty.

CHAPTER
37

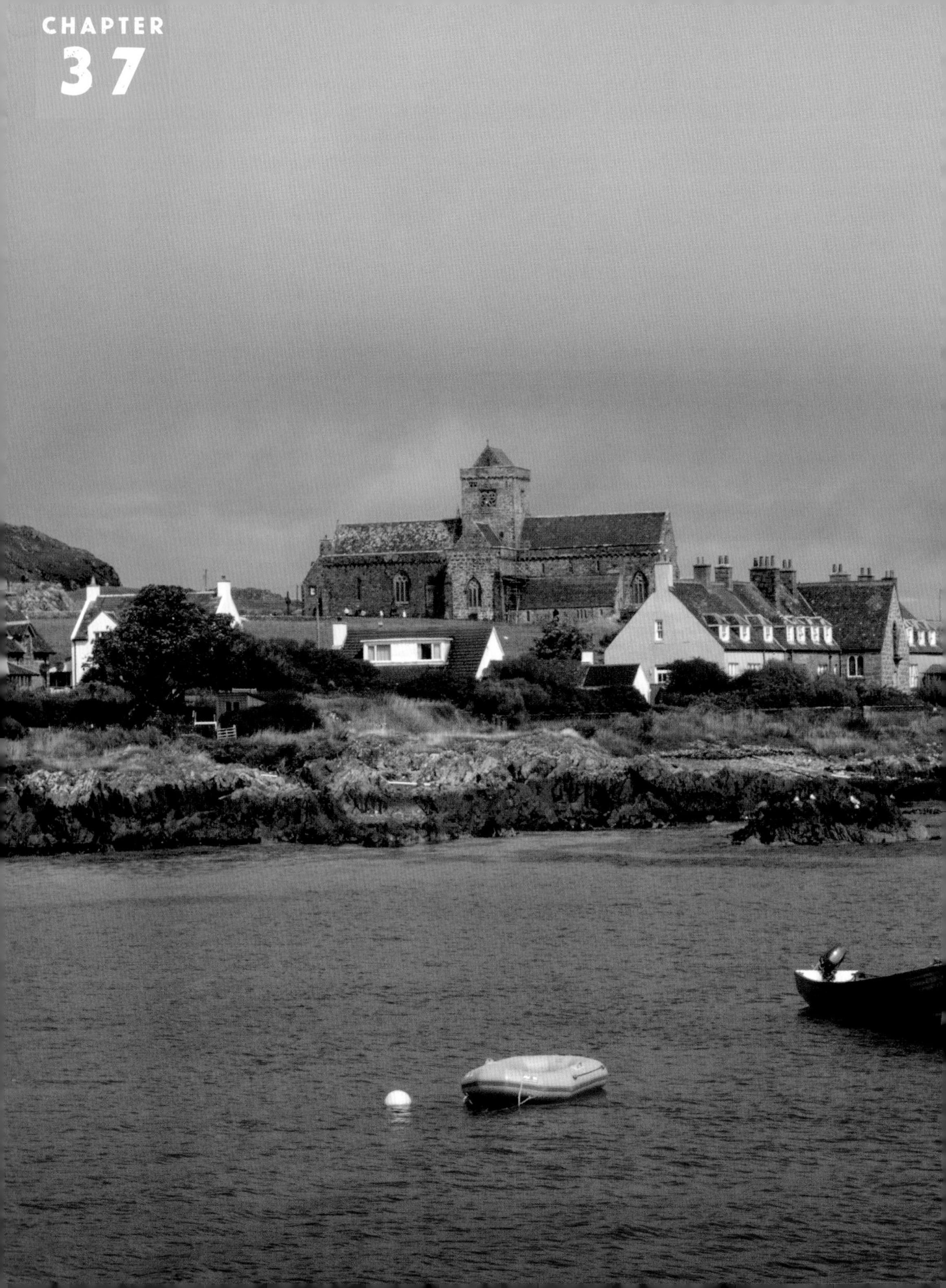

IONA

AN INSPIRING DESTINATION ADORNED WITH BEAUTIFUL CELTIC CROSSES, ROCK POOLS, DEEP GULLIES, AND WHITE-SAND BEACHES

On this sacred island, the great abbey, ancient chapel, and beautiful crosses aren't the only treasures. Iona has several secluded white-sand beaches, secret coves, a beautifully sculpted serpentine cave, and wild, remote headlands to explore. A celebration of all the island's riches, this walk is a rugged, mostly unmarked coastal circuit that ranges from the wild moors of the north to the heather-clad cliffs of the south via the glorious 'Bay at the back of the Ocean'. And there is plenty of time to make a pilgrimage to the famous abbey.

Iona is a tiny, low-lying island off the south-western tip of Mull, just a ten-minute ferry ride across the turbulent waters of the Sound. Although crowds of tourists and pilgrims visit during summer, most don't stray beyond the abbey and the village so you are likely to encounter few others.

The anti-clockwise walk starts from the jetty, heading north along a charming village street to the grand, restored abbey. Little remains of the small timber church and monastic settlement St Columba and his followers founded in 563, yet his small shrine became a major pilgrimage centre and Iona a resting place for Scottish kings including Macbeth. In more recent times, the Labour leader John Smith was buried here. The exquisitely carved high Celtic crosses that stand guard in front of the abbey are amongst the earliest examples of the pagan circle and Christian cross entwined in a single design and are themselves worth the entrance fee.

Given its isolated position and works of art, the abbey was vulnerable to repeated Viking attacks. In the most brutal, the abbey monks were murdered on the shores of Tràigh Bhàn, the 'White Strand of the Monks'. The pretty, round pebbles on this

---

TERRAIN: Easy coastal path; steep, very uneven route down the cliffs; scrambling on the island

STARTING POINT: Iona's jetty Lat/Long 56.3304, -6.39140; GR NM 286 240

DISTANCE: 16km (ascent 445m)

TIME: 6 hours

OS MAP: OS Explorer 373

DIFFICULTY: 4

NAVIGATION: 4 (5 to find St Martin's Cave)

ACCESS: 2

DON'T MISS:
- Discovering superlative rock pools at the northern tip
- Remote and beautiful St Martin's Cave
- Exquisite Celtic high crosses at the abbey
- Searching for Iona marble pebbles at St Columba's Bay
- Serpentine pools for secret swims on the west coast

FACILITIES: None on the route. Cafés, inns, restaurants, general stores, and toilets in Baile Mòr village.

SPECIAL NOTES: Path from village to W of abbey closed during bird-breeding season (April–mid-August). From the jetty take the 2nd road on R to head N up the island.

GETTING THERE: Ferry from mainland to the Isle of Mull then drive to Fionnphort. Bus from Craignure ferry terminal (www.westcoastmotors.co.uk). Once in Fionnphort take the regular 10-minute ferry ride across the Sound of Iona.

CHAPTER 37

IONA

tranquil beach are a mix of pink granite, quartz, green serpentine, and banded gneiss.

Just beyond the strand around the northern tip of the island, the barnacle- and limpet-edged rock pools forming mini-oases of life between the rock strands are a naturalist's dream. There are seaweeds of every shape and colour from huge, frilled ribbons of sugar kelp and long tresses of yellow thongweed, to green bladderwrack and vibrant red hornweed.

Continuing around the north shore, there are views of the sandbar on charming Eilean Annraidh and of Calf Island, with the vertical cliffs of Staffa and Ben Mor visible in the distance. The next beach, Tràigh an t-Suidhe, is dotted with smooth bathing pools carved by wave action on the relatively soft serpentine rocks. From here, the route leaves the well-trodden grass path to explore the wilder northwest of the island. This area, although boggy in places and somewhat inland, has a beauty of its own. The wildlife is undisturbed here and there is a sense of tranquility.

Almost halfway down the west coast, the well-tended greens of the golf course come into view. Just beyond, the idyllic sheltered sands of Port Ban sit at the northern end of the Bay at the Back of the Ocean which then sweeps towards the rugged hills at the southern end of the island. From the end of the beach a short climb leads to the blowhole of Spouting Cave which works best on a low tide and reasonable swell.

The free-range route then continues south to the lovely but hidden St Martin's Cave. The deep gully access is more reminiscent of a tunnel than an open-roofed channel and locating it requires good navigational skills. The cave is stunning, its wave-sculpted walls almost glowing with the vibrant greens and reds of the serpentine rock.

Slightly to the south of the cave, the raised pebble beach at Port Beul-mhòir is perfect for a secret dip: very few visitors venture to this part of the island. The route back to the main path leading to St Columba's Bay is rough and boggy in places but the excursion to the cave and cove makes it well worth the effort.

St Columba's Bay on the southern tip, said to be the landing site of the saint and his fellow monks, is a popular destination. Nevertheless, there is a great sense of peace here, although mine was interrupted when a neighbouring pilgrim asked if he could sit next to me to play his guitar. Visitors here are fascinated by the pebbles on the beach, either adding them to the numerous Celtic patterns on the grass banks or searching among them for the pure translucent greens, known as Mermaid's Tears, or the white-and-green rare Iona marble.

Slightly east of the island's southern tip, the source of the marble is revealed as a small outcrop of rock in the now-derelict quarry. The remote and steep location explains why large-scale extraction was never possible and now all that remains is rusting wheels and pulleys.

The route around the boggy southern tip ends in the 'corncrake habitat' just south of the village. Having spent many hours looking for these rare birds in the wild, it wasn't until I was sitting in the unlikely environment of the Argyll Hotel that I heard one on the lawn. So much for the corncrake's famous reticence. Before leaving the island, a visit to Sandeel Bay just south of the village is a must, if time permits. It is a truly idyllic spot.

There is a Gaelic prediction that those who go to Iona go not once, but three times. On my fourth visit I still found much to explore and concluded that there would always be something new to discover on this island.

DIRECTIONS

» From the jetty (1) take the first R past the post office and houses to Bishop's House. Pass through two wooden gates in the meadows below the abbey (2), cross a small stream and head diagonally L across the field to the island lane. Turn R along the lane past the path up to the island's high point, Dun I (3).

» When the lane sweeps L to the Iona Hostel continue through the gates onto Ardionra Croft and walk across the grassland to Tràigh Bhàn (4) on R. Walk N up the beach.

» Go round the N tip of the island to find rock pools (5) and continue along the base of the dunes to find a faint sand path that crosses a few fence lines to reach Tràigh an t-Suidhe and the serpentine bathing pools (6). At the W end of the beach walk up the rocks and through the dunes to cross a further fence, small beaches, and past a derelict caravan at the base of the rock buttress.

» After 300m take the R fork to continue along the coast. Head towards the low saddle between two buttresses (7), then across marshy land and a small stream to R of the fence. After 700m cross the fence, turn L then after a few metres turn R and walk uphill on the steep, natural path in the rocks.

» At the top continue along the clear sheep track that runs through boggy ground on the plateau. Head SW and walk parallel but not next to the coast. After 1km cross a fence line. The path is less distinct here but generally follows the animal trails between two parallel rock bands.

» After 1km drop down onto an open grazed area and reach small, sandy beach of Port Ban (unmarked on OS map), past the 11th hole of the golf course. Continue S along Camas Cùil an t-Saimh (Bay at the Back of the Ocean) (8).

» Towards the S end of the beach the easy footpath to Port na Curaich (St Columba's Bay) heads uphill to R of the grey bungalow. For St Martin's Cave continue on the coast and across a small stream to the R of the main path. Head uphill in the rougher terrain and find a free-range route, slightly inland from the coast, to Port Beul-mhòir (9). From the grass banks at the top of the beach walk 250m N to reach the steep, narrow gully through the rocks. Follow this to the coast to find St Martin's Cave (10). Alternatively, follow the distinct path from the S end of

Eilean Chalba

Tràigh an t-Suidhe

5

6

Tràigh Bhàn

4

Iona
Hostel

Eilean
nam Ban

3 Dun I

7

Cnoc Urrais

Abbey 2

1 Jetty

Camas Cùil an t-Saimh 8

Iona Campsite

Fionnphort

13

Sound of Iona

Tràigh
Mhòr

St Martin's Cave

Port Beul-mhoir 10
9

Loch
Staoineig

Druim an
Aoineidh

Druim
Dhughaill

11 12

Marble
Quarry
(Dis.)

Port na Curaich

the Camas Cùil an t-Saimh (Bay at the Back of the Ocean) towards Port na Curaich. Just S of the W tip of Loch Staoineig, take a W bearing between two rock buttresses to find the cave.

» Make your way back to link up with the path to Port na Curaich by heading straight out of the gully, passing a small cairn after 100m, and then walking initially uphill across the rough terrain in a SE direction to hit the path after 1.3km.

» At the main path turn R to Port na Curaich (11). After visiting the beach retrace your steps for 200m to find a faint path on R towards the base of the rocks. Follow the rocky path uphill until it widens at the top. Then continue E and downhill across a small stream to the marble quarry (12).

» Leaving the quarry by the same route, take the R fork N through the cleft in the rocks ahead past the only post marker on the route. Continue

on a clear, undulating path bearing NE through boggy terrain.

» Several hundred metres after the village comes into view, drop down on the stone path then go through the gate towards the houses and the corncrake fields (13). Turn R onto the main island road towards the jetty.

CHAPTER 38

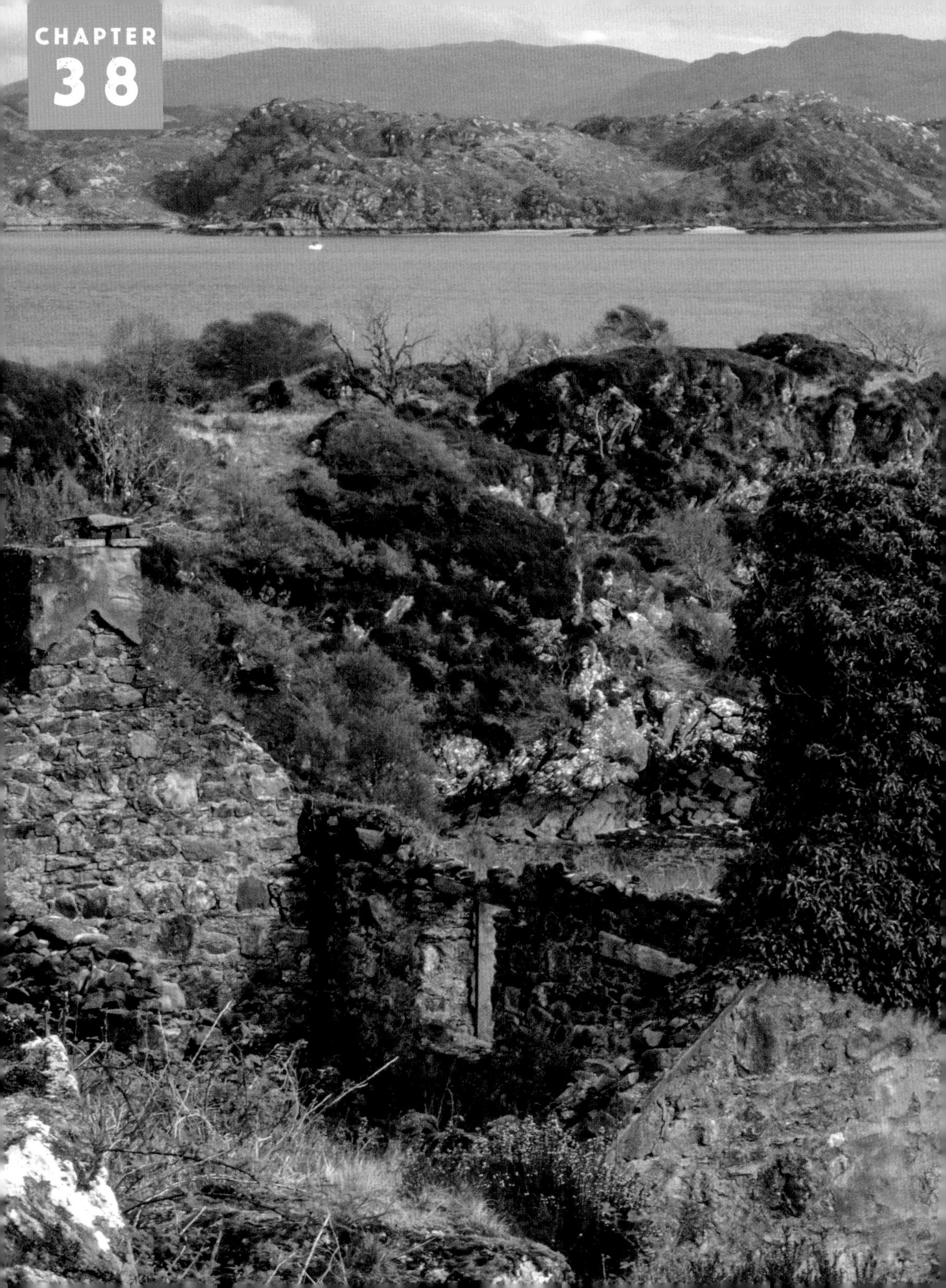

EILEAN SHONA

FAIRYTALE FORESTS, AN ENCHANTING VALLEY, AND SECRET COVES AWAIT ON DISCOVERING THE HIDDEN PATH TO THIS MAGICAL ISLAND

Owned and lovingly restored by Vanessa Branson, Eilean Shona is an island where the bar is set high for adventure. The family keeps a 'Book of Feats' in which alleged achievements include eating a raw jellyfish, swimming ten hours across open water to the Isle of Eigg, and climbing the mountain at midnight.

This walk is not without its challenges. To get to Eilean Shona, you must first negotiate a short tidal crossing to neighbouring Shona Beag – a wild and remote peninsula to the east of the island. The route across Shona Beag is mostly along animal tracks, but from the isthmus connecting it to Eilean Shona, there is a reasonably clear coastal path. Passing through the sublime scenery of the North Channel, the route heads inland, climbing alongside magical Baramore Burn to reach a scenic viewpoint on the flanks of Beinn a' Bhàillidh, before continuing downhill to the south coast.

There are longer and more challenging alternatives to this circular walk including an ascent of Beinn a' Bhaillidh – a 'Marilyn' for those interested in bagging a summit. An extension to Aonach (Shoe Bay), one of the island's two idyllic sandy beaches, is also recommended. For the seasoned islandeer it is also possible – with the right tide and conditions – to rock-hop around the Atlantic shore of the west coast from Baramore Bay to Shoe Bay instead of taking the inland route described.

Eilean Shona is strikingly located at the narrow entrance of Loch Moidart, just south of the rugged Moidart Peninsula. To the west are the isles of Muck, Eigg, and Rum, with Skye to the north. Private and secluded, the island has several restored holiday cottages along with the exclusive main house and gardens, and a permanent population of two. Large

---

TERRAIN: Shona Beag: steep, rough, through bracken. Eilean Shona: tracks, well-marked paths, some boggy

STARTING POINT: Lay-by S of Glenuig. Lat/Long 56.8029, -5.81245; GR NM 673 744

DISTANCE: 22km (ascent 890m)

TIME: 6 hours

OS MAP: OS Explorer 390

DIFFICULTY: 2

NAVIGATION: 3

ACCESS: 3 (5 if going direct to Eilean Shona)

DON'T MISS:
- Swimming and foraging for clams at Shoe Bay
- Picnics, swimming, and dreaming at Baramore
- Ancient and magical woods around the main house

SPECIAL NOTES: Despite the right to roam please respect the privacy of island guests. Call ahead (01967 431249) or knock on the back door of Eilean Shona House or the woodman's bungalow on arrival. To maximise time on the

island depart just before the causeway floods to give yourself 6–12 hours to explore. Crossing on the ebb allows less than 6 hours on the island before the next high tide.

GETTING THERE: On the A861, pass the turn-off on R to the Glenuig Inn. After 3km find a gated entrance to a stone track on the R and space for one vehicle parked considerably (PH38 4NG).

FACILITIES: No facilities; shop and inn at Glenuig.

areas of woodland in the east and around the house feature a collection of ancient and rare pines. From the hills of the interior the views are truly spectacular.

The route itself is very varied. Starting from the main road, just south of Glenuig, a short walk down through the woods leads to the tidal causeway. Hidden from the road, the character and views of Loch Moidart are slowly revealed and foragers will be delighted to find clusters of giant mussels clinging to the causeway rocks.

Once on Shona Beag you'll need good navigation skills and a keen eye for the right animal tracks to take through the wilderness. The route follows an ancient path and you can see the remains of its old walls in the undergrowth. The western descent to the isthmus is steep and there are only a couple of places where this can be achieved safely.

Once over the isthmus to Eilean Shona, you immediately sense that the landscape is cared for. With a full-time woodsman to plant new trees and clear paths, the beauty of the island is sustained. The anti-clockwise route follows the shore of the North Channel, passing the rock buttresses, small caves, and waterfalls at the base of rugged Beinn a' Bhàillidh. Soon the Old Schoolhouse, a remote and romantic gas-lit bolt-hole, comes into view along with off-grid Shepherd's Cottage, its water supplied by its own spring.

The whole of this island is special but tiny Baramore beach on the north coast is truly breathtaking. The grassy banks with views across the water to remote Eilean na h-Oitire on the Moidart Peninsula make the perfect picnic spot. From Baramore follow the glorious inland route to the south shore, or take up the challenge of rock-hopping around the west coast and complete the full coastal route.

Climbing up through the verdant Baramore Burn valley is about as good as it gets. Clear water rushes down past silver birches within a shallow amphitheatre created by the rock walls of the island's mountain. Pockets of wildflowers nestle between the luxuriant moss-covered rocks. Once on the saddle, the views south across the water to the mountains of the Ardnamurchan Peninsula and beyond are magnificent.

Nearing the south coast, the charming path to Shoe Bay on the southwest point weaves its way to secluded white sands sheltered by rocky reefs. At high tide, this spot is known as the blue lagoon, while at low tide the deep white sands are reminiscent of the Caribbean. You might spot otters and if the numbers of succulent clams on the beach are anything to go by, they must be very well fed.

Returning to the main path the descent towards Eilean Shona House passes through a fantasy forest of dense pines, their roots cloaked in luxuriantly thick moss. The feel of the woods is familiar, like the forests in many a childhood fairy tale. A creaking ornamental gate then opens to the private gardens of Eilean Shona House, which the route bypasses but allows tantalising glimpses through the trees of the well-tended gardens.

Down at the pier, there are two wooden boat-houses and stores for kayaks, yachts, and other craft. Every guest's dreams are catered for, from a day's kayaking adventure or one spent simply messing about on the water. Across the South Channel you catch sight of the evocative, turreted ruins of Castle Tioram, once a stronghold of the MacDonald clan. You can explore Eilean Tioram from Dorlin, back on the mainland.

After a day on this island, you can appreciate why the author of Peter Pan, J.M. Barrie, chose it as his summer retreat. Although encounters with Captain Hook are unlikely, it is perfectly possible to spot pine martens, white-tailed sea eagles, otters, red squirrels, and even golden eagles here and simply enjoy the magic.

DIRECTIONS

» From the pull-in, go through the gate and walk downhill through the woods for 1km to reach the causeway (1). Cross up to 3hrs before high tide and 2.5 hours before low tide. Once on Shona Beag, continue uphill along the island's stone track. After 300m, just before the house and almost at the top of the hill, take the diagonal route to R. Walk uphill along the faint grass track through the trees while keeping a lookout for the free-range but distinct uphill route on grass through the bracken. At the high point look ahead to locate the telegraph poles on the skyline and walk towards them, dropping down slightly into some boggier land before ascending again.

» After 600m or so, pass under the telegraph wires when you can clearly see one post to the R and two to the L. Head towards the crags and pass through the saddle (2). Catch sight of a white house on Eilean Shona, which is almost opposite the descent route and find the deer path that zig-zags down through the rocks and silver birch, past the remnants of the old stone wall.

» Towards the bottom of the hill there is a wider grassy stretch and then multiple routes from here to the isthmus. Try the deer path that leads across the boggier ground and initially runs parallel to the N shore of the isthmus. Walk slightly uphill through the small forest and rocks to the S side of the isthmus (3) and Port Thairbeirt Dheas. Cross to Eilean Shona.

» Once across the isthmus, turn R on the stone track and walk uphill, passing white-painted Sawmill Cottage to R. After 200m turn R onto the main island stone track that initially hugs the woody shoreline of the North Channel then passes the foot of steep rock faces with multiple waterfalls.

» Pass the Old Schoolhouse and then Shepherd's Cottage. Just beyond it the track turns into a narrower path that can be boggy before reaching the bay at Baramore (4). Turn uphill to follow the sign for South Shore. For the full circumnavigation (weather- and tide-dependent), continue to Baramore and then around the rocks of the foreshore along the Atlantic Coast to Aonach (Shoe Bay).

» Follow the route beside the waterfall to the col (lowest point between two hills) and then descend

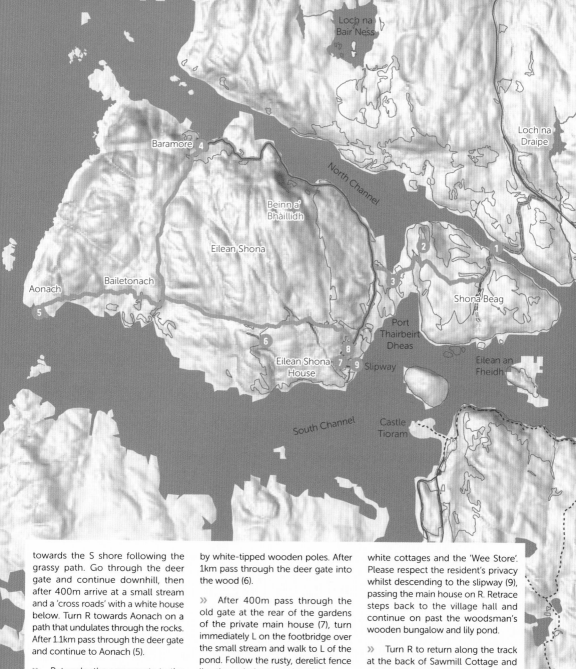

Loch na
Bair Ness

Loch na
Draipe

Baramore **4**

North Channel

Beinn a'
Bhàilidh

Eilean Shona

2   **1**

3

Aonach

Baileatonach

Shona Beag

5

6

Port
Thairbeirt
Dheas

Eilean Shona
House   **8**

7   **9**   Slipway

Eilean an
Fheidh

South Channel

Castle
Tioram

towards the S shore following the grassy path. Go through the deer gate and continue downhill, then after 400m arrive at a small stream and a 'cross roads' with a white house below. Turn R towards Aonach on a path that undulates through the rocks. After 1.1km pass through the deer gate and continue to Aonach (5).

» Return by the same route to the stream crossroads, then turn R along the small path that heads uphill. Climb up to the saddle and then descend through the rocks on the path marked

by white-tipped wooden poles. After 1km pass through the deer gate into the wood (6).

» After 400m pass through the old gate at the rear of the gardens of the private main house (7), turn immediately L on the footbridge over the small stream and walk to L of the pond. Follow the rusty, derelict fence line through the trees downhill.

» Arrive at the rear of the village hall (8) and for an optional detour, turn R onto the main island path past the

white cottages and the 'Wee Store'. Please respect the resident's privacy whilst descending to the slipway (9), passing the main house on R. Retrace steps back to the village hall and continue on past the woodsman's wooden bungalow and lily pond.

» Turn R to return along the track at the back of Sawmill Cottage and retrace the route back across the isthmus to Shona Beag and then return to the causeway.

CHAPTER

39

MUCK

REMOTE ROUTE WITH SPECTACULAR VIEWS ROUND THE BAYS AND ROCKY HEADLANDS OF THE SMALLEST OF THE SMALL ISLES

It's two hours on the ferry but the scones are worth it', according to Lawrence MacEwen, the Laird of Muck, in the foreword to *A Drop in the Ocean*. After spending three days on the island I can not only verify the scone quality but also pronounce the boat trip a true delight. During the two-hour crossing, the skipper of the *MV Sheerwater* pointed out whales, dolphins, basking sharks, and sea eagles.

There is even more natural beauty to see on the free-range coastal circuit, mostly walking along cliff tops with magnificent views to the other Small Isles, the Outer Hebrides, and the mountains of the mainland. The route follows sheep tracks through farm and moorland, with some rough and boggy areas as well as easy scrambling on the foreshore. The ascent of Beinn Airein, the island's high point, is straightforward although the dramatic descent on the western cliff edge is steep. The walk can be completed in a day but given current ferry times, that means an overnight stay. It is the perfect excuse for more exploration as well as absorbing the tranquil vibe of the island.

The smallest in the archipelago known as the Small Islands, Muck is low-lying and cattle and sheep graze the fertile interior. The dramatic coastline features basalt ledges, dolerite dykes, terraced cliffs, and flat grassy cliff tops. The bays are generally rocky, dotted with huge pools and the occasional gem of a white shell beach. The views to the Inner and Outer Hebrides and the mountains of the mainland are stunning from every perspective. The main settlement of Port Mòr in the east is linked to the island's other centre of habitation, the large farm at Gallanach in the west, by the island's short road.

TERRAIN: Grassy cliff tops; marshy ground and rocky foreshore; steep, rocky descent from Beinn Airein

STARTING POINT: MV Sheerwater Jetty on Muck. Lat/Long 56.8336, -6.2273; GR NM 422 793

DISTANCE: 15.7km (ascent 627m)

TIME: 4 hours 30 mins

OS MAP: OS Explorer 397 (or 390)

DIFFICULTY: 3

NAVIGATION: 4

ACCESS: 2

DON'T MISS:
- Chatting to islanders over tea and scones at the café
- Swimming in Mermaid's Pool
- Spectacular Hebridean views from the top of Beinn Airein
- Searching for tiny cowrie shells at Shell Bay

FACILITIES: Café in Port Mòr; toilets and showers at the Community Hall. Some accommodation on the island www.isleofmuck.com.

GETTING THERE: By boat, the MV Sheerwater, from Arisaig (summer months only) on Mondays, Wednesdays, Fridays, and Sundays. www.arisaig.co.uk or 01687 450224. From Mallaig, the CalMac ferry calls on Tuesdays, Thursdays, Fridays, and Saturdays in summer, and Mondays, Wednesdays, Fridays, and Saturdays in winter www.calmac.co.uk or 01687 462403. Note: both routes are for passengers only and cars are not carried.

One of the most striking aspects of a visit here is the warm welcome from the islanders. Immediately on arrival at Port Mòr, greetings and familiar banter are exchanged between the crew and islanders. Everyone pitches in to help with the unloading and loading of baggage as incoming and outgoing visitors change places.

The starting point of the clockwise walk is Port Mòr, the main hamlet on the island built after the original settlement above the inlet at Kiel was cleared. The settlement ruins are a ghostly reminder of the brutal, forced evictions of the Highland Clearances. Most of the island's facilities are found at Port Mòr, including a community centre that is particularly welcoming on a rainy day, and the Green Shed, an arts and crafts outlet, with group accommodation in the bunkhouse. The cheerful café in a romantic old stone croft is a great place to sit with a plate of crab sandwiches, one of the celebrated scones, or a slice of fantastically moist chocolate cake. You can meet the friendly islanders and soak up the unhurried atmosphere of this entrancing island. In season, you might hear the distinctive rasping call of a corncrake behind the café – a call that can make the novelty of spotting this secretive bird wear thin rather quickly.

The free-range route then heads south down the west side of Port Mòr to Caisteal nan Duin Bhàin, a natural rock stack fortified in the Iron Age by the construction of a thick wall around the summit. Along this stretch of coast the seals appear to check on your progress. Surfacing between dives to catch fish, they seem to fix you with their doleful gaze.

Heading west on the south coast, just past the characterful bothy and towards the most southerly point, the deep swimming hole of Mermaid's Pool is a firm favourite with islanders. The limestone-lined rock pools here are full of life and if you delve deeper you may spot one of Britain's corals, the cup coral. A little further west along the foreshore, the sound of dripping water reveals the location of Pigeon's Cave well before you see its entrance, set deep in the cliffs.

After rounding the southerly tip of the island you reach Sloch na Dubhaich (Devil's Cauldron), a vast amphitheatre where the piercing cries of seabirds bounce off its sheer rock walls. Rock climbers make for the high cliffs of An Leachdach that continue northwest: you can spot the metal belay pegs near the edge. In season, fairy rings of mushrooms and toadstools appear in the short grass on top of the cliffs, adding a touch of magic. Ahead, the peak of Beinn Airein looms with the beautiful Jurassic limestone pavement of Camas Mòr at its base.

On a clear day, there are panoramic views from the top of Beinn Airein to Barra and North Uist, Mull and Coll, the An Sgùrr of Eigg, the mountains of Rum, Skye, and the mainland. Visiting golden eagles may be seen prospecting along the cliffs but they don't stay on the island for too long because there are no rabbits to hunt.

The route down from Beinn Airein feels quite exposed with near-vertical drops on the west side, but there is space to descend safely away from the cliff edge. At the base the stunning, seabird-speckled sea stack of Sgorr nan Laogh is worth a stop. The route then continues north up the west coast to reach the turf-roofed Gallanach Bothy, located in splendid isolation overlooking Shell Bay where tiny cowrie shells can be found.

Heading along the north coast, you'll see a Bronze Age stone circle on the peninsula of Àird àn Uan, which leads to Eilean nan Each (Horse Island) – an important site for over 80 species of breeding birds including the island's only puffins. It is accessible on very low tides that occur only a few times a year. After walking around the peninsula, the route continues across the island's largest sandy beach, Gallanach Bay, a popular destination and a favourite anchorage for visiting yachts. The lucky few may spot otters and porpoises in the protected waters of the bay, with fine views of Rum beyond. Gallanach itself has a large farm complex and Gallanach Lodge offers excellent accommodation and food. It is open to non-residents for evening meals and

drinks as long as enough notice is given. For a very different overnight experience, continue a little further east where you'll find a single yurt, part of the welcoming Godag B&B and stunningly located on the northeast shore. From here you can enjoy incredible views of Canna without even getting out of bed, and the energetic Kelly will even cook you breakfast in the morning.

After walking along the east coast, celebrate the end of the route with a refreshing beer or tea and cake at the Port Mòr café; it generally remains open until the boat leaves. The husband-and-wife team, jointly known as Sheddie, are a hoot and I have fond memories of them racing back up the hill on the tricycle to retrieve something for me from their craft store. Small is beautiful couldn't sum up Muck more perfectly.

DIRECTIONS

» From the jetty (1), walk along Port Mòr's road as far as the 'S' bend at the top of the inlet, then take the road to L to pass underneath the old cemetery ruins (2). Take the R fork uphill and continue on the track past the stone cottage. After 0.6km take the sheep path to the L, initially uphill on the rough ground, then walk parallel to the inlet to reach the rocky outcrop at Caisteal nan Duin Bhàin (3).

» Continue parallel to the coastline, crossing a couple of streams. Just before reaching the bothy, take the steep path up to the plateau and continue along the clifftop. To visit Mermaid's Pool (4), after walking 100m or so on the cliff top, descend to the foreshore through a deep inlet.

» Ascend to the clifftops above Sloch na Dubhaich (5) then keep to the cliff edge of An Leachdach (6) to Fang Mor passing through a makeshift gate then descending, crossing a small stream to reach the small rock beach.

» Climb the grass bank to R of the cliff, turn L at the top, continue uphill, cross the stile, and walk parallel to the stone wall to reach the sheep pens. Go through the gate, up and over the bank and across the lazy beds to the fence. Follow it to reach the head of the beach at Camas Mòr (7).

» Go through the metal gate and turn L to ascend Beinn Airein (8). On the plateau walk parallel to the sea cliffs, heading SSE and keeping the trig point to the R. Just before you draw parallel to the trig point at a small marshy cleft, turn L to regain the fence line and descend sharply. At the base, pass the sea stack of Sgorr nan Laogh (9).

» Above the headland of Sròn na Teiste head NW by choosing a contour that will take you above the small cliffs to cross the head of two steep gullies. Continue N to pass the cliff of Rubh' Leam na Làraich (10) and walk up and over a rock outcrop onto the cliff tops above a rock ledge.

» Cross the Gleann Mhàirtein river and keep to the foreshore at the base of the cliffs. Just beyond a sea-filled tunnel (11) penetrates deeply into the rocks. Head up the grass valley for 50m or so to find the path on the right over the dyke. Continue on the cliffs and pass through the gap in the stone wall. Almost 2km from the river join a good track, walking to the R of a group of trees to pass Gallanach Bothy (12).

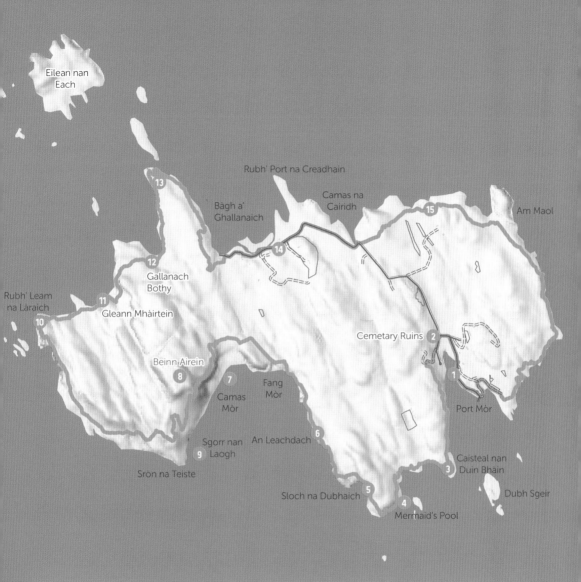

Eilean nan
Each

Rubh' Port na Creadhain

Camas na
Cairidh

Bàgh a'
Ghallanaich

13

Am Maol

15

14

12

Gallanach
Bothy

Rubh' Leam
na Làraich

11

10

Gleann Mhàirtein

Cemetary Ruins

2

1

Beinn Airein

8

7

Fang
Mòr

Camas
Mòr

Port Mòr

6

Sgorr nan
Laogh

An Leachdach

9

Caisteal nan
Duin Bhàin

3

Sròn na Teiste

Dubh Sgeir

Sloch na Dubhaich

5

Mermaid's Pool

4

» Continue along the foreshore towards Eilean nan Each (Horse Island) past the Bronze Age burial circle (13) near the tip of the peninsula. Drop down onto the beach and walk along the west shore of Gallanach Bay towards the Lodge (14) and farm buildings. Find the farm track and follow it to the farm, pass the beach, then continue along the island road.

» At an 'S' bend in the road, pass through the metal gate and cross the field to a further gate. Continue over the fields, stone wall, and stream to find the track around the inlet below Godag House. Pass the yurt (15), then head through the gate towards the salmon farm via sheep pens and a gully.

» Continue E along the N coast crossing a couple of fences before turning down the E coast. About two-thirds of the way down, cross the deep inlet and a small stile on the opposite bank before finding the grass track above Port Mòr. Continue L at the croft and descend to the main island road.

ORONSAY

A SHORT WALK WITH BIG VIEWS, SOARING CLIFFS, LARGE SEA CAVES AND DEEP GULLIES

Living on the Minginish Peninsula on Skye, just across from Oronsay, I had watched this island from afar and thought I knew it. Then I visited and explored its cliffs and rock pools. What I found there I'll never tire of.

The walk follows a clearly marked path to Ullinish Point and the pebbly causeway crossing. Once on the island, the easy free-range route along grassy cliff edges provides plenty of opportunities to explore the impressive sea caves and gullies, while on the shoreline section you'll discover several large rock pools. For the energetic, the short, sharp climb to the south-western tip is rewarded with a stunning panorama of the precipitous Talisker headland, the peaks of the Black Cuillin, and the Old Man of Storr towards the north end of Skye.

Oronsay is derived from the Gaelic word orasaigh, which means island of low tide. There

are several Oronsays in Scotland but this one is spectacularly located in Loch Bracadale on the west coast of the Isle of Skye. Although small in size, this uninhabited, wedge-shaped island offers an adventure-packed walk and a wealth of impressive wildlife. Otters and dolphins in search of a tasty morsel are drawn to the small salmon farm in the loch, and the golden eagles from Talisker Bay and Glen Brittle are often seen soaring overhead.

The route starts from the small settlement of Ullinish and heads across the moorland before reaching the causeway via a steep descent at Ullinish Point through a crack in the rocks. You can enjoy a peaceful swim here towards low tide when the two small sand beaches are revealed. At the southeast end of the causeway a line of stones marks the site of an ancient fish trap.

TERRAIN: Access to Ullinish Point can be boggy; most of the island route is on grassy cliffs

STARTING POINT: Car park, S from the Ullinish loop road. Lat/Long 57.3483, -6.4526; GR NG 322 374

DISTANCE: 6.9km (ascent 224m)

TIME: 2 hours 45 mins

OS MAP: OS Explorer 410

DIFFICULTY: 2

NAVIGATION: 3

ACCESS: 3

DON'T MISS:
- Sea cave and tunnel adventure on the south shore
- Wild camping on the flat grassy area on the north side
- Spectacular views of Outer Hebrides, Skye and Cuillins
- Golden eagles, otters and dolphins
- Sheltered white-sand beaches

SPECIAL NOTES: Walking across the causeway is possible 2 hours either side of high tide.

GETTING THERE: Off the A863 Sligachan to Dunvegan road, follow signs to Ullinish IV56 8FD. At the bottom of this loop road a lane marked 'Oronsay Path' leads towards the car park and island. Bus 6100 Portree to Dunvegan calls at Ullinish Country Lodge.

FACILITIES: No facilities on the island. Ullinish Lodge bar closed to non-residents. Closest shop and café is the Bog Myrtle at Struan, further facilities in Dunvegan.

Once on the island, the flatter land at the north end is dotted with the ruins of ancient sheilings and makes a perfect wild-camping pitch. Taking a clockwise route, you come across huge pools in the rocky 'finger' that points southeast towards the Minginish Peninsula. These are big enough to plunge in and explore with a mask and snorkel.

Walking along the east coast, the indentations in the low cliffs feature steep gullies filled with luxuriant greenery as well as caves. The most impressive is a large sea cave, accessible at low tide, with an amazing arch so tall it feels more like a tunnel. Reds, blues, and greens of mosses and seaweeds add colour and a briny scent while the acoustics amplify the sound of the waterfalls and the tide surging at the entrance. This is in every sense a world apart.

Towards the south-western tip of the island, the rock rises steeply to a 74-metre-high point from which the views are truly spectacular, particularly of the two sea-stacks below. Far to the west, the grey silhouettes of the Outer Hebridean chain of islands are visible on a clear day, and the flat tops of Macleod's Tables and the distinctive sea-stacks of Macleod's Maidens stand guard over the entrance of the loch in the foreground. The island of Wiay lies in-between. Looking east, the jagged peaks of the Cuillins form a dramatic backdrop to the Minginish Peninsula, while to the north, the distinctive shape of the Old Man of Storr stands sentry. Looking south, the steep buttress walls of Talisker rise vertically from the sea.

The return route is equally impressive and features another 70-metre crag perched above the colourful, vertical cliffs. This small island really packs a punch and is well worth adding to the itinerary if you are visiting the Isle of Skye.

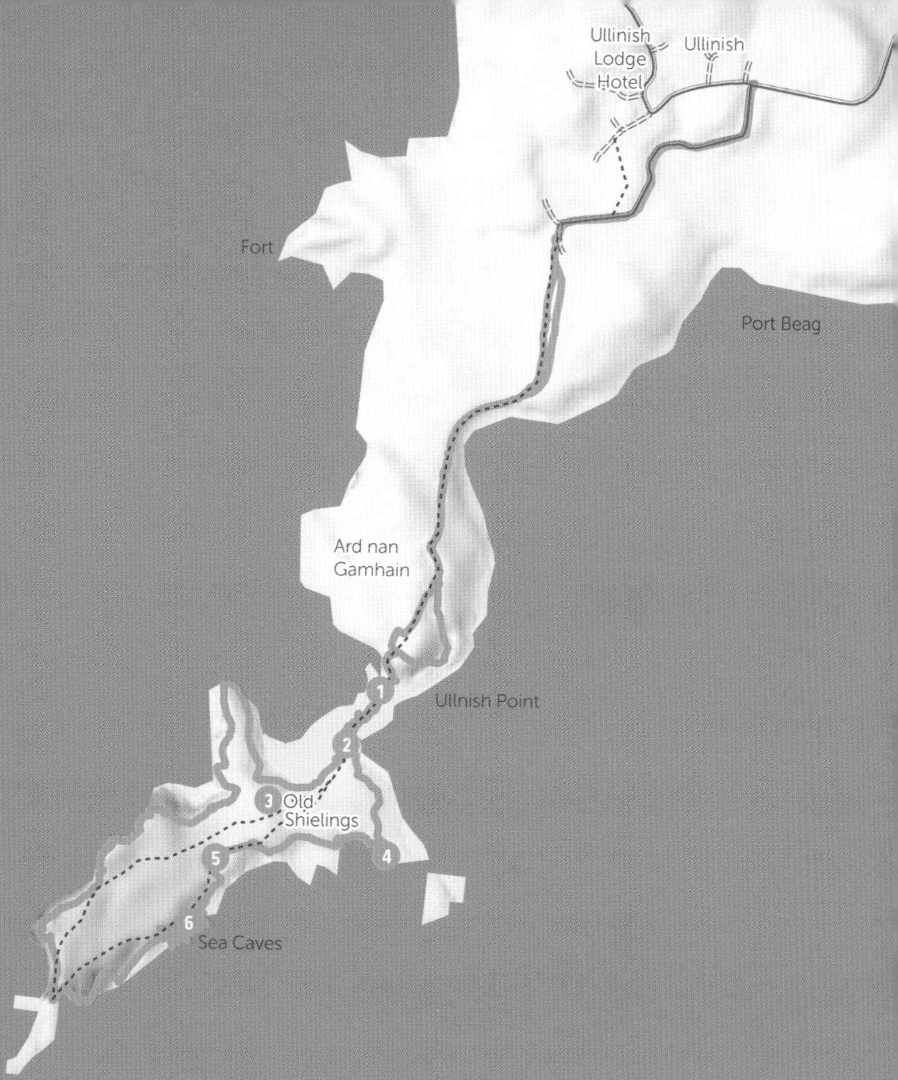

Ullinish
Lodge
Hotel

Ullinish

Port Beag

Fort

Ard nan
Gamhain

1

Ullnish Point

2

3 Old
Shielings

4

5

6

Sea Caves

DIRECTIONS

» Start at the end of the public road and continue through the kissing gate following the footpath signs to Oronsay across the boggy moorland. At the far end of the field, pass through another gate and skirt around the top of a storm beach. Ascend the small, rocky hill and then keep L to avoid boggy ground. Approximately 1.1km from the start, cross the stile and descend through the rock gully to reach the causeway (1).

» Walk 500m across the causeway, past the ancient tidal fish trap (2), onto the N end of the island to find the old shielings (3). Continue clockwise on the shoreline to reach the huge rock pools (4) at the E point, then the deep inlet just beyond (5).

» Continue along the coast and drop down the low cliff to explore the large sea cave below (6). Climb up to the high point on the SW tip, above the two sea stacks. Take the grassy cliff-edge path back to the causeway.

VATERSAY

BEAUTIFUL WILD ISLAND WITH WHITE-SAND BEACHES, TURQUOISE WATERS, AND DRAMATIC COASTAL INLETS TO NAVIGATE

'd almost stepped on an otter in the long grass of the shore. Holding my breath, I watched the beautiful, sleek animal use its paws to wash its face and whiskers. Next to it was the remains of a meal – a pile of empty shells, their soft contents quickly devoured. This special encounter was to be repeated before my time on the island was up.

This is a long walk, mostly along the faint animal paths that criss-cross the machair, turf, rocks, and rough grazing on the edge of Vatersay. There are easy scrambles on each of the headlands as well as beach crossings at three stunning bays – Tràigh Bhàrlais, Tràigh Siar, and Bàgh a' Deas. Along the deeply indented coastline there are deep shafts to explore as well as rock pools brimming with marine life. If the distance is too great, the walk can be split into two shorter sections and the starting point switched to the beach car park on the tombolo.

Lying to the south of Barra, Vatersay is the most southerly inhabited island of the Outer Hebrides and also the most westerly inhabited place in the UK. Between the hilly north and south sections of the island there is a low-level tombolo with two long beaches on either side of the dunes. This thin, sandy grassland strip effectively stops the island being split in half. The friendly main settlement on Vatersay sits at the southern end of the tombolo; the seasonal community café is at its north end.

Before the causeway linked Vatersay to Barra, life was difficult for this outlying community and there were repeated but unsuccessful requests for a connecting bridge. The demise of Bernie, the prize-winning bull, however, seems to have clinched the argument. Beef cattle reared on Vatersay started their journey to market with a 250-metre swim across the sound to Barra but when Bernie didn't

---

TERRAIN: Free-range on faint paths; some easy scrambling and route-finding around steep, rocky inlets

STARTING POINT: S end of causeway. Lat/Long 56.9460, -7.5333; GR NL 637 975

DISTANCE: 22.1km (ascent 546m)

TIME: 7 hours

OS MAP: OS Explorer 452

DIFFICULTY: 2

NAVIGATION: 4

ACCESS: 1

DON'T MISS:
• Spotting otters along Vatersay Sound
• A secluded swim at the stunning Bàgh a' Deas
• Hand-dived scallop pakoras at Café Kisimul on Barra
• Splendid isolation at our most westerly inhabited point

SPECIAL NOTES: Several steep gullies to navigate. Alternative circuit of two shorter walks starts at the Community Hall. The first follows the described route for

the N part of the island. The second route heads S on the tombolo (or Tràigh Siar), then follows the route described.

GETTING THERE: From Barra drive S over the Vatersay causeway and park. Bus W33 from Castlebay, Barra, Monday to Saturday.

FACILITIES: Vatersay Community Hall Café at N end of tombolo for simple refreshments and toilets. Open during summer months only and can sell out quickly.

make it there was an outcry. As a consequence, 220,000 tonnes of rock was quarried and the causeway opened in 1991.

The anti-clockwise route starts at the southern end of the causeway and bears west, along the north shore of the Sound of Vatersay – the prime site for spotting the otters living here year-round. Small piles of fish bones and scales, scattered bodyparts of shellfish, and flattened areas of grass indicate their favourite dining spots.

Towards the northwest tip of the island, the route rounds a rugged headland dotted with boulders before drawing parallel with the tiny islet of Bioruaslum, which is accessible at low tides to view the Neolithic walled fort. Further on, towards the tombolo, there is an interesting scramble at the head of an unnamed inlet before the route heads up the flank of Heiseabhal Mòr.

Walking the length of shell-white, sandy Tràigh Siar (West Beach) is a pleasure for all the senses. You hear the roar of perfect sets of waves breaking on the beach, smell the tangy ozone spray, and feel

the powdery sand beneath bare feet. If you manage to resist a swim here you won't miss out; there are more secluded swims to come. Above the beach a memorial and a cairn of rocks marks the burial site of 350 men, women, and children who drowned in 1853 following the sinking of the sailing ship *Annie Jane* en route from Liverpool to Quebec.

Once over the tombolo and on South Vatersay, the route along the north shore is free-range and rugged and there are steep-sided gullies – Chirein and Grisiabhaig – to navigate on the heavily indented east coast. Once on the south shore, however, you reach the stunning beach of Bàgh a' Deas. Secluded, with impossibly white sand and shallow turquoise sea, this is the place to swim.

Further along the south coast, the route passes the evocative ruins of Eorasdail, a settlement first established in the early 1900s by desperate people from the neighbouring island of Mingulay when life there became unsustainable. Known as the Vatersay Raiders, Mingulay's *cottars* (people without land) were soon joined by others from Barra and they inadvertently became the cause célèbre for land reform in Scotland. The island's absentee landlord took them to court and the Raiders were initially jailed but public outrage persuaded the authorities to purchase the island and divide it into crofts. Eòrasdail was occupied until the 1970s and many of the proud descendants of the Vatersay Raiders still live on the island.

The route continues around the hill of Am Meall, with great views across to Castle Bay on Barra, and returns across the tombolo to the north part of the island via the island lane. Here, the remains of a wrecked aircraft lie scattered near the road. It crashed in 1944 during a training flight from Oban killing three of the nine men on-board.

As I made my way back to the jetty, I couldn't think of a more perfect island walk. This one seemed to have everything, especially when it ended at one of the best curry houses around on neighbouring Barra. The hand-dived scallop pakoras are to die for.

DIRECTIONS

» At the S end of the causeway (1) turn immediately W (R) along the lane, then R again after 660m to follow the lane towards the coast.

» At the end of the track, go through the metal gate and head immediately R towards the shore. After 250m cross the stile over the stock fence then follow the N shoreline, looking out for otters (2) along the faint track around the grass and rock plateau of the headland. Towards the NW tip of the headland, cross the boulder fields.

» When the beach of Tràigh Bhàrlais (3) comes into view go up into the rocks above, at a height of around 40m, for an easy scramble around the headland before dropping onto the beach via an easy grass path.

» Walk across Tràigh Bhàrlais beach to the clear, sandy path uphill, cross the fence and go up between the steepest part of the hill to the L and the nose of the headland at a contour height of 45m. (Using the OS 1:250,000 map a clear contour ring of 10m is marked and the route heads to the R of this on a faint path.) Once around the headland keep to a height of 40–50m.

» Pass the islet of Bioruaslum (4) and then between Bioruaslum and Tràigh Siar cross the top of the inlet at the base of the rocks. Shortly after the inlet head immediately up the bank to avoid the steep drop. Walk across the plateau, on a contour of 60m or so, before heading down on the path towards the beach.

» At Trèseabhaig, cross the boulders at the base of the cliffs via a faint path at a height of around 30m. After 500m go over the stile and follow the clear path along the fence line to the gate for access to the beach of Traigh Siar (5) and walk S along the tombolo, looking out for the Annie Jane Memorial (6). Find the gap in the sand dunes on L with a clearly marked path, go through the gate, and turn R to reach the N shore of the S part of the island. After 200m cross the stile and continue along the coast path that ends at Sloc Mhàrtuin (7). Cross the fence with care by the steep drop to the inlet. Continue on the free-range route around the rocky headland of Rubha Huilis.

» Turn S and navigate the inlet of Sloc Grisiabhaig (8) at a contour of 50m. Turn E to follow the S shore and cross the swimming beach at Bagh a' Deas (9). Continue along the coast, passing a cairn after a further 1km.

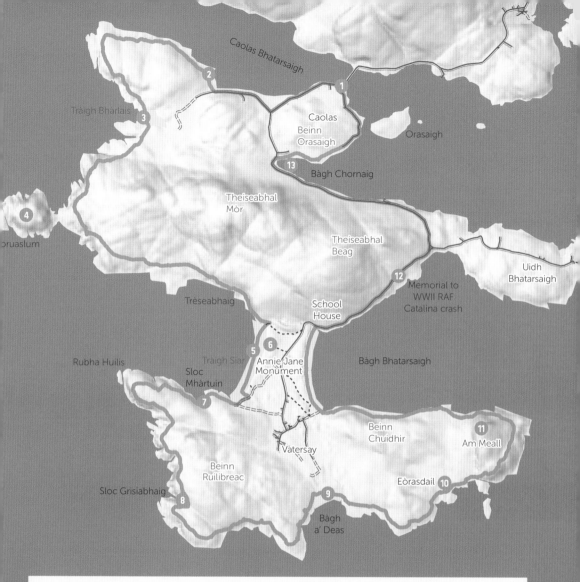

Caolas Bhatarsaigh

2

1

Tràigh Bhàrlais

3

Caolas
Beinn
Orasaigh

Orasaigh

13

Bàgh Chornaig

Theiseabhal
Mòr

4

oruaslum

Theiseabhal
Beag

Uidh
Bhatarsaigh

12

Memorial to
WWII RAF
Catalina crash

Trèseabhaig

School
House

Bàgh Bhatarsaigh

Rubha Huilis

Tràigh Siar

6

Annie Jane
Monument

5

Sloc
Mhàrtuin

7

Beinn
Chuidhir

11

Am Meall

Vatersay

Beinn
Rùilibreac

Eòrasdail

10

Sloc Grisiabhaig

8

9

Bàgh
a' Deas

» Cross a stream and pass the ruined stone cottages of Eòrasdail (10), before crossing the fence line 300m further on and reaching the small beach. At the end of the beach cross the fence, drop into the gully, and continue straight ahead to follow the small track uphill. Continuing through the grass and boulders, find the cleft through the bluff ahead. After 300m, at a height of around 60m, go around Am Meall (11) and head to the N shoreline or follow the markers higher up the flank of Beinn Chuidhir.

» Cross the stile and drop down to the beach to walk N back up the tombolo. At the end of the beach, climb the bank, cross the fence, and turn R on the road to pass the School House and after 1km the aircraft wreckage (12). Continue on the road bearing L and following the Cycling 780 route alongside Bágh Chornaig.

» At the head of Bágh Chornaig (13) cross the bridge and follow the faint path to R on the shore side of the house, crossing the fence after 80m and continue past the remains of a jetty and fishing boats, crossing a rickety stile after a further 120m.

» Pass the houses on a gravel track and arrive back on the road to the causeway.

Cairn Galtar

ERISKAY

A CHALLENGING ROUTE AROUND A RUGGED HEBRIDEAN ISLAND WHERE GOLDEN EAGLES SOAR AND DOLPHINS SWIM OFFSHORE

Rugged and free-range, this anti-clockwise route mostly follows distinct sheep trails. It involves some bushwhacking through bracken on the south and east coasts and bog-hopping over soggy ground. There are also short, easy scrambles to negotiate rocky bluffs and to avoid descending into deeper sea inlets. Once on the north-east coast, there is a fine secluded beach for a swim, then the route continues on single-track roads with some beach walking to complete the circuit.

This is a challenging route but the intrepid islandeer will encounter some wild, unspoilt terrain, stunning white beaches, and be rewarded by sightings of the very best of Hebridean wildlife. Yet it's not just the natural beauty of this island that delights: Eriskay has some great stories for those who want to sip its 'spirited' history.

Coilleag a' Phrionnsa (the Prince's Cockle Strand) on the west coast, is where Bonnie Prince Charlie first stepped foot on Scottish soil in 1745. He had sailed from France to build support for removing George II, the ruling British Protestant king, from the throne. Around the beach you'll see a non-native flower, the sea bindweed. Its seeds are said to have fallen from Bonnie Prince Charlie's pocket when he came ashore.

The island is also the inspiration for Compton Mackenzie's book *Whisky Galore*. When the *SS Politician* ran aground off Ròisinis Point in 1941, her cargo included more than 260,000 bottles of whisky and Jamaican banknotes worth a small fortune. After rescuing the crew, the islanders mounted a highly successful, if unofficial, salvage operation and managed to drink or conceal much of the booty from the authorities. Stories of the

TERRAIN: Free-range on moorland via animal tracks, boggy in parts; easy rock scrambles; island roads

STARTING POINT: Eriskay ferry terminal Lat/Long 57.0706, -7.3076; NF 784 102

DISTANCE: 17km (ascent 660m)

TIME: 5 hours

OS MAP: OS Explorer 453

DIFFICULTY: 3

NAVIGATION: 5

ACCESS: 1

DON'T MISS:
- Wild swimming off the remote beach at the NE tip
- Sea eagles, dolphins, whales, and otters
- Visiting the beach where Bonnie Prince Charlie landed
- Hardy Eriskay ponies, descendants of an ancient breed

SPECIAL NOTES: Good navigational skills and confidence in route-finding needed. On the E coast keep to suggested contour line to avoid steep inlets.

GETTING THERE: By road, cross the causeway from South Uist. Ferry from Barra. Regular bus services from across the Outer Hebrides.

FACILITIES: Toilets at ferry terminal; food at Am Politician and the Eriskay shop in Rubha Ban. Take plenty of water and food for the walk.

ERISKAY

often seen against its skyline. Crofters used these hardy ponies to carry peat and seaweed and after becoming endangered, numbers have slowly improved. The spectacular wildlife continues on the remote, rocky and indented east coast. After a scramble up Meall nan Caorach you may be lucky to spot the flash of a sea eagle's white tail feathers above you on the rocks or hear the gentle 'blow' of dolphins as they take a breath after hunting in Eriskay's bountiful seas. These waters are among the richest of any UK coastal region and you may catch sight of minke whales, Risso's, bottlenose, and white-beaked dolphins, orcas, and porpoises.

good times still roll and a whisky bottle from the wreck can be seen in the island's only pub, the Am Politician – a welcome refreshment stop towards the end of the route.

Wildlife abounds on this small island where golden eagles soar over the ridge of Ben Scrien and the rare Eriskay ponies, descendants of an ancient breed native to the Western Isles of Scotland, are

As I neared the end of my walk, the crystal-clear water of the sandy bay on the northeast tip of the island proved too tempting. Lying peacefully on my back in the still water, a furry head suddenly popped up beside me and I nearly jumped out of my skin. The otter was close enough for me to see the water droplets on its whiskers.

DIRECTIONS

» From the ferry terminal (1), head uphill along the lane, then onto grass bank to skirt R of the house. Continue S along sheep trails to cross the head of the Gleann Fada inlet (2).

» At the S point of the island, ascend the L side of the rocks and continue slightly inland to avoid the rocks of the coast. Keep to the L of Meall nan Caorach, past the saddle (3) with Meall Ainort. Walk L of the bluff and descend through the valley towards the SE corner of Loch a' Chapuill (4).

» Skirting the S of the loch, follow the wooden markers towards the house, passing to the R of it. Follow the path along the inlet of Arcairseid Mhòr then walk along the track past the houses of Arcairseid.

» At the tarmac road turn R and after 300m, at a sharp R bend, continue ahead on the track. Pass the ruined cottage on R and further ruins on the beach.

» Cross the inlet at Sheisinis at low tide or follow the fence line to a stile higher up to cross at high tide. Use the animal tracks to walk N towards the crags, keeping to a height of 20–30m to avoid descending into the various inlets. After 500m, at the last ruin, climb the crag to a height of 60m then cross Glen Stulavaig by walking towards the shore to find the animal crossing point.

» Pass the inlet beyond Rubha Basadearn, following a contour of about 130m to reach Loch Dubhat. Pass to R of the loch, crossing its small stream and keeping to a contour of about 50m to avoid the inlets.

» Climb the fence at the head of Sloc a' Mhaide then go round the NE tip of the island above Sloc Caol to find the swimming beach (5) just beyond. Pass between the ruins of Ròisinis on a faint path over the brow of the hill to reach the tarmac road at Bun a' Mhuilinn. Head downhill through the houses on the shoreline and follow the road until it bends left towards the main village and shop (6) then follow signs for the Am Politician (7).

» Continue past the pub for 400m and just beyond the houses and cemetery take the gravel track on R towards to the coast. After 500m drop down onto the beach at Coilleag a' Phrionnsa (8). Walk the length of the beach before taking the small path up the bank at the S end and continuing along the road to return to the ferry terminal.

Cabhsair Eirisgeigh

Caolas Eirisgeigh

Calbaigh

Haun

Ròisinis

5

Sloc Caol

Rubha Bàn

Bun a'
Mhuillinn

7 6

Sloc a' Mhaide

Ben
Scrien

Loch
Dubhat

Coilleag a'
Phrionnsa

8

Rubha Basadearn

Coilleag

Glen Stulavaig

Pàirceannan

Ferry 1

Arcairseid

Sheisinis

Acarseid Mhòr

Loch a' Chapuill 4

Beinn Stac

2 Gleann Fada

Meall nan
Caorach 3

VALLAY

IMPOSING MANSION RUINS, STUNNING WILD FLOWERS, DESERTED WHITE BEACHES, AND WILD-CAMPING OPPORTUNITIES

The first time I explored this island I couldn't see a great deal through the curtains of Hebridean rain. The ruined, baronial-style mansion was foreboding and the incoming tide menacing, yet it was a completely exhilarating experience and I wanted to return. On my second trip a few years later, the machair quite literally sparkled with the colours of wild flowers and the shallow sea, uplit by the bone-white sands, reflected every shade of shimmering blue-green all the way out to St Kilda. The Hebridean scenery on Vallay is hard to match and a trip here is a must, whatever the weather.

The walk starts with an epic two-kilometre crossing of vast, tidal Tràigh Bhàlaigh – Vallay Strand. Once on the island, the free-range route follows animal tracks through the machair alongside the sandy foreshore of the south and east, before con-

tinuing on an undulating path over the dunes that back the white crescent beaches of the north coast.

Vallay sits off the northwest coast of North Uist in the Outer Hebrides. It was first settled in Neolithic times and inhabited until the middle of last century so there are plenty of ruins to discover. To the south is a sheltered lagoon, to the north are wild Atlantic beaches with views extending to St Kilda and Harris. This is definitely a coastline of contrasts. Inland, horned Highland cattle bring to mind the Vikings that once invaded these shores. Vallay is a remote and secret destination for nature lovers and pioneering outdoor enthusiasts – walkers, swimmers, surfers, kitesurfers, and windsurfers – although you'll rarely see another soul.

The clockwise walk starts by crossing Vallay Strand between North Uist and Vallay. The shallow lagoon doesn't always completely drain and leaves

---

TERRAIN: Tidal sands; grassy foreshore and dune tracks

STARTING POINT: Pull-in at Àird Glas. Lat/Long 57.6361, -7.3972; GR NF 780 735

DISTANCE: 15.7km (ascent 251m)

TIME: 4 hours

OS MAP: OS Explorer 454

DIFFICULTY: 2

NAVIGATION: 3

ACCESS: 4

DON'T MISS:
- Epic crossing over vast tidal sands
- Extraordinary machair with abundant flora and fauna
- Deserted white-shell beaches for swimming or surfing
- Panoramic views to distant St Kilda
- Wild camping and spotting otters

SPECIAL NOTES: Access is 4 hours either side of low tide, but wind and spring times will reduce this window.

GETTING THERE: Drive W from Sollas on the A865 and about 2.5km beyond Malacleit find Aird Glas, opposite a forestry plantation, with parking space for 2 cars to the side of the track. Cross Valley Strand towards the mansion.

FACILITIES: No facilities on the island; café and shop in nearby Sollas.

The clockwise route around the island begins below Vallay House and continues west along the sandy foreshore and machair. During my July visit, the sheer variety of wild flowers was a delight. Bright red poppies sat among the purples, whites, and blues of orchids, clover, ox-eye daisies, harebells, campanulas, and scabious. The hum of bumble-bees, including the great yellow bumblebee, filled the air and the fertile grassland was alive with day-flying moths, butterflies, and hundreds of other insects. Birds rustled amongst the tall stems and against a background of piping oystercatchers and honking geese I heard a corn bunting – a sound like jangling keys.

After rounding the western tip, the views out to the St Kilda archipelago are breathtaking. You are looking at the remotest part of Britain, more than 60 kilometres away over rough seas and accessible only when weather conditions permit safe passage.

The north coast of Vallay is a string of gloriously deserted white-shell beaches delineated by rocky strands. Small areas of flattened grass and piles of shells mark the dining spots of the resident otters. Depending on the sea conditions this coastline is either a swimmer's or a surfer's dream, and it features a majestic backdrop: the mountains of Harris and the islands of Pabbay and Taransay. About halfway along the north coast it is possible to cross to the tidal islet of Orasaigh if there is time – another reason to wild-camp overnight.

The machair route continues around the eastern tip of the island to return along the south coast. Passing two standing stones, you reach the remains of a medieval chapel, Teampull Mhuir.

a few small pools and channels to cross. It's worth starting out early and doing some shallow wading to allow enough time to complete the route and enjoy what the island has to offer. For the adventurous, more time can be spent on the island by taking a picnic and marooning yourself over the high tide. There are also plenty of places to wild-camp overnight.

After passing the smaller islands of Torogaigh and Stangram in the Valley Strand, you cross over to the island almost opposite ruined Valley House and the gable-roofed farm. Entering the dilapidated property itself is not recommended but there is plenty to see through the windows – colourfully tiled fireplaces, rich-red painted walls, and ornate ceilings. Images of the previous owner, Erskine Beveridge, sitting by the fire and writing notes on the day's archaeological finds spring to mind.

Beveridge, a wealthy textile merchant and skilled amateur photographer, travelled across Scotland with a plate camera. The hundreds of images he took between 1880 and 1919 record Scotland's rural heritage and the life of small, remote communities. They were published in Wanderings with a Camera. On his death, his son George inherited Vallay but drowned in 1945 while sailing back from North Uist. A memorial to him stands on the west coast.

As the tide started to flood back in, I returned to North Uist feeling the island had revealed its secrets. Looking back at Vallay from a distance, it seemed to have merged with the sea and sky – just waiting for the next person to discover what a truly magical place it is.

Rubha

Camas Mòr

Camas na Criche

Orasaigh

4

Cuil na Muice

Bàgh nan Craobhag

Tràigh Himiligh

5

Ceann Uachdarach

3

Standing Stones 6

Vallay / Bhalaigh

2

Tràigh Iar

Dùn Thomaidh

1

Stangram

Tràigh Bhàlaigh

Torogaigh

Loch Fada na Gearrachun

Loch na Gearrachun

Loch Eig

DIRECTIONS

» From the pull-in walk 200m along the farm track to the coast and follow the tracks left by vehicles, heading almost due N. Keep to the R of the two smaller islands of Torogaigh and Stangram and aim for the ruined buildings on the island.

» After 2.9km arrive on the foreshore of Vallay, just below the main house (1). Walk W on the foreshore or follow animal tracks on the low grass banks of the S coast. There are numerous opportunities to make a detour to the memorial (2).

» Pass the walls of Dùn Thomaidh opposite a small fishing jetty on North Uist to continue round the western tip at Rubha and Camas Mòr. From here walk over the shingle bank past the beacon and take any one of the various animal tracks E through the sand dunes.

» Reach the huge beach at Camas na Criche (3) and after 1km climb up onto the rocks at the end to cross the fence on the rocks. Walk along the sands of Bàgh nan Craobhag and across the S end of Orasaigh (4).

» At the end of Cuil na Muice beach climb up onto the rocks, cross to the beach of Tràigh Himiligh (5) and follow the animal tracks through the dunes and to the E tip of the island. Follow the shoreline, passing the standing stones (6) and continue to head W. After 600m pass between two parallel fences and exit via the metal gate onto the sands to return to the ruined buildings. Retrace your steps across Tràigh Bhàlaigh.

BERNERAY

A MAGICAL HEBRIDEAN WALK ON MACHAIR, ROCKY FORESHORE, AND ALONG THREE MILES OF PERFECT, WHITE SANDY BEACH

Bailing rainwater out of my rucksack, I reflected on my last trip to this same beach. The sun was beating down and the miles of bone-white sand were more reminiscent of the Caribbean. Yet today, the stormy sea was spectacular and the different layers of grey in the heavy sky quite extraordinary. As a soggy lunchtime oatcake plopped into my lap, I heard a gentle puff from the ocean, followed by several more. I looked up and saw a pod of dolphins feeding just a few metres away. They stayed there for ten minutes or so before moving on, like a fleeting glimpse of sunshine.

The wildlife certainly adds variety to a splendid clockwise walk along the machair and shoreline of this iconic Hebridean island. From the ferry terminal, the route crosses Loch Bhuirgh to reach one of the most magnificent beaches in the UK – rain or

shine. From here there are options to climb to the high point of Beinn Shlèibhe for bird's-eye views of the islands of Lewis Sound. The walk finishes with an easy stroll along the east coast, passing traditional thatched buildings, seal-watching spots, and winding up at a great café.

Berneray lies south of Harris and a causeway links it to the northern coast of North Uist. Cottages and crofts are dotted along the east coast and around the harbour of Loch a' Bàigh. The Atlantic-facing half of the island is flat and rimmed by steep dunes, the backdrop to over 5 km's of perfect white-sand beach.

After crossing the shell-dotted foreshore of Loch Bhuirgh, which completely empties on a low tide, the route along the machair of the south coast passes the memorial to Angus MacAskill. He is entered in the *Guinness Book of World Records*

TERRAIN: Faint paths through machair and along beach

STARTING POINT: Ferry terminal. Lat/Long 57.7025, -7.1802; GR NF 915 798

DISTANCE: 18.7km (ascent 200m)

TIME: 4 hours (plus 30 mins to ascend Beinn Shlèibhe)

OS MAP: OS Explorer 454

DIFFICULTY: 2

NAVIGATION: 3

ACCESS: 1

DON'T MISS:
- Wild camping and skinny-dipping on miles of perfect white beach
- Home-made cakes at the Berneray Bistro after a fabulous walk
- Views over the Harris Sound from Beinn Shlèibhe

GETTING THERE: By road along short causeway from North Uist. Ferry from Harris and Lewis.

FACILITIES: Food and supplies at Berneray Shop and Bistro; toilets at ferry terminal, youth hostel, and harbour.

as the tallest non-pathological giant in recorded history. Born in Berneray, Angus and his family were forcibly evicted and he grew up in Nova Scotia – and didn't really stop, reaching a grand height of 2.36 metres. Tales of his superhuman strength included lifting a fully-grown horse. He joined a travelling show in America as part of a double act with General Tom Thumb, the shortest man of the time. Together they must have made quite a sight.

A little further on the route turns northeast at Rubha Bhoisnis, the start of five kilometres of white sandy bliss where the horizontal stripes of cobalt sea, white sand, and green machair stretch out like a vast Hebridean flag. Rust-coloured seaweed and feeding birds that follow the ebb and flow of the waves are the only interruptions to this vast expanse of white. No wonder the Thai Tourist Board used a photo of this beach to market one of their own. Bird cries and the powerful Atlantic surf are the only sounds along this stretch of paradise. It is truly spellbinding.

The beach does finally come to an end, yet when you look back through the haze created by the surf it is almost impossible to see where you started along this sandy trek. The route continues through a gap in the dunes then onwards around the northern tip where the short deviation inland to climb Beinn Shlèibhe is recommended.

Continuing south along the east coast, you swiftly cross the beach at Beasdaire and reach the youth hostel – two traditional thatched black-houses with wonderful views that welcome travellers from far and wide. Peter Clarke, chairman of the Gatliff Hebridean Hostels Trust, describes it as a place where 'the passage of time and the outside world quickly become of no concern'. Sitting on the beach, surrounded by wild beauty, you couldn't agree more. Otters frequent the foreshore (there's one woven into the thatch on the hostel roof) and your patience might be rewarded with a sighting.

Close by, the derelict blackhouse is worth exploring. Roofed with peat and still featuring the old bed, kitchen, fireplace, and wood panelling, the dwelling offers a window into island life of the past.

Further south, down the main island road, the route passes the post office, a seal-watching site, and the harbour in Loch a' Bàigh before reaching the Berneray Shop and Bistro just a few minutes before the ferry port. This is a great place to top up on local produce, sample delicious home-made cakes, and wait for the evening treat of its sumptuous local seafood.

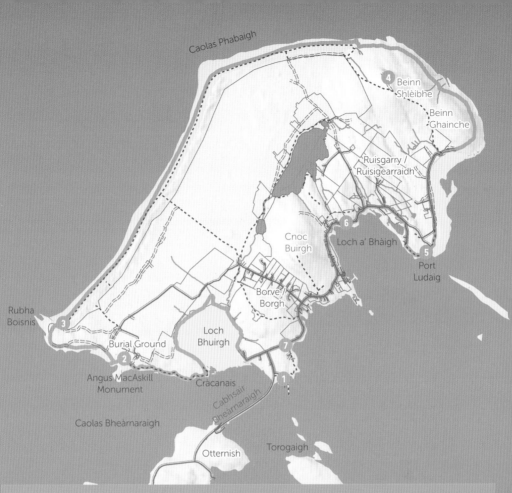

Caolas Phabaigh

4 Beinn
Shlèibhe

Beinn
Ghainche

Ruisgarry /
Ruisigearraidh

6

Cnoc
Buirgh   Loch a' Bhàigh

5

Port
Ludaig

Rubha
Boisnis

3

Borve/
Borgh

Loch
Bhuirgh

Burial Ground   7

2

Angus MacAskill   Cràcanais
Monument
Cabhsair
Bheàrnaraigh   1

Caolas Bheàrnaraigh

Otternish   Torogaigh

DIRECTIONS

» From the ferry slipway (1) follow the road out, turn R, then turn L after 260m towards a small group of houses. After a further 320m, almost parallel with a ruin on the right, go through the metal gate on L and follow the track to the beach of Loch Bhuirgh. Pass in front of the house on the track without walking up its drive, then walk around the beach to reach Cràcanais on SW side of the mouth of the loch. Use the easiest route to navigate around the bay and the streams at the N end, depending on the state of the tide.

» At the wreck of a boat follow the small path onto the machair and

continue around the headland at Cracanais. Pass the burial ground at Sheabie, and the memorial to Angus MacAskill (2).

» Cross the fence line near the shore and after 1km drop down onto the beach (3). Continue along it for about 5.5km until more rocks start to appear and a prominent post directs you into the dunes. At the top of the bank take the path to L along the coast towards Rogh. To climb Beinn Shlèibhe (4), at the top of the dune follow the yellow-topped posts uphill.

» After rounding the north end of the island, keeping to about 35m

above sea level, head down towards the building below. Follow the sandy track past Tir-nan-og, to reach the main island road and continue S along the tarmac road.

» Follow the faint grass track, passing the shore side of the house to visit the youth hostel and blackhouse (5) near Port Ludaig. Continue the loop back to the tarmac road, past the old school. Turn L at the main island road and continue along it past the church and the seal-watching point (6) to reach the Berneray Shop and Bistro (7). Turn L, following the road signed 'Sound of Harris Ferry and North Uist' to complete the walk.

CHAPTER

45

TARANSAY

PRISTINE, TALCUM-POWDER WHITE BEACHES, REMOTE WILD CAMPING, AND SECLUDED SWIMMING ON A TRUE CASTAWAY ISLAND

Landing on the beach after a calm kayak crossing of the turquoise waters of the Sound of Taransay, the heat and brightness of the white sands radiated upwards and gentle waves lapped the shore. My immediate feeling was that I'd arrived at one of the most beautiful islands in the world. In the bay the fairy terns plunged daintily into the water, while gulls and oystercatchers nested in the dunes. Inland daisies, thrift, celandines, and sundew studded the machair and from the purple heather on the hillside came the industrious sounds of bees foraging for sweet nectar. That this is an island for nature is in no doubt.

This completely free-range walk follows the animal tracks that circumnavigate the island's outer edge. It includes stunning beach crossings, a magnificent rock arch, mysterious ruins, and far-reaching views to the blue peaks of Harris. The island is a patchwork of hard rock, grass and machair, heather moorland on the higher slopes, and boggy ground in the north. Consequently, the route is rugged, undulating, and crosses a mix of terrains. And it is utterly enchanting.

Taransay lies 3 kilometres from Harris across the Sound of Taransay in the Outer Hebrides. Uninhabited since the 1970s, the island has plenty of ruins and place names that offer pointers to what life may have been like dating back to Pagan, Christian, and Viking times. Geographically, the island is in two fairly distinct parts that are joined by the beautifully secluded, sandy isthmus at the head of Loch na h-Ùidhe. The larger landmass to the east of the isthmus, which is dominated by the bulk of Beinn Rà, is the location of the landing beach and the pre-Clearance townships of Paibeil, Uidh, and Raah. The smaller, wilder west side, known as Àird Mhànais, is

---

TERRAIN: Undulating bog, rock and grass; mostly following animal tracks or finding free-range routes

STARTING POINT: Landing beach near Paibeil. Lat/Long 57.8844, -7.0074; GR NG 033 993

DISTANCE: 21.7km (ascent 507m)

TIME: 6 hours

OS MAP: OS Explorer 455

DIFFICULTY: 2

NAVIGATION: 4

ACCESS: 5

DON'T MISS:
- Exploring the stunning sea arch at Roagh
- Wild camping above four deserted white beaches
- Searching for the sticky sundews in the machair
- Swimming in solitude from pristine talc-white beaches

SPECIAL NOTES: Privately owned. Right to roam allows access but limited during deer-stalking season Aug – Oct. Friendly advice from West Harris Trust 01859 503900.

GETTING THERE: Kayak or private boat from Seilebost Beach (Lat/Long 57.8668, -6.9555) on Harris following a bearing of 298 degrees.

FACILITIES: No facilities or water on the island. Closest restaurant is fabulous Machair Kitchen at Talla na Mara Community Enterprise Centre south of Horgabost on the A859.

shaped by the low peaks of Bualabhal and Hear-rabhal, and along the north coast at Roagh is the spectacular rock arch.

The clockwise walk starts at the landing beach between the two rocky headlands of Sgonn and Sgeir a' Bhuallt, the latter meaning 'Smitten Rock' and said to mark the site of a massacre. An invading Lewis clan slaughtered Taransay's inhabitants but were, in turn, attacked and killed by the islanders of Berneray when they fled to this rock.

The first point of interest after the landing beach is Paibeil at Taransay's most southerly point. Once the main settlement, there are now only a few buildings in various states of repair including a long barn, farmhouse, and school chalet. The latter two were renovated as part of the BBC's reality TV series Castaway 2000, which revolved around the challenges faced by the 36 men, women and children recruited to live on this remote uninhabited island for a year. Their task was to build a sustainable, self-sufficient community from scratch and the series marked the beginning of Ben Fogle's fame.

Paibeil is also the site of two early chapels that are shrouded in local legend. St Taran's, in the beach landing area, is marked by a rectangular hollow and the remains of ancient, turf-covered walls. Of St Keith's, located just south of Paibeil 'village', just grassy mounds and foundation walls remain. In the shore below the chapel foundations, erosion continually exposes new material from shell middens, making it a great place to explore.

Ancient tradition stipulated that a man must not be buried in St Taran's, nor a woman in St Keith's, yet a mixed burial took place in one of the graveyards. According to local legend, the following morning one of the bodies was found lying out on the ground beside the grave.

The bay slightly to the south-west of Paibeil is known as Miosadar and was the site of a small village before the sea broke through to leave a sand cliff of up to 3.5 metres high. On the face of the cliff a beautiful prehistoric midden full of empty shells and pottery has been revealed. New material emerges and can often be seen in the sand.

Just west of Paibeil, Allt a' Mhuilinn (the Mill Burn) joins the sea. From its source at Loch an Dùin, it tumbles down through two more lochs, Loch Sionadail and Cromlach. The stream can be followed, as an additional walk, up to Loch an Duin where there is a small fort on an islet near the shore. Further along the coast, just before the isthmus on a grassy slope above the beach, are the remains of the settlement of Uidh and a standing stone known as Clach an Teampuill — a tall pillar of gneiss with a bold cross carved on one face.

Beyond the brilliant white beaches of the isthmus, on the western part of Taransay, Àird Vanish is a wild and lonely area of rocks, moor, and sea caves with the twin peaks of Hearrabhal and Bualabhal. Turning north from its most southerly point at Rubha Sgeirigin, you leave the relatively sheltered Sound of Taransay to encounter the full force of the Atlantic and a more eroded landscape. There are few places shielded from the wind and waves here except for Bagh a' Chàigeal where the people of Harris once stopped off with their horses, en route to the forest of North Harris for the summer grazing. The highlight of this undulating section of the walk is the magnificent natural rock arch at Roagh. On a high tide the water boils in the chasm far below and the pounding reverberates through your body. You can literally feel the energy in this highly charged place.

Crossing the isthmus back to the eastern part of the island, you are offered a fascinating insight into island life of the past. On the hillsides behind Camas Chleiteir and at the northernmost tip, Rubha nan Totag, the ridge-and-furrow lines of lazy beds indicate how root vegetable and grains were cultivated. The multiple sheilings and ruins of long-houses, barns, byres, and corn-drying kilns along the north-east coast are testament to the harsh life of crofters on Taransay.

The final section of the walk is marked by the spectacular sandspit at Corran Rà, the setting for the film *The Rocket Post*. Based on the true story of German Gerhard Zucker, the film recreates his attempts at sending mail between the Scottish islands by rocket just before World War II. The producers chose this beautiful spot on Taransay over Scarp, the true location of the story.

Taransay is now the largest of the Scottish islands without a permanent population and has, thankfully, remained distinctly wild, pristine, and free.

DIRECTIONS

» From the landing beach (1), E of Paibeil, walk across the grass at the top of the beach towards the houses. After 500m or so pass the first building and continue between the farm buildings (2) towards the coast. After a further 500m pass to R of the small pond and continue over the mixed grassy, rocky, and marshy ground to negotiate the various enclosures and dykes.

» Cross the stream of Allt a' Mhuilinn. Just before crossing the isthmus pass the ruins of the old township of Uidhh (3) and the standing stone on the grassy bank. After a further 200m cross the beach at Loch na h-Ùidhe.

» Reaching the point near Lainis (4), look out for seals on the rock in the bay and continue along the undulating faint animal paths around the S of Àird Mhànais (5).

» Head towards the island's SW tip, Rubha Sgeirigin, go around the headland, and continue N over the increasingly rocky and undulating ground. After 800m reach the first high point of the walk, Bualabhal (39m). Descend into the valley.

» At Bagh a' Chàigeal (6) continue straight ahead to avoid walking around the headland of Àird Tro, and start to head uphill, keeping parallel to the coast towards the second high point of the walk.

» At the rock arch (7) near Roagh, head inland and walk around its S side and then descend towards the shore to N. At the beach, Tràigh a' Siar, cross back over the isthmus continuing for 160m before an easy scramble up the rocks at the far side of the beach. Continue along the coastline, crossing multiple streams running down from the hills and lochs above.

» Once round the N tip of the island, Rubha nan Totag (8), bear slightly inland and take a zig-zag route up the steep mixed grass and rocks to a contour height of approximately 35m to walk safely around the headland.

» Just S of Tolm (9), start to descend over boggy ground and find the best free-range route to avoid the wetter areas. After 700m or so, pass the ruined buildings and sheep-pen walls and continue S passing further ruins.

» Find one of the many faint paths through the hilly sand dunes to reach the beach and sand spit at Corran Rà (10) and return to the landing beach.

GREAT BERNERA

CROSS THE BRIDGE OVER THE ATLANTIC TO DISCOVER ONE OF THE BEST BEACHES IN THE HEBRIDES

This is a full coastal circuit with wild free-range sections that link quiet lanes and footpaths. One section follows the Great Bernera Trail to explore the remote peninsula of Valasay, then the route continues to the northern tip of the island where the highlights are the Iron Age village and magnificent beach at Bostadh. Walking through low-lying, glaciated landscapes and passing the chain of inland lochs, you reach Breaclete, which offers a history lesson on rebellion in its excellent museum as well as good refreshments. The route ends with a wild walk to a restored Norse mill and the birthplace of lobster farming.

Great Bernera, off the west coast of Lewis, is an island with a passionate history and strong community life. Until recently it was owned by the late and extravagantly named Count Robin de la Lanne-Mirrlees, a popular laird and island resident.

His flamboyant lifestyle and knowledge of heraldry influenced Ian Fleming in developing an alter ego for James Bond in *On Her Majesty's Secret Service*.

The fierce community spirit that pervades this island is apparent from the very start of the walk. Fearing for their economic survival without a direct link to Lewis, the population came together to demand a causeway. The bridge was indeed built in 1953, but only when the islanders threatened to blow up the adjacent cliffs and build one themselves.

On the clockwise walk, immediately after the bridge you reach a fascinating alignment of stones known as Callanish VIII and marked on the OS map as Tursachan. The tall standing stones unusually form a semi-circle – possibly a unique arrangement – on a steep, rocky slope ending in a cliff. Its purpose and its significance are not known. Beyond

---

TERRAIN: Quiet lanes and footpaths; free-range over rough, boggy ground

STARTING POINT: Lay-by, Bernera Bridge. Lat/Long 58.2056, -6.8282; GR NB 165 342

DISTANCE: 24.3km (ascent 741m)

TIME: 6 hours

OS MAP: OS Explorer 458

DIFFICULTY: 3

NAVIGATION: 4

ACCESS: 1

DON'T MISS:
- Swimming off Bosta Beach to the sound of the tidal bell
- Fascinating Iron Age village site and replica Norse mill
- Crofting history and great cakes at the community centre
- Discovering a stone-built landmark in fishing history

GETTING THERE: A859 from Stornoway, Isle of Lewis, towards Tarbert. After 7 miles turn R on the A858 following signs for Bernera and Uig. At Garynahine turn L onto the B8011 and after 3 miles turn R for Bernera. Continue on B8059 for 6 miles to cross the road bridge and reach the lay-by.

FACILITIES: Small village store; cafe and toilets in the community centre at Breaclete.

the stones the route traverses boggy land and you will need some route-finding skills to reach the island lane to Valasay.

Leaving the tarmac road behind, the route crosses over the narrow stone footbridge, which serves two beautifully isolated houses. The tidal stretch between Caolas Bhalasaigh and the sea loch of Tòb Bhalasaigh is particularly rich in marine life. In the sheltered lagoon there is a rare mix of seaweeds, as well as sponges, sea stars, brittle stars, and molluscs. You may also see coral and anemones. With such an abundance of food, it isn't surprising that otters frequent the shores of the loch and with luck, you'll spot them. There are also wonderful views from this peninsula. To the west, beyond the islands of Bhàcsaigh and Pabaigh Mòr, the stunning white sands on the reef headland of Lewis are clearly visible.

The route through Valasay to Tobson follows the waymarked Great Bernera Trail through moorland and foreshore past stone ruins, slipways, and old lobster ponds. Passing through the outskirts of the village the route then heads uphill on a marked path to reach the valley and beach at Bostadh. Here, in 1993, a great winter storm uncovered stonework within the sand dunes and subsequent excavations revealed them to be Iron Age dwellings, some virtually intact. Although they themselves could not be preserved an impressive, thatched-roofed replica allows visitors to experience building techniques and living conditions of the time. Some of the finds are also displayed in the local museum at Breaclete.

On a strand of rocks towards the east of the beach, the tide and time bell is one of a number that have been installed around the coast of Britain as part of a project to celebrate and reinforce connections between different parts of the country, the land and the sea, and between people and their environment. The movement of the waves against the bell creates a constantly changing sound. This is a glorious beach to swim from, with the right tides and swell.

The route back to Breaclete follows the tarmac road. From the top of the rise after the cemetery you can see the Flannan Isles across to the west side of Lewis. The road continues through croft land and moorland and along the tranquil banks of the lochs. At the Tobson crossroads, a cairn commemorates the Bernera riot of 1874 by the island's crofters, which resulted in three of them standing trial. The eventual passing of the Crofters Land Act in 1886 granted all crofters throughout Scotland secure tenancies as well as fair rents. The cairn was constructed using stones from every croft on the island, plus coping stones from the dwellings of the three ringleaders.

The community centre at Breaclete is a great place to stop for refreshments and find out more about the island. From here the route heads east to the scenically located replica of a Norse Mill. Water power from a stream was used to grind corn in this small, beautifully thatched, stone building.

Beyond the mill, the free-range route traverses peatland, rocks and beaches to reach the impressive 19th-century lobster pond on the east side of Loch Riosaigh a couple of kilometres north of the jetty at Dubh Thòb. The brainchild of local fisherman Murdo Morrison who went to Australia to earn the money for construction, it was to transform the lobster-fishing trade. Previously, many fishermen who sent live lobsters to London's Billingsgate would receive a telegram from their agent stating, 'All dead on arrival', which meant no pay. Once the tidal pond was built, lobsters could be kept alive until the prices were right and they were in the best condition to travel. It's great fun to rock-hop across this milestone in fishing history.

From the pond, the route continues southeast over rolling moorland before you reach the road at the jetty at Dubh Thob and return via Kirkibost to the bridge over the Atlantic.

DIRECTIONS

》 From the Great Bernera end of the road bridge (1) follow the unmarked route and immediately pass through the semi-circle of standing stones (2), then head W over rough ground to the pier at Tacleit. From here take the single-track road N, crossing an interesting stone bridge (3) to arrive at Valasay.

》 On Valasay (4), follow the blue and purple signs of the Great Bernera Trail through wild countryside to Tobson (5), then on to beautiful Bostadh Beach (6) to see the tide bell and the site of the Iron Age houses.

》 Return S via the single-track road past the memorial (7) to the Bernera Riot at the Tobson junction. Continue to Breaclete, stopping for refreshments at the community centre (8) and a visit to the museum.

》 Leaving the community centre, continue along the road, turn L to pass the cenotaph, then turn R at the tip of Loch Breacleit onto a small lane, continuing to its end. Take the narrow but well-defined path (to L of the house) to reach the intact, thatch-roofed Norse Mill (9) on the banks of Loch Riosaigh.

》 Continue E around Loch Riosaigh and up through the bluffs of Cnoc Righseodh to visit the giant lobster pond (10) on the far side of the loch. Cross the wall for an interesting excursion before heading directly E across the undulating grassland and old peat workings to reach the E coast of Àird Mhor.

》 Head S along the coast on distinct sheep tracks to the jetty at Dubh Thòb (11) to end this free-range section of the walk. From here, return to the starting point via the network of well-signed, single-track roads.

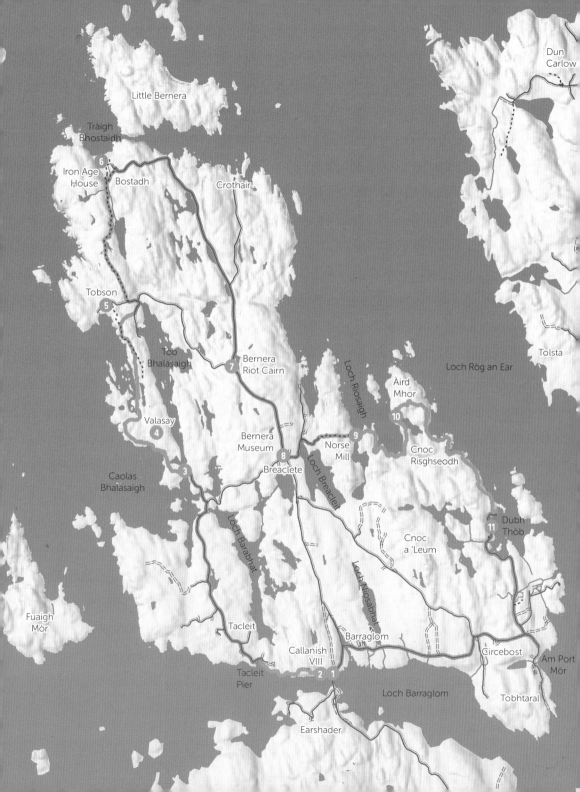

Dun Carlow

Little Bernera

Tràigh Bhostaidh

⑥ Iron Age House

Bostadh

Crothair

Tobson

⑤

Tolsta

Tòb Bhalasaigh

⑦ Bernera Riot Cairn

Loch Rìosaigh

Loch Ròg an Ear

Àird Mhor

⑩

Valasay

④

Bernera Museum

⑧ Breaclete

⑨ Norse Mill

Cnoc Risghseodh

Caolas Bhalasaigh

③

Loch Breacleit

Cnoc a 'Leum

Dubh Thòb ⑪

Loch Barabhat

Fuaigh Mòr

Loch Niosabhat

Tacleit

Barraglom

Circebost

Am Port Mòr

Tacleit Pier

Callanish VIII

② ①

Loch Barraglom

Tobhtaral

Earshader

SOUTH WALLS

EXHILARATING CLIFFTOP WALK PAST TOWERING SEA STACKS ON A QUIET ISLAND WITH A SECRET FORESHORE AND WONDERFUL WILDLIFE RESERVE

Standing on top of the cliff and looking down into the depths of the gloup – a collapsed sea cave – many metres below, the rise and fall of the sea at the base sent hollow gurgling sounds upwards, tempting me closer to see if my torch beam would reach the source. Saving myself for the exploration of the other gloup, the geos (gullies), sea arches, and stacks, I withdrew but not without a huge rush of adrenaline. This island had more than earned its place in this book.

Walking the quiet lanes of the north of the island, then passing through the main village and ferry terminal of Longhope, the route soon becomes wilder, following tracks and shoreline. After navigating the rocky foreshore section beneath the low cliffs and Martello tower of the east coast, you reach the white sands of Kirk Bay and perhaps stop for a refreshing dip. Climbing up to Cantick Head, the footpath follows the clifftop and the route takes in the spectacular geology of the south coast with fabulous views of the other islands of the Pentland Firth and beyond.

South Walls is joined to the southern tip of Hoy in the Orkney Archipelago by a causeway, The Ayre, built on top of the sandbanks. The island's small population is concentrated at Longhope, with a scattering of houses in the low-lying north. The south of the island is wild and remote with some incredible geological features, many within a wildlife reserve well known for its flora and nesting seabirds. Most visitors to the south-west islands of Orkney tend to stick to Hoy and since few visit South Walls, it remains peaceful and a stunning location for a clockwise walk.

Although there are fewer wartime relics in South Walls compared to the surrounding islands,

TERRAIN: Undulating grass track with some route-finding; flat rocks on the foreshore; island lane

STARTING POINT: East end of The Ayre. Lat/Long 58.7853, -3.2274; GR ND 291 893

DISTANCE: 18.9km (ascent 200m)

TIME: 4 hours 30 mins

OS MAP: OS Explorer 462

DIFFICULTY: 2

NAVIGATION: 3

ACCESS: 2

DON'T MISS:
• Sea stacks, caves, and two huge gloups with blowholes
• Porpoises, dolphins, and basking sharks at Cantick Head
• Rare pink Scottish primrose (May) in the wildlife reserve
• Panoramas of the Orcadian islands and Pentland Firth

SPECIAL NOTES: Foreshore section of the walk is best undertaken on lower tides. This walk can be combined with walks on the larger island of Hoy.

GETTING THERE: Ferry from Houton terminal (mainland) to either Longhope or Lyness on Hoy, then Hoy and Walls Community bus (01856 701356) or taxi to the start.

FACILITIES: Traditional inn, the Royal, at Longhope, also Stromabank Hotel has a public bar and food. General store at Longhope (closed Sunday); public toilet at Longhope Pier; café at Lyness museum on Hoy near the ferry terminal.

the island did play its part in protecting Scapa Flow –'the stopper in the North Sea bottle'. This strategically important stretch of water was the Royal Navy's main anchorage in both world wars. Yet South Wall's role in coastal defence dates even further back. The early 19th-century Martello tower on the northeast shore was built in response to threats from Napoleonic forces and American privateers. More about the history of the island and its military role can be found at the excellent Scapa Flow Visitor Centre and Museum at Lyness, opposite the ferry terminal on Hoy.

The whole east coast route to Osmondwall is along the foreshore and passes beneath the low cliffs. They are easily climbed if you need to get around the trickier coastal sections at mid-tide. At the cemetery at Osmondwall, a bronze figure of a lifeboatman commemorates the eight crewmen of the Longhope Lifeboat who lost their lives during a rescue in 1969.

The highlight of this walk is the section from the south-eastern tip and along the south coast. From Cantick Head, the perilous expanse of Pentland Firth lies to the south and to the north-east, the Sound of Hoxa forms the southern entrance to Scapa Flow. Porpoises, seals, whales, dolphins, orcas, and basking sharks are regularly spotted from this lofty vantage point that also boasts some of the best views on Orkney. Closer to South Walls are the islands of Flotta (with its flare stack), Switha, Swona, Stroma, and South Ronaldsay, while the statuesque

outline of Duncansby Head is further south on the mainland. The lighthouse is still active, although the buildings are now used for holiday accommodation.

On the south coast, which has some of the most spectacular coastal scenery in Britain, powerful seas have pounded the cliffs to form several spectacular geological features. The wave erosion of the fault lines in these cliffs has created steep-sided geos, the cry of seabirds echoing eerily from their depths. One of the most spectacular is the Birsi Geo. Other striking features are the soaring rock arches, some of which have collapsed to form sea stacks, such as The Candle just south of Snelsetter. But perhaps the most spectacular sights are the two gloups – caves where the roof has collapsed to expose the sea surging across the cave floor below. During high seas they become magnificent blowholes and seeing spray blasted out of their tops is quite a surreal experience when walking towards them on the cliff. Further west of the blowholes you reach the small island, appropriately named The Axe.

Many of these geological features are within the Hill of White Hamars Scottish Wildlife Trust Reserve. More than 180 different species of wild flower have been recorded here, including the rare purple Scottish primrose. This is also one of the best sites on Orkney for spotting butterflies.

On this relatively undiscovered island there is a treasure trove of natural wonders to explore. Make sure you visit if you are planning a trip to Hoy – South Walls will be the icing on the cake.

DIRECTIONS

» From the car park at the east end of The Ayre (1), walk along the lane towards Longhope. After 2km reach Longhope (2), passing the ferry terminal, inn, shop, and lifeboat museum. Continue along the lane for 3.1km to where the road turns R, then drop down onto the beach and continue on the foreshore (or to avoid the foreshore section turn R on the road and follow it to Osmondwall). Follow the mixed beach and rocks around the Point of Hackness (3), beneath the Martello tower (4) and Crowtaing, and continue via the flat rocks along Kirk Hope (5).

» At the cemetery (6) and church of Osmondwall, walk across the beach head to find the track that works its way uphill to the lighthouse.

» Just before Cantick Head lighthouse building (7), go over the stile to reach the coastal path. Pass beneath the walls of the lighthouse complex and continue to climb steadily uphill to head W along the S coast. After 1.2km drop down to Hesti Geo (8) and the grassy mound of an ancient broch (fort), and then around the steep-sided West Geo (9).

» Pass the first of two large gloups (10), just east of Snelsetter. After 0.5km, opposite the path that leads to Snelsetter, find the large sea stack known as The Candle (11).

» Walk around Birsi Geo (12) and continue over the various stiles and fences of the Hill of White Hamars reserve (13).

» Reach the small islet, The Axe (14), and continue to the highest point of the walk before skirting around Aith Head (15). Continue downhill towards the car park crossing the stiles and a small footbridge.

CHAPTER
4 8

FLOTTA

A SENTINEL ISLAND IN THE PEACEFUL WATERS OF SCAPA FLOW WITH SEA STACKS, SEABIRDS, AND FASCINATING WARTIME RELICS

This low-lying Orkney island between Hoy and South Ronaldsay doesn't broadcast its natural and historic wonders. Perhaps, after two friendly 'invasions' by thousands of Royal Navy personnel during the two world wars, followed by the construction of a giant North Sea oil terminal, this gentle island has seen enough activity. But now the secret of Flotta is out.

This coastal circuit follows the easy Flotta Trail on a generally unmarked path that takes in the impressive and beautiful coastal formations and stunning sea vistas. Orkney was Britain's chief naval base during both world wars and sailors not confined to ships lived and worked on Flotta. The route takes in the vast array of atmospheric wartime ruins still visible on the island. If ferry times permit, extend the route to spot the wildlife on the remote and wild Golta. The access, through one of the

country's most important oil distribution terminals, is fascinating.

Flotta, at the southern entrance of Scapa Flow, is one of the circle of islands that protects this stunning natural harbour from the ravages of the North Sea. Its skyline is dominated by the glowing flare stack of the oil terminal and a huge wind turbine, both towering above any other structure in Orkney. By contrast, the rest of the island is heathland or is still farmed with lush grass meadows sloping gently to the sea.

The anti-clockwise walk starts from Gibraltar Pier where the island's wartime history is immediately obvious. Not only the control centre for Scapa Flow, the island also provided entertainment for the thousands of servicemen billeted here. The ruins of the Naval Cinema stand starkly against the backdrop of the conifer woodland planted during

---

TERRAIN: Grass paths and tracks; quiet island roads

STARTING POINT: Flotta ferry terminal. Lat/Long 58.8379, -3.1285; GR ND 349 950

DISTANCE: 18.9km (ascent 270m)

TIME: 4 hours 30 mins (including the short route on Golta)

OS MAP: OS Explorer 462

DIFFICULTY: 1

NAVIGATION: 2

ACCESS: 2

DON'T MISS:
- Stunning views of the archipelago and Scapa Flow
- Sea stacks, geos, and puffins (in season) off Stanger Head
- Flotta penguins and other bizarre metal creatures
- Fascinating wartime structures and relics

SPECIAL NOTES: For access to Golta contact Flotta Terminal Security on 01856 884359 before visiting and after exit.

GETTING THERE: Ferry from Lyness (Hoy) or Houton (mainland) www.orkneyferries.co.uk, 01856 872044.

FACILITIES: Toilets at the ferry terminal; community centre offers hot and cold refreshments (seasonal opening times, 01856 701219). General store next to the museum.

World War II. The six holes in its rear wall mark the location of projection equipment, and the sloping ledges on the side walls reveal the position of the balconies.

Walking south along the west coast, more wartime relics dot the landscape. One enterprising islander converts military debris into art that displays humour and skill. The bagpipe-playing Flotta penguins near Rotten Gutter are a personal favourite.

Further south, the wild heather-clad beauty of West Hill, where skuas breed, is enhanced by fabulous sea vistas across Fara to the looming mountains of Hoy. Looking south, there are views of the lighthouse on Cantick Head, South Walls, and to the island of Switha.

The southwest coastal route is interspersed with rusting mounted anti-aircraft guns and missiles. At the ruins of the coastal artillery battery at Innan Neb, remains of gun emplacements, the old barrage balloon mooring site, and a water reservoir await. A set of concrete steps isolated in the landscape indicates the entrance to a long-lost building, while a decaying Nissen hut contains rusting beds and other domestic bric-a-brac. Eerie and deserted, the headland is a reminder of those who served on this island.

After walking around Kirk Bay, the route climbs to the Port War Signal Station above Stanger Head on the island's southeast tip and the sheer scale of the wartime operation is slowly revealed. Built to control shipping movements into and out of Scapa Flow and now in ruins, the station is an atmospheric place to explore.

The extension of the walk south to Stanger Head itself is recommended to view the dramatic sea stacks, geos, and blowholes of the Cletts. In season, fulmars wheel far below and puffins, shags, razorbills, and guillemots hunt to feed chicks in cliff nests and burrows at this fabulous location. The crevices and cracks of the cliffs also support an unusual fern, the sea spleenwort. It is the only member of the fern family that can tolerate this harsh, salty environment.

Heading north along the east coast, you can visit the Buchanan Battery and enjoy views across the Sound of Hoxa to South Ronaldsay. Here the chain of smaller islands is connected by the Churchill Barriers that form the road link to Kirkwall in the north.

Turning west around Pan Hope, a detour to the Flotta Heritage Centre is worthwhile for the insights offered into island life. Slightly further east the welcoming seasonal community centre in Whome is a good place to stop for refreshments and view the tapestries that depict island life through the ages.

If ferry times permit, the extension through the oil terminal to the wilds of Golta is memorable. The island's north coast was the Navy's main recreation area and featured a golf course, on which George V and Admiral Jellicoe played, as well as tennis courts, a large boxing venue, and an officers' club. Nature has now taken over this wild and remote spot.

The walk past the oil terminal itself is quite an experience. This strategically important North Sea facility processes oil and gas from the Piper, Claymore, and Tartan oilfields for onward transfer. The walk around the fenced perimeter of this chemistry set of sprawling pipework, processing units, columns, tanks, and huge flare stack is a glimpse into another world. The silent operation of the plant is broken only by the shrieks of gulls that have somehow built nests here.

Back at the Gibraltar Pier, seals sometimes entertain departing visitors and oil workers who time their departure from work with the ferry's arrival almost to the minute. Back on Mainland Orkney, the wind turbine and flare stack are the only Flotta landmarks still visible, the beauty of the island cloaked once again to all but those in the know.

DIRECTIONS

≫ From the ferry terminal at Gibraltar Pier (1), walk up to the road (the entrance to the oil terminal is straight ahead) and turn R. After 200m take the track to R, passing the ruins of the Naval Cinema (2) and Sutherland Pier. Continue on the track along the coast for 3.8km past the disused airstrip, Flotta penguins (3), and over the heathland to Innan Neb (4).

≫ After 800m meet the lane, then just in front of the barns at Balaclava turn R along the grassy footpath at the side of the fence. Continue around Kirk Bay on the grassy path. Turn R along the farm track in front of the stone barn and after 200 metres turn R again at the junction to pass the ruined stone cottage with its picnic bench. Continue on the lane and immediately after the church (5) turn R along the side of the churchyard, to reach the coast after a further 100m. Continue along the coast towards Stanger Head, turning inland to walk uphill towards Port War Signal Station (6).

≫ Continue along the track past the small lake on the L to a junction. For the extension to view the stack and caves off Stanger Head (7) turn R, then R again after 300m. Return to the junction using the same route and then continue straight ahead on the single-track road.

≫ After 800m, take a detour on a R-hand bend at the bottom of the hill to view the Buchanan Battery (8). Go back to the road and after 400m take the sharp L turn to walk parallel to Pan Hope towards the main village at Whome. After a further 400m find the shop and museum (9) along the lane to R then, a little further on, the community centre and refreshments (10).

≫ Continue along the main island road (B9045) for 1.4km to take the extension for Golta. Go through the gate on R and follow the lane towards and past the oil terminal (11) onto Golta (12). You now have two options: if time is short follow the path past the terminal buildings to Sands Taing (3.7km); or take the longer (8km) route. Passing between the flare stacks to the N of Golta, the latter follows the N coast to St Vincent jetty and beyond to the north-eastern tip of the island at Roan Head to view the submarine cables used in World War II. Return through the terminal, let security know that you have left the area, and continue on the road towards Gibraltar Pier.

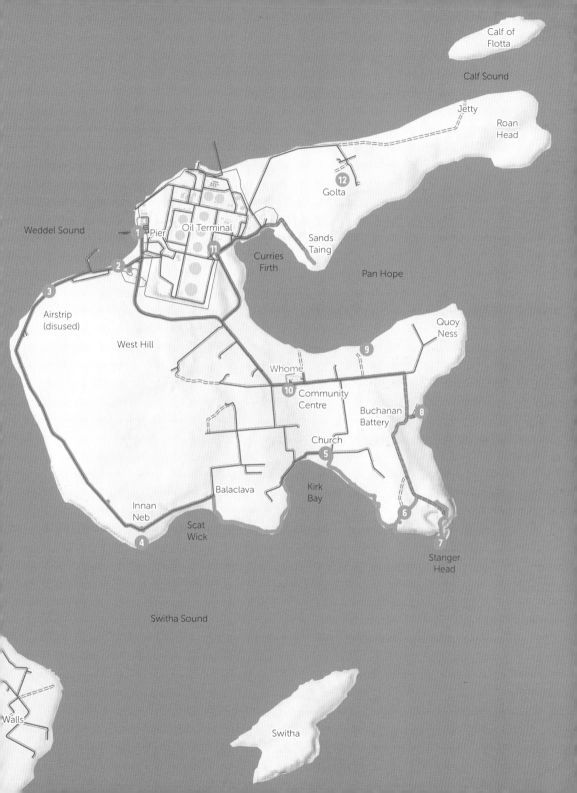

Calf of
Flotta

Calf Sound

Jetty

Roan
Head

Weddel Sound

1 Pier

Oil Terminal

11

Curries
Firth

Sands
Taing

12
Golta

Pan Hope

2

3

Airstrip
(disused)

West Hill

Quoy
Ness

9

Whome

10 Community
Centre

Buchanan
Battery

8

Church

5

Balaclava

Kirk
Bay

Innan
Neb

Scat
Wick

4

6

7 Stanger
Head

Switha Sound

Walls

Switha

PAPA WESTRAY

TAKE THE WORLD'S SHORTEST SCHEDULED FLIGHT TO A REMOTE AND VERY WILD ISLAND WITH THE BIGGEST OF HEARTS

The energy at the northern tip of Papa Westray, where two great oceans meet, will overload every one of your senses and is one of my favourite places in the world. The boiling waters whip the swirling colonies of seabirds into a frenzy as they fish with lethal precision. Over North Hill, where the seabird shrieks compete with the roar of the tidal race, the aerial acrobatics of aggressive skuas force other migrant seabirds to drop their catch. Underfoot, delicate herbs and wild flowers add a vibrant splash of colour to this rare and elemental maritime environment. The unmarked but straightforward coastal route passes near to everything the island has to offer. Nothing is too far away on Papa.

Papa Westray, known as Papay to those who adore it, is one of Orkney's smallest islands and lies some 41 km north of Kirkwall. It is just under 2 kilo-metres from Westray, its larger sister island and the departure point for the world's shortest scheduled flight at just two minutes. Papay has a wealth of archaeological sites, including significant Neolithic and medieval ruins, wildlife thrives on its heaths and rugged coasts, and its beaches are unspoilt and peaceful.

Although a remote and challenging environment to live in, the island has a vibrant community, invigorated by the Papay Development Trust. There is a hostel and shop, and several events running throughout the year – all of them open to visitors. These include a weekly 'pub' and café, film and dance nights, and the Fun Weekend with a BBQ, ceilidh, games, and sports that include a 'carty race doon the New Hooses Brae'. The Trust has also recruited a Papay Ranger to lead tours and co-ordinate a programme of activities for visitors

---

TERRAIN: Easy rock and grass paths

STARTING POINT: Knap of Howar near airport and hostel. Lat/Long 59.3495, -2.9109; GR HY 483 518. Or from the ferry jetty in Moclett if arriving by boat

DISTANCE: 20.1km (ascent 176m)

TIME: 5 hours

OS MAP: OS Explorer 464

DIFFICULTY: 2

NAVIGATION: 3

ACCESS: 2

DON'T MISS:
- Arrival on the world's shortest scheduled flight
- Two oceans meeting at the northern tip of the island
- Community coffee morning for home-bakes and chats
- Rare Scottish primrose and spectacular seabirds

SPECIAL NOTES: North Hill access restricted in nesting season, Apr–Aug. RSPB guided walks May–Aug. For Holm of Papay visits call the Ranger 01857 644224.

GETTING THERE: Two direct ferry sailings from Kirkwall per week. In summer daily ferries to Westray then minibus connection to short sea crossing to Papay on the Golden Mariana. Orkney Ferries 01856 872044.

FACILITIES: Excellent coffee morning Wed 10.30–11.45, St Ann's Community Room; at Beltane House hostel, 'pub' on Sat from 8pm; also well-stocked, community-run shop. Toilets at ferry pier, hostel, and the Kelp Store.

and islanders, including regular trips to the Holm of Papay. Island life here is full and rich.

The walk can be started in a number of places but the most convenient if you are staying at the hostel or arriving by plane is the Knap of Howar on the west coast. This stone settlement was built around 3,800 BC, making the buildings the earliest north European homes still standing. A narrow passage leads to the interior where there are hearths, pits, stores, and stone benches to sit on and ponder life in Neolithic times.

Continuing south down the west coast, the gentle southern section of the walk crosses the flowering machair around the Bay of Moclett and the white beach at Bothican before reaching the ferry terminal (a good alternative start point for the walk). From here, the route leads to the low cliffs at the Head of Moclett, which is an excellent spot to see puffins.

Turning north up the east coast, St Tredwell's Loch is fringed with yellow flag iris in early summer and a haven for wildfowl. The medieval remains are those of a chapel that was once a renowned pilgrimage centre, said to offer miraculous cures for eye ailments. An old mill can be found a little further on at the head of the loch at Mill Point.

Further north along the east coast is South Wick's old stone pier. The 18th-century buildings, once the old kelp and coal stores, now house a heritage and craft centre. Across the water to the east, the Holm of Papay is well worth a visit to see the three cairns, thought to be Neolithic burial sites. The most striking, at the southern end of the island, has an impressive 20-metre subterranean chamber with shapes carved into the walls, and a narrow entrance passage with 12 side areas. Descent into the chamber is now down a ladder via a new opening in the roof, built to preserve the tomb. It's quite an adventure if you are staying on Papay for more than a day.

At North Wick, the large, white-sand bay is perfect for a secluded dip before you reach the wild and windswept northern third of Papay, which is an RSPB reserve. Breeding 'bonxies' (great skuas), Arctic skuas, Arctic terns, curlew, and dunlin populate the maritime heath whilst the low cliffs of Fowl Craig, undercut by sea caves and natural arches, are the summer residence for all four of Britain's auks – guillemot, razorbill, puffin, and black guillemot. Sadly, this is the also the spot where the last of Britain's great auks was shot in 1813. Today a miniature sculpture stands as a memorial to this 75cm-tall flightless bird known as the 'penguin of the north'. When I visited on a cold early spring day, some kind soul had kitted it out with a knitted scarf and hat.

Before you leave the heathland, look out for the tiny pink flowers of the rare Scottish primrose, which blooms twice – in May and July – amongst the many other delicate herbs and wild flowers that flourish here. Turning south down the west coast, the large rock flags that jut into the sea form huge rock pools that are fun to explore, and there are fine views across Papa Sound to the sands of Rackwick in the north of neighbouring Westray.

Further south 12th-century St Boniface's Church, one of the oldest Christian sites in North Scotland, was among few to survive the Reformation. It is a simple but very atmospheric place. Exploration reveals a Norse hogback gravestone and two early Christian cross-slabs, which indicate the site was once of great significance. The lichen-covered headstones of drowned sailors are a reminder of the perilous seas around Orkney.

I have returned to Papay time and time again, never tiring of its raw beauty and its friendly island ways.

DIRECTIONS

» From the airport, leave the airfield and turn R along the lane, pass the war memorial and turn R along the track that runs through the S end of the farm complex at Holland to reach the Knap of Howar (1). Walk S along the W coast, after 900m reach the end of the lane at Backaskaill and continue along the coast and after another 300m, the route passes below the farm buildings. Cross various stiles, walls, and fences to walk through the fields.

» Reach the SW tip of the island at Vest Ness and continue around the Bay of Moclett through the machair. Walk across Bothican Beach and then take the minor road towards the pier.

» At the pier (2), continue along the lane and then through the gate and track below a house to the SE point of the island at the Head of Moclett (3) – a good spot for puffins. Continue N on the E coast via the grassy coast path along the cliff tops.

» After 2.6 km, just before the ruins of the mill, find the faint path inland to visit St Tredwell's Chapel (4) on the loch. Return and continue on the coast between the ruins of the mill (5), then take the track to L of the house.

» At the junction with the road turn L for refreshments at the community café (6) or hostel (7). Otherwise, continue straight over the lane and head N past Southwick Pier (8) then stay on the small lane for 2.3km to reach North Via.

» Access the beach at North Wick (9), avoiding the private lane to the house, and walk onto the grass bank at its N end. Continue around the coast past the large pool of Loch of the Taing. Pass through some old sheepfolds and then follow the faint path uphill along the steep cliffs, crossing the walls via stiles. Towards Fowl Craig look out for the miniature great auk sculpture (10).

» Continue to the N tip of the island at Fowl Flag (11), walk round on the grassy clifftop, then climb to the highest point of the walk near John's Boat. Continue S along the extensive flagstones of the W coast for some great rock-pooling and swimming opportunities at Geo of Odderaber (12). After another 2.6km reach St Boniface's Church (13) and then head S for a further 1km to return to the Knap of Howar.

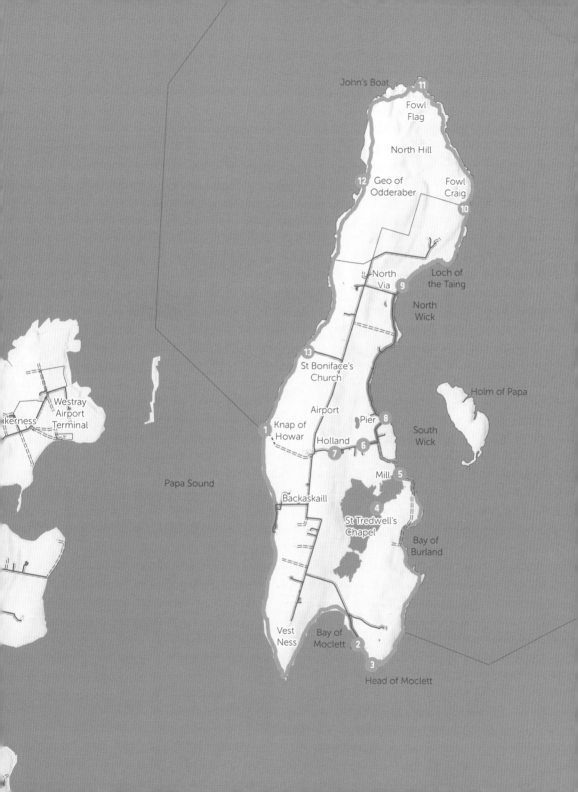

John's Boat

Fowl
Flag

North Hill

12 Geo of
Odderaber

Fowl
Craig

10

Loch of
the Taing

North Via **9**

North
Wick

13

St Boniface's
Church

Airport

Pier **8**

Knap of **1**
Howar

Holland

6

7

South
Wick

Mill **5**

Backaskaill

4

St Tredwell's
Chapel

Bay of
Burland

Holm of Papa

Westray
Airport
Terminal

kerness

Papa Sound

Vest
Ness

Bay of
Moclett

2

3

Head of Moclett

NORTH RONALDSAY

A SPECIAL, FAR-FLUNG ISLAND WITH SUPERB WILDLIFE, INCLUDING WALL-NESTING FULMARS, SEAWEED-EATING SHEEP, AND VISITING ORCAS

Have you ever played North Ronaldsay's Game of Stones?', I was asked during my overnight stop here. 'The rules are simple. Go to the beach. Select a flat stone. Place on the wall. Leave a few holes. Don't trap your fingers. Repeat.'

I had chosen the week of the North Ronaldsay Sheep Festival to explore the island and soon got caught up in its mix of conservation, great music, dance, and food. Here I met an eclectic bunch of people from across the globe, committed to keeping the only example of community farming in the UK alive by maintaining the wall that keeps the island's famed seaweed-eating sheep on the shore.

The route I planned was a flat, pebble- and rock-strewn grassy foreshore walk following the 19-kilometre stone wall of the sheep dyke. The anticlockwise route follows the infinite white sands

of two bays, visits excellent Iron Age ruins and is perfectly punctuated halfway around by the tasty local food and visitor centre of the lighthouse complex.

North Ronaldsay is the northernmost island in the Orkney Archipelago and has a definite 'outer-isle' feel. Remote, low-lying, and exposed, it is populated by 40 or so sturdy islanders who uphold many of the island's traditions, such as singing around the island's standing stone on New Year's Eve and keeping the old Norn dialect alive. The rocks of its north and west coasts are grey-blue flags and the tallest land-based lighthouse in Britain stands at its northern tip. The long, crescent-shaped white-sand beach of Linklet Bay occupies the west coast, while at the far end of extensive, sandy South Bay on the southernmost tip at Point of Burrian is an Iron Age broch (fort). Inland the island is extensively

---

TERRAIN: Easy sheep trails along the foreshore

STARTING POINT: Ferry jetty. Lat/Long 59.3559, -2.4412. GR HY 750 522

DISTANCE: 20.1km (ascent: 184m)

TIME: 6 hours

OS MAP: OS Explorer 465

DIFFICULTY: 2

NAVIGATION: 3

ACCESS: 2

DON'T MISS:
- Tasting the mutton pie at the lighthouse café
- Visiting the Bird Observatory and meeting the wardens
- Taking part in the annual Sheep Festival
- Fascinating lighthouse tour in the company of the keeper

GETTING THERE: By ferry from Kirkwall (Tuesday & Friday in summer). Check sailings the afternoon before in case of rescheduling. Sunday excursion sailings also operate in summer. www.orkneyferries.co.uk. Loganair flights from Kirkwall operate daily www.loganair.co.uk.

FACILITIES: Accommodation, hot food, and grocery shop at the Bird Observatory. Self-catering accommodation and a great café at the lighthouse.

cultivated and its quiet lanes are fringed with wild flowers and stone cottages.

There are four ever-present features on this anti-clockwise route – the feral sheep, the stone dyke, abundant birdlife, and a huge lighthouse. The feral sheep live on the foreshore and you'll see them everywhere, seaweed dangling from their mouths as they munch their way around the coastline. (The only other seaweed-eating creature in the world is, apparently, a lizard from the Galápagos.) The gamey and iodine-rich mutton from the sheep is on the menu at high-end hotels, such as the Ritz and Savoy, and it was served to The Queen on her Diamond Jubilee. Horned and looking more like goats, the nimble sheep traverse the rocks at high tide to find kelp washed ashore during the storms. At low tide they sleep. Their double fleeces in shades of cream, pale-grey, chocolate-brown, and black are spun on the island and the wool is sold far and wide.

The stone dyke, now listed by Historic Scotland, was built to prevent the sheep from eating the inland grass and crops. It may be the longest, continuous dry-stone construction in the world and its two metre height is designed to deters the 'loupers' – high-jumping sheep. Collectively owned by the crofters since the 1800s, the wall is maintained and managed by the island's Sheep Court. Maintenance is a never-ending task because winter storms lash this low-lying island leaving many parts of the wall in ruins. Further evidence of the communal nature of sheep farming here is the presence of nine circular 'punds', or pens, that you pass on the northeast coastal section of the walk. On very high tides, sheep are rounded up for counting, health checks, and sheering – a practice still known as 'punding'.

The dyke is also important for fulmars. During breeding season they nest in its shelter and chicks dot its rocky foundations, particularly on the west coast. But don't be fooled by their fluffy cuteness. They soon turn into hissing puffballs, launching the foulest-smelling vomit over a surprisingly long distance towards anyone who unwittingly wanders into their space.

The fulmar is just one of the many bird species on North Ronaldsay, which is one of the country's best-bird watching locations during the spring and autumn migration periods. The Bird Observatory in the south-west of the island, which offers accommodation and a shop, has super-friendly staff and is a great place to learn about birdlife. It was established in 1987 to conduct long-term monitoring of bird populations and migration, and there is a good chance of accompanying the wardens as they work. A firm favourite for those staying here is a trek to the nets on the beach in the dead of night to free captured storm petrels and ring them for monitoring purposes. The wardens also know a great deal about the island's large population of seals, passing orca and whales, and the occasional lost Arctic walrus.

On the island's north-eastern tip, the lighthouse café makes an excellent refreshment stop and serves North Ronaldsay mutton pie as well as cupcakes of every persuasion. The lighthouse itself, which replaced the Old Beacon at Dennis Head, is built on rocks at the Point of Sinsoss and has 176 steps. From the top, the views are superb and you can see most of the walking route. On a clear day, Fair Isle in the Shetlands – much further to the north – is in sight. The real treat though is meeting Billy Muir. Keeper of the light for 50 years, this firefighter, air traffic controller, and handyman extraordinaire is a mainstay of the island and his tales of shipwrecks, lost treasure, and gigantic waves enliven any tour. Yet Billy's are not the only yarns that are spun on the island: among the converted lighthouse buildings is a shop selling the local wool and hand-knitted items.

You may not be a fan of sheep, birds, and stone walls at the start of this walk but by the end of it you'll be smitten.

DIRECTIONS

» From the ferry port (1), pass the harbour buildings and continue for 480m beyond the small junction on L signed to the North Ronaldsay Bird Observatory (2). Climb over the fence to South Bay Beach (3) then walk for 900m along the sands to reach the flat rocks. Continue for a further 300m to reach the start of the bank on the shore side of the dyke.

» After 1km reach the Iron Age broch (4) at the S tip of the island, Point of Burrian, and find the small lake near Viggay a further 1.7km on. Go round the headland of Bride's Ness and cross the rocky expanse of North and South Taing.

» Cross the beach at Nesstoun, keeping to the beachside of the dyke, and after a further 1.5km reach the golf course (5). Continue on the sandy path close to the shore and then walk parallel to the rocky ledges at Snash Ness. Follow the track, next to the dyke, go around the house, then turn R onto the lane.

» Continuing along the lane to where it bears L, next to the house on the R, take the path back to the shore and continue along the dyke. Reach the old stone fishing huts and pier (6) after 1.3 km.

» At the Old Beacon (7) continue around Dennis Loch, past the ruined sheep pens (8) and after 1km reach the foghorn (9) and walk up the concrete path to the main lighthouse buildings for refreshments. Return to the coast and walk around the grassy headland at Point of Sinsoss, keeping inland of the small loch. Continue on the shore side of the fragmented dyke along the bay of Garso Wick to Garso.

» At Westness, just before the house on the shoreline, turn inland along the track and then R at the crossroads. Continue straight along the lane to Ancumtoun and after 420m, at a sharp L bend in the road, take the path immediately to R, back to the shore. Turn L and continue down the coast along the layered rocks of the foreshore, keeping to R of the dyke.

» Pass numerous geos and the airfield (10) to reach Loch Gretchen and find the standing stone (11) 150m to E. Continue around the outer edge of the dyke and return to the pier.